JOURNEYS

Practice Book

Grade 4

HOUGHTON MIFFLIN HARCOURT
School Publishers

Printed in the U.S.A.

ISBN 10: 0-54-724642-0
ISBN 13: 978-0-54-724642-0

21 0928 17 16
4500580659

Contents

Name ________________________ Date ____________

Story Structure

Read the story below.

A Bark in the Night

As the sun began to set, Matt and his Mama sat reading books. Ernie, their pug dog, was snoring on the couch. It was getting colder outside and the sky had turned gray.

"Looks like we're in for quite a storm!" Mama said. The storm rolled in fast and strong. Rain started pounding the windows as lightning and thunder crashed in the sky.

"Don't be afraid, Matt," Mama said. Suddenly, Ernie jumped off the couch, barking furiously as he ran into the kitchen. Ernie rarely barked. Matt grabbed Mama's hand as they chased after Ernie.

Mama turned on the kitchen light. To their surprise, the door opened and Daddy walked in.

"Hi, honey! You're home early," Mama said. Ernie's barking stopped instantly when he saw it was Daddy, and everyone laughed with relief.

"See Ernie, there was nothing to worry about!" said Matt. He was secretly relieved it was just Daddy's return that caused Ernie's barking.

They all went back into the living room and sat in their chairs. Ernie curled up into his spot on the couch. Soon he was snoring. By then, the storm had settled into a drizzle, and all was calm again.

Complete the Story Map to show the important elements in the story.

Characters	Setting Time: Place:
Plot	

Name ______________________ Date ____________

Because of Winn-Dixie
Comprehension:
Story Structure

Story Structure

Read the story below.

An Unlikely Friend

I was home sick from school the day the Holmes family moved in. It was just before the school year ended, and I was missing the school picnic!

I stared out the window, feeling sorry for myself. Then I saw a girl come out of the new house on the block. She looked about my age, and she was kicking a soccer ball. It was black with red pentagons—just like the ball I lost last week!

I ran to the door and yelled, "Hey! What are you doing with that ball?"

The girl waved. I was furious. "Where'd you get that ball?" I demanded.

The girl stopped kicking the ball and headed my way. I was scared. I didn't know what I'd say, but I wanted my ball back. Before I could say anything, she started talking.

"Hi!" she said. "I'm Kate. Do you like soccer? Want to play?"

I grabbed the ball. Then I saw it wasn't mine after all. It was older, and "KATE" was on it in old ink.

"Sure!" I said. "I can't come out today because I'm home sick. But maybe tomorrow?"

"Great!" said Kate. "It'll be good to have a friend on the block."

"Yeah," I said sheepishly. "Glad to meet you, Kate."

Analyze the story to answer the questions about story structure. Use a Story Map to organize your thoughts.

1. What is the narrator's conflict, or problem, at the beginning?

____

____

2. How does the narrator resolve her problem?

____

____

Name ______________________________ Date ____________

Prefixes *re-*, *un-*, and *dis-*

disagree	return	reappear	unlikely
dislike	review	unfair	unable

Read each sentence. Complete the sentence with a word from above.

1. I need a receipt to ____________ the shirt that doesn't fit.
2. It is ____________ that I will know everyone at the party.
3. My brother and I usually ____________ about whose turn it is to take out the garbage.
4. Our class had to ____________ the ideas from the lesson before we took the test.
5. My sister loves talking on the phone, but I ____________ it.
6. I think it is ____________ that I have to do chores on my birthday.
7. Sometimes cleaning your room can cause a missing toy to ____________ .
8. He was ____________ to go to the party because he was sick.

Name ______________________ Date ____________

Short *a* and Long *a*

Basic Read the paragraphs. Write the Basic Words that best complete the sentences.

I spent a week of my summer vacation at my grandmother's house. At first I was (1) _____ that I would be bored, but I had a lot of fun. Every morning I helped my grandmother in her studio, where she paints pictures that would (2) _____ you.

I helped her (3) _____ some of the paintings that will go on (4) _____ soon. I also made a sign to put outside when the paintings are ready to sell. I used poster board and a black (5) _____ to make the sign. The most fun I had was creating my own painting. I learned how to apply paint to a canvas with a knife (6) _____ . I wore a smock so I wouldn't get a (7) _____ on my clothes. Grandma says that my painting was much improved from ones I've done in the (8) _____ .

On my last night there, Grandma took me out for a (9) _____ dinner. I know for a (10) _____ that I will be back to visit my grandmother next summer.

1. ____________________ 6. ____________________
2. ____________________ 7. ____________________
3. ____________________ 8. ____________________
4. ____________________ 9. ____________________
5. ____________________ 10. ____________________

Challenge 11–14. Read the headline. On a separate sheet of paper, write about it, using four of the Challenge Words.

EASTSIDE SCHOOL TRACK TEAM SETS NEW RECORDS

Spelling Words

1. blade
2. gray
3. past
4. afraid
5. magic
6. delay
7. amaze
8. drain
9. maybe
10. break
11. sale
12. hang
13. stain
14. glass
15. raft
16. jail
17. crayon
18. fact
19. stale
20. steak

Challenge

fraction
trait
champion
activity
graceful

Name ______________________ Date ____________

Spelling Word Sort

Write each Basic Word beside the correct heading.

/ă/ spelled *a* followed by a consonant	Basic Words: Challenge Words: Possible Selection Words:
/ā/ spelled *a*-consonant-*e*	Basic Words: Challenge Words:
/ā/ spelled *ai*	Basic Words: Challenge Words: Possible Selection Words:
/ā/ spelled *ay*	Basic Words: Possible Selection Words:
/ā/ spelled *ea*	Basic Words:

Challenge Add the Challenge Words to your Word Sort.

Connect to Reading Look through *Because of Winn-Dixie*. Find words that have the /ă/ and /ā/ spelling patterns on this page. Add them to your Word Sort.

Spelling Words

1. blade
2. gray
3. past
4. afraid
5. magic
6. delay
7. amaze
8. drain
9. maybe
10. break
11. sale
12. hang
13. stain
14. glass
15. raft
16. jail
17. crayon
18. fact
19. stale
20. steak

Challenge

fraction
trait
champion
activity
graceful

Name ______________________ Date ____________

Proofreading for Spelling

Find the misspelled words and circle them. Write them correctly on the lines below.

The Avid Reader Bookstore is a popular place in town. The owner, Mr. Orville, unpacks a box of new books. He says he is afriad the weather will deley delivery, and some of the books on salee are on back order. The good news is that the book that Jenny wants to read about the magik raeft that goes down the kitchen drane and ends up in the middle of the ocean is not one on back order. But maibe Amanda will have to wait another week for the book about the cowboy who lands in jale for being falsely accused of stealing a graye mustang.

By the end of the day, Mr. Orville is ready for a glas of lemonade and a cookie. He's careful carrying the pitcher so he doesn't drop and braik it. The cold lemonade is refreshing, but the staile cookie has to go!

1. ____________ 7. ____________
2. ____________ 8. ____________
3. ____________ 9. ____________
4. ____________ 10. ____________
5. ____________ 11. ____________
6. ____________ 12. ____________

Spelling Words

1. blade
2. gray
3. past
4. afraid
5. magic
6. delay
7. amaze
8. drain
9. maybe
10. break
11. sale
12. hang
13. stain
14. glass
15. raft
16. jail
17. crayon
18. fact
19. stale
20. steak

Challenge

fraction
trait
champion
activity
graceful

Name ______________________ Date ____________

Lesson 1
PRACTICE BOOK

Because of Winn-Dixie
Grammar: Complete Sentences

Simple Subjects and Simple Predicates

A sentence is a group of words that tells a complete thought. The subject tells whom or what the sentence is about. The predicate tells what the subject does or is. A **simple subject** is the main word that tells whom or what the sentence is about. A **simple predicate** is the verb that tells what the subject is or does.

simple subject **simple predicate**
The trip to the supermarket takes five minutes.

Thinking Question
What is the main word that tells whom or what the sentence is about? What is the main word that tells what the subject is or does?

1–4. Write the simple subject on the line.

1. Mr. Mota left his dog Chase outside the supermarket. ______________
2. The automatic doors opened. ______________
3. Mr. Mota's list had many items on it. ______________
4. The dog outside the door watched Mr. Mota through the window. ______________

5–8. Underline the simple subject once and the simple predicate twice.

5. Soup cans fell to the ground.
6. Mr. Mota sampled some cheese at the deli.
7. He bought some doggie treats for Chase.
8. The friendly cashier smiled.

Name ______________________ Date ____________

Because of Winn-Dixie
Grammar: Complete Sentences

Sentence Fragments

A sentence must have a subject and a predicate to tell a complete thought. A **sentence fragment** is missing a subject, a predicate, or sometimes both.

fragment
Helped set up the tents at the campsite.

Thinking Question
Does this group of words have a subject that tells whom or what the sentence is about and a predicate that tells what happens or says something about the subject?

1–4. Write *sentence* if the group of words is a sentence. Write *fragment* if the group of words is not a sentence.

1. A bear wandered into our campsite. ______________
2. Sniffed around the tents for food. ______________
3. Have a sharp sense of smell. ______________
4. The hungry bear would not leave. ______________

5–8. Write *subject* if the fragment is missing the part of the sentence that tells *whom* or *what*. Write *predicate* if the fragment is missing the part of the sentence that tells *what happens* or *what is*.

5. The huge bear. ______________
6. Was attracted by the smell of the food. ______________
7. Rummaged through a large cooler. ______________
8. A loud roar from another bear in the distance.

____

Name ______________________ Date ____________

Writing Complete Sentences

Because of Winn-Dixie
Grammar:
Complete Sentences

To change a sentence fragment to a complete sentence, first identify what information is missing. Then write a new sentence.

fragment	**complete sentence**
Gave us Ringo	The people who train guide dogs gave us Ringo.
My sister Anna	My sister Anna can't see very well.

Thinking Question
Does each sentence I write express a complete thought with a simple subject and a simple predicate?

1–8. Change each fragment to a complete sentence.

1. One day, my sister Anna.

____

2. She slowly.

____

3. In the doorway, Ringo.

____

4. Her dog for years.

____

5. Listened to the sounds outside the door.

____

6. A steady, light rain.

____

7. She lovingly.

____

8. The dog at her side.

____

Name ______________________ Date ____________

Contractions

Contractions with *not*	
We could not wait to see the puppies. They were not barking.	We couldn't wait to see the puppies. They weren't barking.

1–6. Write the contractions for the word or words in parentheses.

1. (did not) We ______________ want a cat.
2. (would not) Mom ______________ let us get a dog until we took a pet care class.
3. (cannot) Ben ______________ have certain pets because of his allergies.
4. (do not) Some dogs ______________ have long tails.
5. (have not) These dogs ______________ gone for a walk today.
6. (could not) We ______________ choose between the two puppies.

7–10. Look at the underlined contractions. Write each contraction correctly on the line. Then write the words that make up the contraction.

7. Scruffy isnt comfortable in his new home yet. ______________
8. He ha'snt been sleeping at night. ______________
9. Mom and Dad are'nt too happy about that. ______________
10. I wo'nt wake Scruffy up when he is napping. ______________

Name ______________________ Date ____________

Sentence Fluency

You can fix a fragment by combining it with a complete sentence or another fragment.

Sentence and Fragment	Complete Sentence
Becky's family moved to Milliston. In the middle of the summer.	Becky's family moved to Milliston in the middle of the summer.
Fragments	**Complete Sentence**
The town of Milliston. Has a lively youth center.	The town of Milliston has a lively youth center.

1–6. Rewrite each item to be one complete sentence with a subject and a predicate.

1. Becky was worried. About making new friends.

____

2. A flyer at the supermarket. Listed the youth center's summer events.

____

3. A girl on Becky's street. Invited Becky to a party at the center.

____

4. All of the other children welcomed Becky. To the neighborhood.

____

5. Although she was new in town. Becky felt right at home.

____

6. And a game of basketball outside. The children played tag.

____

Name ______________________ Date ____________

Focus Trait: Ideas
Using Vivid Details

A. Read each uninteresting sentence. Add vivid details to fill in the blanks and make each sentence more interesting.

Uninteresting Sentence	Sentence with Vivid Details
1. Some kittens slept in a box.	The ____________ kittens slept ____________ in a ____________ box.
2. After the kittens woke up, we watched them play.	After the kittens ____________ ____________, we watched them ____________.

B. Read each uninteresting sentence. Rewrite each sentence using vivid details.

Pair/Share **Work with a partner to brainstorm vivid details.**

Uninteresting Sentence	Sentence with Vivid Details
3. Winn-Dixie looked in the window.	
4. Miss Franny was scared.	
5. Winn-Dixie smiled at Miss Franny.	

Name ______________________ Date ____________

Author's Purpose

Read the selection below.

Sitting for Freedom

Rosa Parks was a brave woman who stood up for her rights and the rights of countless others in the 1950s. At a time when African Americans were not allowed to attend the same schools, drink out of the same water fountains, or eat at the same restaurants as white people, Mrs. Parks decided to fight discrimination and injustice.

In 1955, Mrs. Parks refused to give up her seat on a Montgomery, Alabama, bus to a white man. At the time, this was against the law. She was arrested and fined by police. Many people were so angry that she was arrested that they refused to ride the bus anymore. The bus company lost money, and the law was eventually changed.

Mrs. Parks stood behind her belief in equality and freedom for all. She inspired many people to work peacefully for civil rights. Her bravery helped transform a nation. The impact of her simple and powerful act is still felt today.

Though discrimination still exists, many people now realize the value of equality and how important it is to treat people with dignity and fairness.

Mrs. Parks remains a strong example of what it means to fight for your beliefs, stay true to who you are, and never give up.

Complete the Inference Map below to show text details that explain the author's purpose.

Text Detail	Text Detail	Text Detail

Purpose

Name ______________________________ Date ______________

Author's Purpose and Viewpoint

My Brother Martin
Comprehension:
Author's Purpose

Read the selection below.

A Movement of the People

The Civil Rights Movement has many famous heroes, including Martin Luther King, Jr. Yet it was powerful only because ordinary people showed courage and determination.

In the fall of 1957, nine brave teenagers risked great harm in order to enroll in a high school in Little Rock, Arkansas, that was attended only by white students.

In 1960, college students across the country sat at lunch counters to protest against unfair treatment of African Americans.

On March 7, 1965, whole families began marching in Selma, Alabama, to demand voting rights for African Americans. They faced conflict and violence. However, they did not give up because they believed in their right to vote.

Without brave citizens like these, the Civil Rights Movement would never have become so strong.

Analyze the selection to evaluate the author's viewpoint. Use an Inference Map like the one shown here to organize your thoughts. Then write your answers to the questions below.

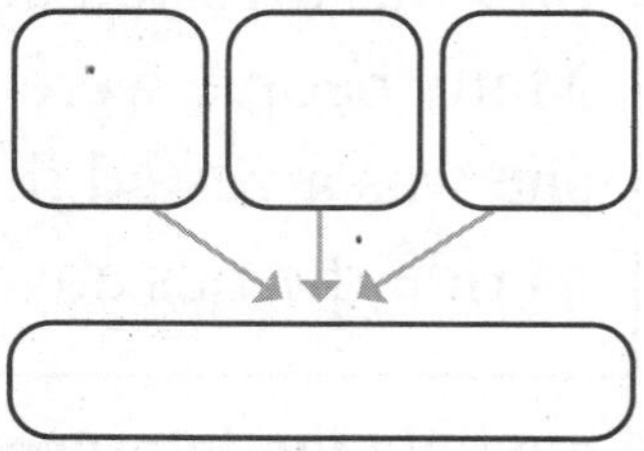

1. What is the author's viewpoint about the Civil Rights Movement?

____

____

2. How does the author support this viewpoint?

____

____

Name ______________________ Date ____________

Prefixes *in-*, *im-*, *il-*, and *ir-*

injustice irresponsible impolite insecure
illegal imperfect irreplaceable

Read each underlined word. Use the meaning of the prefix to help you understand the meaning of the word. Then complete the sentence in a way that makes sense.

1. I know I am irresponsible when I

____.

2. It is impolite to

____.

3. The law says it is illegal to

____.

4. I feel insecure when I

____.

5. The imperfect pair of pants had

____.

6. Losing something that is irreplaceable

____.

7. One example of an injustice is

____.

Name________________________ Date____________

Short *e* and Long *e*

Basic Write the Basic Word that best fits each clue.

1. inexpensive ____________
2. a desire for more than one needs ____________
3. a large animal ____________
4. direction where the sun sets ____________
5. shine brightly ____________
6. a small spot ____________
7. rising at a very sharp angle ____________
8. leader ____________
9. water in the form of a gas ____________
10. to think ____________
11. a place for books or other items ____________

Challenge 12–14. Write a paragraph about a place where you like to go to eat. Tell what you like about it. Use three Challenge Words. Write on a separate sheet of paper.

Spelling Words

1. west
2. steep
3. member
4. gleam
5. fresh
6. freedom
7. speed
8. steam
9. beast
10. believe
11. speck
12. kept
13. cheap
14. pretend
15. greed
16. shelf
17. least
18. eager
19. reason
20. chief

Challenge

echo
menu
creature
reveal
restaurant

Name ______________________ Date ____________

My Brother Martin
Spelling: Short *e* and Long *e*

Spelling Word Sort

Write each Basic Word beside the correct heading.

/ĕ/ spelled *e* followed by a consonant	Basic Words: Challenge Words: Possible Selection Words:
/ē/ spelled *ea*	Basic Words: Challenge Words: Possible Selection Words:
/ē/ spelled *ee*	Basic Words: Possible Selection Words:
Other spellings for /ē/	Basic Words:

Spelling Words

1. west
2. steep
3. member
4. gleam
5. fresh
6. freedom
7. speed
8. steam
9. beast
10. believe
11. speck
12. kept
13. cheap
14. pretend
15. greed
16. shelf
17. least
18. eager
19. reason
20. chief

Challenge

echo
menu
creature
reveal
restaurant

Challenge Add the Challenge Words to your Word Sort.

Connect to Reading Look through *My Brother Martin*. Find words that have /ĕ/ and /ē/. Add them to your Word Sort.

Name________________________________ Date____________

Lesson 2
PRACTICE BOOK

My Brother Martin
Spelling: Short *e* and Long *e*

Proofreading for Spelling

Find the misspelled words and circle them. Write them correctly on the lines below.

Many years ago, Africans were forced to come to the United States as slaves. They lived without fredom. Many people were against slavery. They, at leest, were eagre to spead change and worked hard to free slaves.

Slavery was abolished, but change was slow. When Dr. Martin Luther King, Jr. was a boy, his mother explained that she could no longer preten to beleeve that as a menber of the Atlanta community, she could eat at any restaurant in the city or stroll in the park and enjoy the freshh air. The reasen she gave was that some states still had unfair laws that kepp black people and white people separate.

Though Dr. King paid a steap price for working for equality, his contributions would offer a gleem of hope that change would come.

1. ____________________ 7. ____________________
2. ____________________ 8. ____________________
3. ____________________ 9. ____________________
4. ____________________ 10. ____________________
5. ____________________ 11. ____________________
6. ____________________ 12. ____________________

Spelling Words

1. west
2. steep
3. member
4. gleam
5. fresh
6. freedom
7. speed
8. steam
9. beast
10. believe
11. speck
12. kept
13. cheap
14. pretend
15. greed
16. shelf
17. least
18. eager
19. reason
20. chief

Challenge

echo
menu
creature
reveal
restaurant

Name ____________________ Date __________

Complete Subjects

Every sentence has a **subject** and a **predicate**. The subject tells whom or what the sentence is about. All the words in the subject make up the **complete subject**. A complete subject can be one word or several words.

complete subject
My older brother played the piano after dinner.
Music is awesome.

Thinking Question
Which words tell whom or what the sentence is about?

1–8. In each sentence, the simple subject, or main word in the subject, is underlined. Write the complete subject.

1. Each person in our family plays a musical instrument.

____

2. Ms. Louisa Arnold is our piano teacher.

____

3. This popular jazz song has difficult notes.

____

4. It is fun to play, though. ____________________

5. The talented pianist plays up and down the keyboard.

____

6. My two sisters try to imitate the finger movements.

____

7. The guitarist in our family is my mother.

____

8. She strums the strings of her electric guitar.

____

Name ______________________ Date __________

Lesson 2
PRACTICE BOOK

My Brother Martin
Grammar: Subjects and Predicates

Complete Predicates

The predicate of a sentence tells what the subject does or is. All the words in the predicate make up the complete predicate. A **complete predicate** can be one verb or it can include descriptive words.

complete predicate

Mr. Sanders's work takes him away from home.

Thinking Question
Which words tell what the subject does or is?

1–8. The simple predicate, or main verb, of each sentence is underlined. Write the complete predicate.

1. Mr. Sanders traveled to Sacramento for a business meeting.

____

2. The flight arrived exactly on time.

____

3. A taxi driver drove him to the hotel downtown.

____

4. My grandparents watched us for the week.

____

5. Our parents are away on business.

____

6. My grandfather told us some funny stories.

____

7. We all cooked dinner together.

____

8. We made spaghetti with meatballs, my favorite meal.

____

Name ______________________ Date ____________

Compound Subjects and Compound Predicates

When a sentence has two or more simple subjects, it has a **compound subject.** When a sentence has two or more simple predicates, it has a **compound predicate.**

compound subject

Men and women respected Martin Luther King, Jr.

compound predicate

People sang, marched, and prayed.

Thinking Question
What word is used to combine the compound subject? What word is used to combine the compound predicate?

1–4. Underline the compound subject.

1. Students and teachers at Wilson School listened to Dr. King's speech.
2. Martha and Nina had not heard it before.
3. African American men and women did not have rights.
4. Mothers, fathers, and grandparents were hopeful for their children.

5–8. Underline the compound predicate.

5. M.L. studied hard and graduated early.
6. In Boston, he met and married Coretta Scott.
7. Dr. King traveled and spoke all over America.
8. He won the Nobel Prize and used the money to fight for freedom.

Name ______________________ Date ____________

Contractions

A **contraction** is a short way to write two words. An **apostrophe** takes the place of a letter or letters in a contraction.

contractions

She will	she'll
has not	hasn't
I have	I've

1–4. Write the contraction of the underlined words on the line.

1. They will share their stories. ______________
2. Caitlin should have written a report. ______________
3. I am going to write about kindness. ______________
4. I will write a report about Dr. Martin Luther King Jr. ______________

5–8. Write the words that make up the underlined contraction on the line.

5. People said that they'd march in the streets. ______________
6. Rosa Parks wouldn't sit in the back of the bus. ______________
7. Dr. King thought that people shouldn't ride the bus anymore.

   ____

8. Every adult in America should've voted. ______________

Name ______________________ Date ____________

Sentence Fluency

Short, Choppy Sentences	Combined Sentence with a Compound Subject
Rudy grew up in Dallas. Her brothers grew up in Dallas.	Rudy and her brothers grew up in Dallas.

1–6. Combine the sentences by joining the subjects with the word *and* to form a compound subject. Write the new sentence on the line.

1. Trees surrounded our yard. Bushes surrounded our yard.

____

2. Mother played in a neighborhood band. Daddy played in a neighborhood band.

____

3. Marty practiced the piano after school. I practiced the piano after school.

____

4. My mother sang in the church choir. My Aunt Jo sang in the church choir.

____

5. Friends visited our house often. Relatives visited our house often.

____

6. Our parents protected us from harm. Our grandparents protected us from harm.

____

Name ____________________ Date ____________

Focus Trait: Word Choice

Words That Express Feelings

A. Read each sentence about the story. Look at the underlined words used to express feelings. Then rewrite the sentence using vivid words and details.

Poor Word Choice	Vivid Word Choice
1. M. L. and A. D. <u>did not like</u> learning to play the piano.	
2. Many people <u>cared</u> about equal rights.	

B. Read each sentence about the story. Rewrite it, using vivid words that capture the characters' feelings.

Pair/Share **Work with a partner to brainstorm vivid words for your sentences.**

3. M. L. wanted people to treat each other better.	
4. M. L. was a kind person.	
5. M. L. admired his father's actions.	

Name ______________________ Date ____________

Cause and Effect

Read the selection below.

On Second Thought

Zach was so excited when he heard about Michael's party that he couldn't wait to get home and tell his mom. When she asked what time the party was to start, Zach hesitated. "I don't know," he confessed. "He hasn't actually invited me yet."

The next few days at school, Michael never said a word. By Thursday, Zach decided to just ask him about the party. Michael stammered, "Well . . . uhh . . . I can't invite you, but I can't tell you why. I'm sorry."

Zach was crushed. The whole way home, he tried not to cry.

On Friday, Zach tried to avoid Michael. But Michael came up to him after lunch and asked, "Can I talk to you?" Zach smiled and nodded.

"I'm sorry about the party. I'd invited Chad, and I know he doesn't know you. But you're my friend, too, and I really want you there. Chad can come and get to know you if he wants to, right?" Michael said.

Zach agreed to go to the party, and he and Michael became friends again. Chad saw what a great guy Zach was, and they became friends, too!

Complete the T-Map to show the cause-and-effect relationships in the selection. Write complete sentences.

Cause	Effect
	Zach is excited and rushes home to tell his mom.
Michael tells Zach he can't invite him.	
	Zach tries to avoid Michael at school.
	Zach and Michael become friends again.

Name ______________________ Date ____________

Cause and Effect

Read the story below.

Big Sis

Jasmine hated taking her little brother with her everywhere. Amiel was embarrassing. He danced in public for no reason. He sang, too. He said whatever came into his head. She didn't want to be a responsible big sister every minute of every day, but she had no choice.

"Amiel, wake up!" said Jasmine, tugging her little brother's arm. "Don't stand here daydreaming. We've got to get to the bus stop!"

"Okay," chirped Amiel. He began to dance in place. "Let's go, Jasmine, let's go: cha, cha. Let's go..."

"Stop that!" ordered Jasmine. "Let's go!" She started to pull Amiel across the street. Suddenly Amiel stopped dancing and pulled her back onto the curb, just as a truck whizzed by.

Amiel looked up at Jasmine, his little face quiet and his eyes serious. He exhaled deeply. Then he said, "Okay. *Now*, let's go!"

Jasmine stood frozen with shock for a moment. She could still feel the whoosh of the truck that had plowed past. Then she threw her arms around her brother. "Oh, Amiel!" she cried. "I'll never rush you again!"

Use a T-Map like the one shown here to organize cause-and-effect relationships in the story. Then answer the questions below.

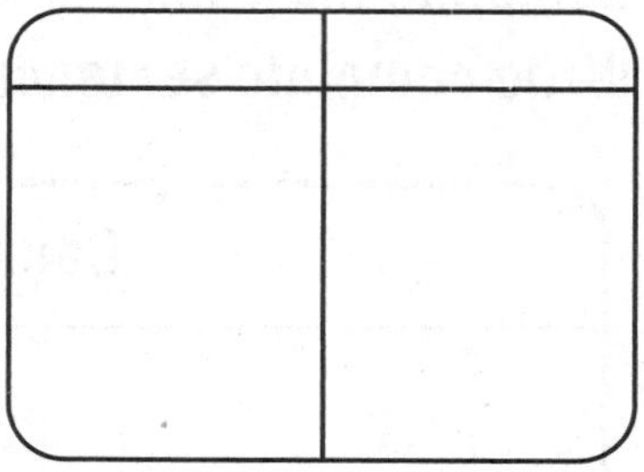

1. How do you think Jasmine feels in the first part of the story? What event(s) cause her to feel this way?

____

____

2. Explain why Jasmine throws her arms around Amiel at the end of the story. Is her action a cause or an effect?

____

____

Name ____________________ Date __________

Using Context

energetic	generous	relative	grateful
homesick	negative	thoughtful	

Complete each sentence with a word from above. Use context clues to help you.

1. While on vacation, I was __________ and missed my friends.
2. The man was __________ a passenger on his train had found his wallet.
3. The boy was being __________ when he brought his mom breakfast in bed.
4. Another name for your uncle is your __________ .
5. When I get out my dog's leash to go for a walk, he gets very __________ and wags his tail.
6. I received a __________ gift from my sister.
7. Tripping and falling in the mud on my way to school was a __________ experience.

Name ______________________ Date ____________

Short *i* and Long *i*

Basic **Read the paragraph. Write the Basic Word that best replaces the underlined word or words in the sentences.**

As I walk through the zoo, I (1) repeat to myself to visit the new monkey house. It is made of glass and red hard clay block. There was a damp (3) coolness in the old monkey house. Now the monkeys (4) reside in a comfortable environment. There is a (5) trench between the trees and the glass that separates visitors from the monkeys. As I stand outside the glass, I give a (6) loud breath when I don't see any monkeys. I am about to (7) conclude that the monkeys are not in their new home yet, when I look up in the trees. The monkeys look down at me, and I smile with (8) happiness. I can't wait to tell my family about my zoo visit when we have dinner (9) this evening.

1. ______________ 6. ______________
2. ______________ 7. ______________
3. ______________ 8. ______________
4. ______________ 9. ______________
5. ______________

Challenge 10–12. **Write some rules that visitors to a zoo might need to follow. Use three of the Challenge Words. Write on a separate sheet of paper.**

Spelling Words

1. skill
2. crime
3. grind
4. tonight
5. brick
6. flight
7. live
8. chill
9. delight
10. build
11. ditch
12. decide
13. witness
14. wind
15. district
16. inch
17. sigh
18. fright
19. remind
20. split

Challenge

ignorant
recognize
advice
twilight
rigid

Name ______________________ Date ____________

Spelling Word Sort

Write each Basic Word beside the correct heading.

/ ĭ / spelled *i* followed by a consonant	**Basic Words:** **Challenge Words:** **Possible Selection Words:**
/ ĭ / spelled *ui*	**Basic Words:**
/ ī / spelled *i*-consonant-*e*	**Basic Words:** **Challenge Words:**
/ ī / spelled *igh*	**Basic Words:** **Challenge Words:** **Possible Selection Words:**
/ ī / spelled *i* followed by a consonant	**Basic Words:**
can be pronounced / ĭ / or / ī /	**Basic Words:**

Spelling Words

1. skill
2. crime
3. grind
4. tonight
5. brick
6. flight
7. live
8. chill
9. delight
10. build
11. ditch
12. decide
13. witness
14. wind
15. district
16. inch
17. sigh
18. fright
19. remind
20. split

Challenge

ignorant
recognize
advice
twilight
rigid

Challenge Add the Challenge Words to your Word Sort.

Connect to Reading Look through *How Tía Lola Came to Stay.* Find words that have / ĭ / and / ī /. Add them to your Word Sort.

Name ______________________ Date __________

Proofreading for Spelling

Find the misspelled words and circle them. Write them correctly on the lines below.

Miguel had fun visiting his friend in New York, but he almost missed the fligt back home to Vermont; the wend blew the ticket out of his hand and he had to chase it. On the drive home from the airport, his mother told him that there is an unsolved crimme in town. Someone damaged the brik wall by the entrance to the school districk office. Workers are going to bild the wall again. Becky, Miguel's neighbor, said she was a witniss to what happened, but she hadn't named who did it.

When Becky finally talked, she gave everyone a frite. She said her car slid on the ice and came within an inche of going in a detch. Instead, she had to grinde against the steering wheel, and her car hit the wall. We're glad Becky wasn't hurt, and Becky learned that driving is a skil.

1. ______________
2. ______________
3. ______________
4. ______________
5. ______________
6. ______________
7. ______________
8. ______________
9. ______________
10. ______________
11. ______________
12. ______________

Spelling Words

1. skill
2. crime
3. grind
4. tonight
5. brick
6. flight
7. live
8. chill
9. delight
10. build
11. ditch
12. decide
13. witness
14. wind
15. district
16. inch
17. sigh
18. fright
19. remind
20. split

Challenge

ignorant
recognize
advice
twilight
rigid

Name ______________________ Date ____________

Declarative and Interrogative Sentences

A sentence that makes a statement is a **declarative sentence**. It ends with a period. A sentence that asks a question is an **interrogative sentence**. It ends with a question mark. Every sentence begins with a capital letter.

declarative sentence	**interrogative sentence**
The skies are gray and cloudy.	Do you think it will snow?

Thinking Question
Does the sentence make a statement? Does the sentence ask a question?

1–10. Add the correct end mark. Write *declarative* or *interrogative*.

1. Did you hear the weather forecast ________________
2. My aunt Rita says that she can smell snow in the air ________________
3. It looks like snow to me, too ________________
4. How many inches of snow will we get ________________
5. I think I see a few snowflakes ________________
6. The temperature is dropping quickly ________________
7. Where is the snow shovel ________________
8. The snow is piling up on the sidewalks ________________
9. Do you want to help me build a snowman ________________
10. Can you find an old scarf and hat for our snowman ________________

Name ____________________ Date __________

Imperative and Exclamatory Sentences

A sentence that gives a command is an **imperative sentence**. It ends with a period. A sentence that shows strong feeling is an **exclamatory sentence**. It ends with an exclamation point.

imperative sentence	**exclamatory sentence**
Be polite to Aunt Susan.	How important good manners are!

Thinking Question
Does the sentence give a command? Does the sentence show strong feeling?

1–10. Add the correct end mark. Write *imperative* or *exclamatory*.

1. I can't wait for Aunt Sue to get here ______________
2. What a wonderful babysitter she is ______________
3. Set the table for dinner ______________
4. Use the word *please* when asking for something ______________
5. Put your dishes in the sink after you finish eating ______________
6. How yummy this ice cream is ______________
7. Come into the den to watch a movie ______________
8. How funny that movie was ______________
9. Get ready for bed now ______________
10. I don't want to go to bed yet ______________

Name ______________________ Date ____________

Kinds of Sentences

A **declarative sentence** makes a statement and ends with a period. An **interrogative sentence** asks a question and ends with a question mark. An **imperative sentence** gives a command and ends with a period. An **exclamatory sentence** shows strong feeling and ends with an exclamation point.

There is a lot of traffic on this road.
Did you look both ways before crossing?
Be careful at this corner.
There should be a crossing guard here!

Thinking Question
What is the purpose of the sentence? What punctuation should be used?

1–10. Add the correct end mark. Write *declarative*, *interrogative*, *imperative*, or *exclamatory* on the line.

1. Play some music ______________
2. What was the name of that song ______________
3. Bring me my maracas, please ______________
4. She is an excellent singer ______________
5. I wish I could sing well ______________
6. That was a great concert ______________
7. Is anyone else hungry for dinner ______________
8. Go somewhere nice to celebrate ______________
9. Do you like Mexican food ______________
10. I love all kinds of food ______________

Name ______________________ Date ____________

Contractions

Two Words	Contraction
I am already homesick.	**I'm** already homesick.
We are going away for the entire summer.	**We're** going away for the entire summer.
You will have a great time.	**You'll** have a great time.

1–5. Write the contractions for the underlined words.

1. You are going to miss summer baseball. ____________
2. I have heard that summers are hot in the islands. ____________
3. My grandmother said it is hot and humid every day. ____________
4. Mom said we will be close to the beach. ____________
5. She is looking forward to being with my grandparents. ____________

6–10. This note has five mistakes in the use of contractions. Underline the mistakes and write the contractions correctly on the line below.

Hi Cody,

Iv'e been on the island for a week, and I'm having a great time. My cousins are so cool. Theyr'e baseball nuts, like you and me. W'eve bought tickets to a baseball game. I can e-mail you some pictures. Your'e going to laugh when you see me in the straw hat. Its going to be a great summer after all.

Bye for now,
David

____

Name ______________________________ Date ____________

Sentence Fluency

Statements	Varying Sentence Types
My mom makes great burritos. They are delicious. I am learning how to make burritos myself. You can come over and try them.	My mom makes great burritos. How delicious they are! Can you believe I am learning to make burritos myself? Come over and try them.

Activity Change each underlined statement to a question, a command, or an exclamation. The word in parentheses ( ) tells you which kind of sentence to write. Write the sentences on the lines.

A good meal and a good deed can go together. (question) You can come to our annual Friends and Family Picnic at the King School. (command) Last year we raised more than two hundred dollars for our town's food bank. We all had a delicious meal. (exclamation)

This year we are raising money for hurricane victims in the Dominican Republic. This is a great chance to help others. (exclamation) Come share your family traditions and foods. You can share one of your special recipes for others to try. (command)

You can join us on June 15. (question)

1. ____
2. ____
3. ____
4. ____
5. ____
6. ____

Name ______________________ Date ______________

How Tía Lola Came to Stay
Writing: Write to Express

Focus Trait: Voice

Natural Speech

Weak Dialogue	Natural Speech
"The weather is very cold."	"Brr, it's cold outside!"

A. Read each line of dialogue. Rewrite the underlined phrases to make them sound more natural.

1. "Dress warmly because there is a great deal of snow outside."	"__________ because there is a ________ of snow outside."
2. "Would you like to go inside and have a cup of cocoa?"	"______ go inside and ______________."

B. Read each line of dialogue. Rewrite it to make it sound more natural.

Pair/Share **Work with a partner to brainstorm words for your dialogue.**

3. "I am happy with the way our snowman looks."	
4. "I want to go sledding tomorrow if there is still snow on the ground."	
5. "It would be nice to invite some other people to come with us."	

Name ______________________ Date ____________

Theme

Read the selection below.

Best Friends

David sat by the living room window wishing he could go outside. He had been sick all week, and he was tired of his fever and stuffy nose.

He wondered what his friends Ahmed and Liam were doing. They had speaking parts in the school's Autumn Leaf Festival. Ahmed was going to be an oak leaf, and Liam was playing a maple leaf.

"I should be playing my trumpet in the band," David told his mother. "This is the best festival of the year!"

Three blocks away, the festival was about to begin. David could hear the bass drum thumping away. He was missing all the fun!

"Don't be sad," his mother said with a wink. "There might be a surprise for you right around the corner."

Three blocks away, David's friends were making their own plan. It included David and required the mayor's permission. The mayor said yes!

After the parade marched around the town square, the marchers took a detour. They marched right by David's house. He saw his two best friends waving at him.

Ahmed and Liam are awesome friends, thought David.

Fill in the Inference Map to show how setting, characters, and characters' actions help you identify the theme of the selection.

Setting

Characters

Characters' Actions

Theme:

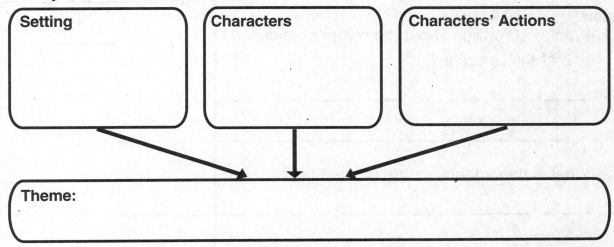

Name ______________________ Date ____________

Theme

Read the selection below.

The Lot

We have two baseball teams, the *Hawks* and the *Ravens*. In the summer, we play every day except Sundays. After we trampled Mrs. Norbert's garden, though, we had to find a new place to play. The empty lot at the corner of Oak Street seemed like the perfect spot.

For four days, we worked from morning until night. We cleaned up the junk and cut the grass. On the second day, a man stopped by and watched us from his truck. On the fifth day, he walked over to talk to us.

"I own this lot," he said, "and I don't remember giving you permission to use it."

"Sorry, Sir," said Neil, "we thought no one would care if we played here."

"Well, I do care. I think you should all go home now," the man said.

The next day, there was a dump truck and a steamroller at the lot. A week later there was grass, a baseball diamond, and a fence! The owner of the lot called us over to him.

"You kids helped me decide what to do with this place," he said. "You're welcome to play here as much as you want IF you promise to take care of the lot."

Complete an Inference Map like the one shown here to help you figure out the theme of the selection. Then answer the questions below.

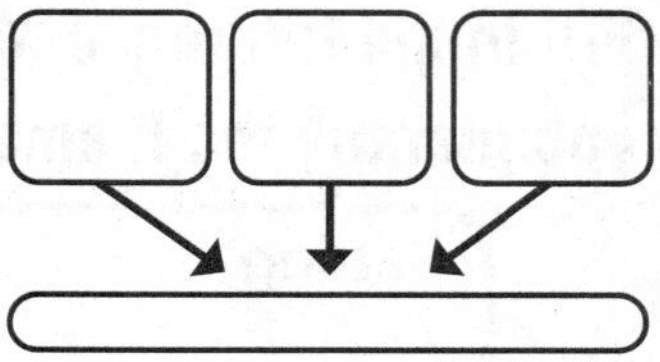

1. What is surprising about the owner's actions at the end of the selection?

____

____

2. What is the author's theme or message?

____

Name ______________________ Date ____________

Prefixes *non-* and *mis-*

misplace	mistreat	nonfiction
misspelled	misjudged	nonsense
misunderstood	nonbeliever	nonstop

Complete each phrase to make a complete sentence. In items 1–7, use your own words to complete the sentences in a way that makes sense. In items 8–9, choose a word from the box to complete the sentences.

1. To make sure I don't turn in an assignment with misspelled words, I ______________________.
2. I am a nonbeliever in ______________________.
3. If I misunderstood what was said, I ______________________.
4. The most important thing I have ever misplaced was my ______________________.
5. When you mistreat your belongings, they ______________________.
6. My favorite nonfiction book is ______________________.
7. One time I misjudged ______________________.
8. My sister Tina talks ______________ on her phone with friends from school.
9. My dad thinks that buying a new school bag every year is ______________.

Name ______________________ Date ____________

Short *o* and Long *o*

Basic **Write the Basic Word that completes each analogy.**

1. *Soup* is to *lunch* as ____________ is to *breakfast.*
2. *Typed* is to *e-mail* as ____________ is to *letter.*
3. *Shout* is to *yell* as *brag* is to ____________ .
4. *Near* is to *close* as *distant* is to ____________ .
5. *Normal* is to *usual* as *strange* is to ____________ .
6. *Lose* is to *lost* as ____________ is to *found.*
7. *Climb* is to *hill* as ____________ is to *problem.*
8. *Approve* is to *disapprove* as *praise* is to ____________ .
9. *Teacher* is to *students* as ____________ is to *guests.*
10. *Surf* is to *wave* as *ski* is to ____________ .

Challenge 11–14. **Write a paragraph about taking an ocean voyage to another country. Tell about your trip on the ocean. Use four of the Challenge Words. Write on a separate sheet of paper.**

Spelling Words

1. block
2. shown
3. oatmeal
4. wrote
5. fellow
6. scold
7. coast
8. odd
9. locate
10. slope
11. throat
12. host
13. online
14. shock
15. solve
16. known
17. remote
18. stock
19. boast
20. globe

Challenge

bonus
approach
motion
continent
accomplish

Name ______________________________ Date ____________

Spelling Word Sort

Write each Basic Word beside the correct heading.

/ŏ/ spelled *o* followed by a consonant	**Basic Words:** **Challenge Words:** **Possible Selection Words:**
/ō/ spelled *o*-consonant-*e*	**Basic Words:** **Possible Selection Words:**
/ō/ spelled *oa*	**Basic Words:** **Challenge Words:**
/ō/ spelled *ow*	**Basic Words:** **Possible Selection Words:**
/ō/ spelled *o* followed by a consonant	**Basic Words:** **Challenge Words:** **Possible Selection Words:**

Challenge Add the Challenge Words to your Word Sort.

Connect to Reading Look through *The Power of W.O.W.!* Find words that have /ŏ/ and /ō/. Add them to your Word Sort.

Spelling Words

1. block
2. shown
3. oatmeal
4. wrote
5. fellow
6. scold
7. coast
8. odd
9. locate
10. slope
11. throat
12. host
13. online
14. shock
15. solve
16. known
17. remote
18. stock
19. boast
20. globe

Challenge

bonus
approach
motion
continent
accomplish

Name ______________________ Date ____________

Proofreading for Spelling

Find the misspelled words and circle them. Write them correctly on the lines below.

People were in shok when they heard the news that Tim was involved in the disappearance of the ancient weaving from the local museum. Tim seemed like a nice enough feloe who was knowne and recognized by several of the volunteers at the gift shop. He wroat a silly note to enclose with the toy blok kit he bought for his nephew. He also tried to loccate a gloab for his niece, but there were none in stoc.

Tim did boaste about planning a trip to the coest of South America but said he had to postpone it because of a sore throte. Then he asked about the weavers' video shon during the day. Needless to say, the museum staff was surprised when the security video showed Tim taking the ancient weaving and then covering up with it while he took a nap in the back!

1. ______________ 7. ______________
2. ______________ 8. ______________
3. ______________ 9. ______________
4. ______________ 10. ______________
5. ______________ 11. ______________
6. ______________ 12. ______________

Spelling Words

1. block
2. shown
3. oatmeal
4. wrote
5. fellow
6. scold
7. coast
8. odd
9. locate
10. slope
11. throat
12. host
13. online
14. shock
15. solve
16. known
17. remote
18. stock
19. boast
20. globe

Challenge

bonus
approach
motion
continent
accomplish

Name ______________________ Date ____________

Simple and Compound Sentences

A **simple sentence** has one complete thought. It has a subject that tells who or what the sentence is about. It has a verb that tells what the subject does.

subject **verb**
Markos <u>plays</u> baseball.

A **compound sentence** has two or more complete thoughts joined together. The separate ideas can be joined with a comma (,) and a conjunction.

Mother <u>felt</u> happy**, so** she <u>sang</u> a song.

Thinking Question
What will you always find in a simple sentence? What will you always find in a compound sentence?

1–6. Write *S* on the line if it is a simple sentence. Write *C* on the line if it is a compound sentence.

1. ___ Ana and Bruce ate eggs and drank milk for breakfast.
2. ___ My baby sister was tired, so she took a nap.
3. ___ I like baseball, but my brother likes basketball.
4. ___ I want to go swimming and hiking today.
5. ___ Mom cheers for the Packers, but Dad prefers the Bears.
6. ___ Lee spread butter and jelly on his biscuit.

Name _______________________ Date ___________

Subject and Verb Agreement

Agreement means that the sentence parts match. The subject of a sentence must match the verb. A **singular** subject needs a singular verb. **Plural** subjects need a plural verb.

singular subject and **singular verb**
Daisy plays the violin.

plural subject and **plural verb**
Chip and Tim play guitars.

Thinking Question
What kind of verb agrees with a singular subject? What kind of subject agrees with a plural verb?

1–8. Circle the correct verb or verbs in each sentence.

1. Andy and Brian (is, are) going to the movies.
2. Mom and Dad (was, were) at Grandmother's all day.
3. Sammy (enjoy, enjoys) baking cookies for her friends.
4. My friends really (like, likes) to eat my cookies!
5. Mary and I (work, works) at the food pantry every Saturday.
6. Sylvia and her cousins, Jude and Hugh, (is, are) lifeguards.
7. Dori (think, thinks) that we should (collect, collects) food for the homeless.
8. "I (agrees, agree)," said Mr. Jackson, "and Miss Brown (do, does), too."

Name ______________________________ Date ____________

Combining Simple Sentences

Try these methods to combine short, choppy sentences or to fix run-on sentences.
1. Combine the subjects.
2. Combine the verbs.
3. Connect the ideas with a comma (,) and a conjunction such as *or*, *for*, *and*, *nor*, *but*, *yet*, or *so*.

poor sentences
June likes to sing. June draws well.
June likes to sing June draws well.

compound sentences
June likes to sing, and she also draws well.

Thinking Question
What punctuation is used to combine the simple sentences? What conjunction is used to combine the simple sentences?

1–5. Rewrite each sentence to avoid short, choppy sentences and run-on sentences.

1. Carla put on her skates. Carla skated across the pond.

____

2. Jen is collecting food for the food bank.
Fran is collecting food for the food bank.

____

3. Jen collects food for the food bank.
She helps people.

____

4. Nathan and Aaron are taller than Ed.
Nathan and Aaron are not as tall as Jim.

____

5. I slept for two hours. I am still tired.

____

Name ______________________ Date __________

Making Comparisons

You can use different forms of adjectives to compare two or more people, places, or things. To compare two things, add *-er* to an adjective. To compare three or more things, add *-est* to an adjective.

Compare two things: Granite is **harder** than chalk.
Compare three or more things: Diamonds are the **hardest** gemstone of all.

However, some adjectives with two syllables, and all adjectives with more than two syllables use *more* or *most* instead of *-er* or *-est*. All adjectives use *less* or *least*.

Compare two things: I think social studies is **more interesting** than English.

I think subtraction is **less difficult** than multiplication.
Compare three or more things: I think math is the **most interesting** subject in school.

I think addition is the **least difficult** of all.

1–8. Complete each sentence by writing the correct form of the adjective shown in parentheses.

1. An elephant is ______________ than a mouse. (large)
2. This dress is the ______________ one in the store. (beautiful)
3. Jenny didn't spill her water because she was ______________ than her sister. (careful)
4. Bill is the ______________ student in class. (tall)
5. I didn't have much money, so I bought the ______________ item on the menu. (expensive)
6. A feather is ______________ than a stone. (light)
7. Ahmed was the ______________ runner at the track meet. (fast)
8. Traffic is ______________ in the country than in the city. (heavy)

Name ______________________ Date ____________

Sentence Fluency

Two Sentences with the Same Subject	Sentences Combined Using a Comma and a Conjunction
Dora got on her bike. Dora rode her bike down the street.	Dora got on her bike, <u>and</u> she rode down the street.

1–5. Combine each pair of simple sentences using a comma and a conjunction.

1. Next month is my tenth birthday. I can't wait to get an allowance.

____

2. Olivia was sick today. We brought her books to her after school.

____

3. Every year our class does a project to help the community. This year will not be different.

____

____

4. Gary called his friends. They were at football practice.

____

5. Dad had to cook dinner. Bridget watched her little sister.

____

Name ______________________ Date ____________

Lesson 4
PRACTICE BOOK

The Power of W.O.W.!
Writing: Write to Express

Focus Trait: Ideas

Why Events and Actions Happen

Good writers tell or hint at why events happen and why characters act the way they do. The plot helps direct the actions of the characters. A plot has a beginning, middle, and end.

Plot Event or Action	Reason Why
The Words on Wheels program is in its last week.	The library has no more money to pay for gas and buy books.

Read each event or action from *The Power of W.O.W.!* Then give the reason why it happened.

Plot Event or Action	Reason Why
1. Ileana, Shane, and Jason decide to have a car wash.	
2. Ileana does not accept a donation from her uncle, Mr. Diaz.	
3. A television news van comes to the car wash.	
4. The car wash becomes busier and the kids begin making more money.	

Name ______________________ Date ____________

Understanding Characters

Read the selection below.

The Helper

The Star family is a group of ordinary people with an ordinary life. Dad works at a store, and Mom works in an office. Bea and Arno go to school. CeeCee, their dog, stays at home. When she hears a Star at the door, she races over to say hello.

Everyone has chores to do at home. CeeCee's job is to pick up her toys and put them in a basket when told to "pick up."

On Friday, the family hurried home to get ready for a camping trip. Everyone rushed around getting packed. Clothes were stuffed into duffels. Dirty clothes were thrown at the hamper, but some missed.

Mom ordered carryout food for supper, but everyone forgot about CeeCee. She had to make a "CLANG" with her dish to get her food.

At last, it was time for bed.

"CeeCee, pick up," said Dad, as he turned off the lights.

The next morning no one could find his or her shoes, keys, purses, or duffels. They looked everywhere.

"Where's my stuff?" whined Bea.

"Ha!" laughed Dad. "Look at the dog's basket!"

CeeCee had picked up all the things they had left around and put them in her basket. She glanced over from where she lay in front of the door, her leash in her mouth.

"Good girl!" said Dad. "Now let's go camping."

Fill in the Column Chart to tell about CeeCee. Then answer the question below.

Thoughts and Feelings	Actions	Relationships with Others

Why did CeeCee put the family's things in her basket?

____

Understanding Characters

Read the selection below.

The Brothers

Marty and Mikey are twin brothers. They look alike and they sound alike. In every other way, however, they are not alike at all.

Marty is a vegetarian, but Mikey eats meat. Marty drinks nonfat milk and eats nonfat ice cream. Mikey drinks whole milk and hates nonfat ice cream.

Marty wakes up every day at 7:00 A.M., even if he stays up late. Mikey goes to bed early, or he will sleep until 9:00 A.M.

Marty talks nonstop. Mikey waits until his brother finishes talking, so he doesn't get to say a lot.

With all of these differences, the twins have never been able to fool family or close friends for long. Then one Friday night, Marty had a plan to confuse their new sitter. One twin kept the sitter busy all night. He complained that his carrots were not crunchy enough and asked a million questions about a show they were watching. The other twin left his vegetables on his plate and went to bed right after dinner.

When the parents came home, they asked the sitter how the night went.

"Well, thanks for the tips! That Mikey is a good sport," she laughed. "I have a feeling he may be extra tired in the morning."

Fill in a Column Chart like the one shown here to describe either Marty or Mikey. Then answer the questions below.

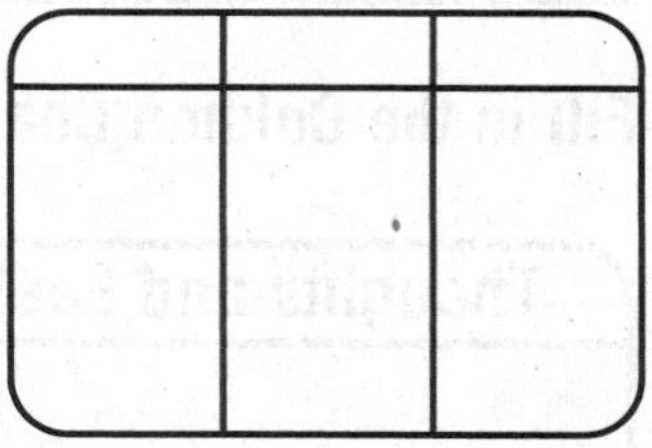

1. Which twin probably kept the sitter busy all night? Support your answer with text details.

____

____

2. Do you think the sitter was correct about who was who? Explain why you think so.

____

Name ______________________ Date __________

Use a Dictionary

dispose, *v.* to throw away
harbor, *n.* a sheltered body of water where ships can anchor safely
mineral, *n.* a natural substance, such as diamonds or coal, that is not plant or animal
mine, *v.* to dig a tunnel or hole in order to find minerals
valuable, *adj.* worth a lot of money

1–4. Choose a word from the sample dictionary entries above to complete each sentence.

1. When silver was discovered in Colorado, thousands of people went West to ______________ for it and get rich.
2. Like gold, silver is rare, so even a little bit is ______________ .
3. If the silver is buried deep, miners must move a lot of earth and ______________ of it safely.
4. Silver is just one important ______________ . Others include coal, iron, and copper.

5–7. Use the given word in a sentence. You may use a dictionary to check the word meanings.

5. errand

____

6. popular

____

7. trampled

____

Name ______________________ Date ____________

Homophones

Stormalong
Spelling: Homophones

Basic Write the Basic Word that best completes each sentence.

1. I cannot ______________ for my grandmother's birthday party.
2. We are going to celebrate in two ______________ with a picnic.
3. I hope that my sprained ankle will ______________ by then.
4. Organizing the party has been a real ______________.
5. People have ______________ gifts from all over the country.
6. I ______________ that my uncle is buying a piñata.
7. I asked my grandmother not to ______________ at the presents in the closet.
8. I bought Grandmother a spinning weather ______________.
9. She can put it on the ______________ of the roof.
10. Most of the guests will be adults. I will be the only ______________.

Challenge 11–14. Write a short article for your school about holding a book sale to help get money for new school playground equipment. Use four Challenge Words. Write on a separate sheet of paper.

Spelling Words

1. wait
2. weight
3. heard
4. herd
5. days
6. daze
7. heel
8. heal
9. peak
10. peek
11. sent
12. cent
13. scent
14. feet
15. feat
16. vain
17. vane
18. vein
19. miner
20. minor

Challenge

raise
raze
rays
principal
principle

Name ________________________ Date ____________

Lesson 5
PRACTICE BOOK

Stormalong
Spelling: Homophones

Spelling Word Sort

Write each Basic Word beside the correct heading.

/ā/ sound	**Basic Words:** **Challenge Words:** **Possible Selection Words:**
/ĕ/ sound	**Basic Words:**
/ē/ sound	**Basic Words:** **Possible Selection Words:**
/ī/ sound	**Basic Words:**
Other homophones	**Basic Words:** **Challenge Words:** **Possible Selection Words:**

Spelling Words

1. wait
2. weight
3. heard
4. herd
5. days
6. daze
7. heel
8. heal
9. peak
10. peek
11. sent
12. cent
13. scent
14. feet
15. feat
16. vain
17. vane
18. vein
19. miner
20. minor

Challenge

raise
raze
rays
principal
principle

Challenge Add the Challenge Words to your Word Sort.

Connect to Reading Look through *Stormalong*. Find words that sound alike but have different spellings and meanings. Add them to your Word Sort.

Name ______________________ Date ____________

Proofreading for Spelling

Find the misspelled words and circle them. Write them correctly on the lines below.

To swim with manatees, you need a guide and snorkeling gear, including fins for your feete that fit your hele comfortably. You might feel like a minar in all of the gear, but the gear is necessary. Sometimes your search for manatees is in vian and all you experience is the secnt of the sea, but often you can get a piek at the giant sea cows moving slowly through the water if you wate long enough. You'll find you can stop on a cint when you see a manatee, and you can be so excited you'll feel like a vien might pop. Swimming with a hurd of manatees can put you in a daiz. A manatee's wieght can reach 3,000 pounds, and it can be 13 feet long. If you ever get to swim with these gentle giants, you will be very lucky!

1. ______________ 7. ______________
2. ______________ 8. ______________
3. ______________ 9. ______________
4. ______________ 10. ______________
5. ______________ 11. ______________
6. ______________ 12. ______________

Spelling Words

1. wait
2. weight
3. heard
4. herd
5. days
6. daze
7. heel
8. heal
9. peak
10. peek
11. sent
12. cent
13. scent
14. feet
15. feat
16. vain
17. vane
18. vein
19. miner
20. minor

Challenge

raise
raze
rays
principal
principle

Nouns

A **noun** is a word that names a person, place, or thing. A **common noun** names any person, place, or thing. A **proper noun** names a particular person, place, or thing. Capitalize proper nouns.

common noun: man
proper noun: David Smith

Thinking Question
Does the word name a person, place, or thing?

1–6. Write the nouns in each sentence, and tell whether each is common or proper.

1. Life at sea can be adventurous.

   ____

2. The sailors called the dog Sharkey because he loved dangerous activities. ____________________

   ____

3. The name of the ship is *Clipper*. ____________________

   ____

4. *Clipper* sailed to Europe, China, and Australia.

   ____

   ____

5. Every morning the crew hoisted the anchor.

   ____

6. Captain Jones safely sailed the ship through Hurricane Alice and returned to London. ____________________

   ____

Name _______________ Date _______________

Singular and Plural Nouns

A **plural noun** names more than one person, place, or thing. How do you make a noun plural?

Add –*s*	**Add –*es***
ship, ships	bush, bushes
key, keys	fox, foxes

Change *y* to *i*, add –*es*	**Change *f* to *v*, add –*es***
city, cities	self, selves

The **waves** came up over the side of the boat.

Thinking Question
Does the noun in the sentence name more than one person, place, or thing?

1–5. Write the plural form of each noun.

1. storm _______________
2. wave _______________
3. day _______________
4. lady _______________
5. leaf _______________

6–10. Write the plural form of the noun in parentheses to complete each sentence.

6. (sailor) All the _______________ work to keep the ship in top shape.
7. (duty) Every sailor has many _______________ to perform.
8. (table) The sailors eat at _______________ nailed to the floor.
9. (boy) Some of the crew started working on a ship when they were young _______________.
10. (wave) Sailing over the high _______________ can make you feel sick.

Name ______________________________ Date ____________

Irregular Plural Nouns

Some nouns have special plural forms. These words do not follow a spelling pattern. You must remember the singular and plural form of irregular nouns.

There is a family of **geese** swimming in the lake. Tiny **mice** search through the tall grass along the bank looking for food.

Thinking Question
Does the noun have a special plural form?

1–4. Write the plural form of each noun.

1. woman ________________ **3.** deer ________________

2. child ________________ **4.** tooth ________________

5–10. Write the plural form of the noun in parentheses to complete each sentence.

5. (foot) Alfred Bulltop Stormalong was eighteen ______________ tall when he was just a baby.

6. (person) After the baby drank barrels and barrels of milk, it took ten ________________ to pat him on the back.

7. (child) Stormalong was much taller than all the other ________________ his age.

8. (tooth) He probably used a giant toothbrush to brush his ______________ .

9. (foot) His ______________ must have been enormous!

10. (potato) When Stormy left his life as a sailor, he became a farmer and grew ______________ .

Name ______________________________ Date ____________

Writing Quotations

Capitalize the first word of a quotation. If a quotation comes at the end of the sentence, place a comma and a space before the first quotation mark. Place end punctuation before the last quotation mark.

Jesse said, "Would you like to hear the conversation I wrote between a young manatee, a sea turtle, and a squid?"

Rosalie said, "Please read it to me."

1–6. Write these sentences correctly. Add commas, capital letters, end marks, and quotation marks where they are needed.

1. Manatee said, "this rope is not that tasty"

   ____

2. Sea Turtle asked, Why are you chewing on it then?

   ____

3. Manatee replied "well, I'll chew on anything that floats by."

   ____

4. Sea Turtle said Here is our friend Squid.

   ____

5. Manatee asked "can you help me grab that plant"

   ____

6. Squid exclaimed sure! I bet it tastes better than that rope.

   ____

Name ______________________ Date __________

Word Choice

Less Exact Nouns	More Exact Nouns
The boys signed up for a tour of the river.	The campers signed up for a tour of Rainbow River.

1–8. Rewrite each sentence. Change the underlined words to exact nouns.

1. This summer, some children and I are going to sailing camp.

____

2. We are looking forward to many exciting things.

____

3. Sailing a boat through water is a real challenge.

____

4. The early morning air can be chilly, so everyone wears warm clothes.

____

5. From time to time, someone spots animals in the open water.

____

6. One morning, a boy sees a dolphin and her calf swimming nearby.

____

7. It takes a lot of work to sail a boat.

____

8. At noontime, we catch a strong wind and speed toward shore.

____

Name ______________________ Date ____________

Focus Trait: Organization

Beginning a Story

A. Identify the character and setting in the story opening. Then make a prediction about what the story problem might be.

1. Sui Li crept down the stairs. She opened the cellar door and stepped in. She smelled dust and dampness. Her flashlight gave off light. The door shut behind her.

Character: ______________________

Setting: ______________________

Story Problem: ______________________

B. Read each story opening. Then write sentences to introduce a story problem.

2. The waves slapped against the side of the sailboat, harder and harder. Tom's father said, "Look at how dark the sky is getting!".

____

____

____

3. The cave seemed miles wide. Amber stared in amazement at the strange rock formations.

____

____

____

4. James looked up and down the empty street. He called out into the silence, "Is anybody there?"

____

____

____

Name ____________________ Date ____________

Compare and Contrast

Read the selection below.

Lesson Learned

Princess Maria was kind, friendly, and very smart. Her sister, Princess Bella, was beautiful and popular. Since she was not very nice to Maria, they didn't always get along well.

As the Winter Wonder Ball approached, Maria realized that she didn't have a ride to the ball. Her sister had a fancy sports car, but Maria knew she wouldn't let her drive it.

On the other hand, Bella didn't have a gown to wear, and she knew that Maria knew how to sew. In fact, she was making her own gown.

Bella was too proud to wear a handmade dress, but all the fanciest stores had no dresses left.

Bella had no choice but to ask her sister for help. Kind Maria agreed to make her sister's dress. When she finished, Bella couldn't believe how beautiful the gown was.

Bella hugged her sister and thanked her. She apologized for not being very nice in the beginning, and she even drove Maria to the ball.

Both sisters looked fabulous! They were the prettiest girls at the ball, and they had a wonderful time. Most importantly, they were glad that they learned to work together!

Complete the Venn Diagram to compare and contrast the two princesses and infer what they learned.

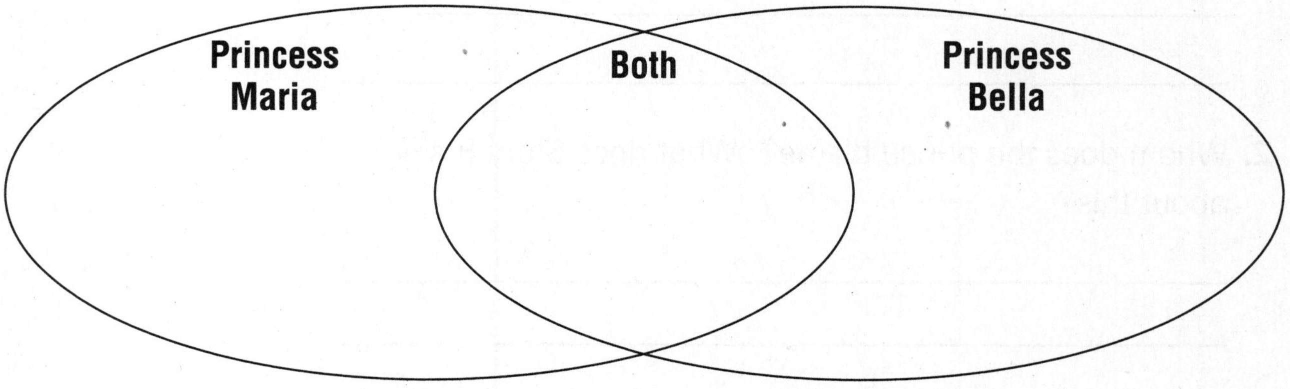

Name ______________________________ Date ____________

Compare and Contrast

Read the selections below.

How It Happened

Story A

You may be wondering how I came to be sitting here on this rock, croaking like a frog. Well, I was minding my own business and fishing when I Iooked up and saw an ugly witch fall head first in the pond. She called for help, and when I cleared my throat to keep from laughing she turned me into a frog!

What an ill-tempered witch!

Story B

You may be wondering how the prince came to such a poor end. Well, I was gathering herbs for the sick when I tripped over his fishing rod and fell in the pond. As I spluttered and splashed and almost drowned, he simply snorted and croaked with laughter. The more he snorted and croaked, the more he began to look like a frog!

I guess wishes do come true.

Compare and contrast details from the stories. Use a Venn Diagram like the one here to organize your thoughts. Then write your answers below. Use complete sentences.

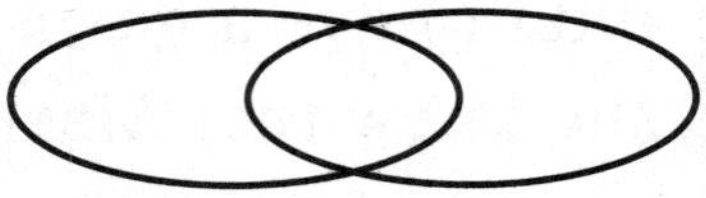

1. What main fact do both narrators agree upon? Support your answer with details from the selection.

____

____

____

2. Whom does the prince blame? What does Story B say about this?

____

____

Name ______________________ Date __________

Suffixes *-y*, *-ous*

adventurous	handy	rocky
glorious	cloudy	chilly
scary	wondrous	glamorous

Complete each sentence with a word from above.

1. A pencil is a ______________ thing to have when you are taking a test.
2. The ______________ princess wore an expensive gown and jewels to the ball.
3. The ______________ skier raced down a steep mountain.
4. The ______________ sky made the air seem even more ______________ .
5. The climb up the ______________ cliff was difficult and tiring.
6. The ______________ monster frightened the villagers.
7. At the end of the day we watched a ______________ sunset.
8. Their mouths dropped open at the ______________ sight.

Name ______________________ Date ____________

Vowel Sounds: /ŭ/, /yo͞o/, and /o͞o/

Basic Read the paragraph. Write the Basic Words that best complete the sentences.

The puppy running through the grocery store was the first (1) ____________ something was wrong. Diana stood next to the (2) ____________ and vegetable section. She looked at a (3) ____________ of bananas but chose an orange instead. Suddenly, the (4) ____________ dog jumped into Diana's cart! It tore open a loaf of bread, causing a (5) ____________ to fly into Diana's face. Startled, Diana squeezed the orange, and (6) ____________ exploded over Diana and a nearby man. He was (7) ____________ to Diana. He began to (8) ____________ with her. He said it was her fault that his business (9) ____________ was ruined! One worker had to (10) ____________ the dog. The cleaning (11) ____________ had to mop the floor.

Challenge 12–14. Write sentences that tell about jobs that people might have. Use three Challenge Words. Write on a separate sheet of paper.

Spelling Words

1. bunch
2. fruit
3. argue
4. crumb
5. crew
6. tune
7. juice
8. refuse
9. truth
10. young
11. clue
12. trunk
13. amuse
14. suit
15. rude
16. trust
17. dew
18. stuck
19. rescue
20. brush

Challenge

computer
mustard
tissue
customer
attitude

Name ______________________ Date ____________

Once Upon a Cool Motorcycle Dude
Spelling: Vowel Sounds /ŭ/, /yo͞o/, and /o͞o/

Spelling Word Sort

Write each Basic Word beside the correct heading.

/ŭ/ spelled *u* followed by a consonant	Basic Words: Challenge Words: Possible Selection Words:
Other spellings for /ŭ/	Basic Words:
/yo͞o/ and /o͞o/ spelled *u*-consonant-*e*	Basic Words: Challenge Words: Possible Selection Words:
/yo͞o/ and /o͞o/ spelled *ue*	Basic Words: Challenge Words:
/yo͞o/ and /o͞o/ spelled *ui*	Basic Words:
/o͞o/ spelled *ew*	Basic Words: Possible Selection Words:
Other spellings for /yo͞o/ and /o͞o/	Basic Words: Challenge Words:

Challenge Add the Challenge Words to your Word Sort.

Connect to Reading Look through ***Once Upon a Cool Motorcycle Dude***. Find more words that have the /ŭ/, /yo͞o/, and /o͞o/ spelling patterns on this page. Add them to your Word Sort.

Spelling Words

1. bunch
2. fruit
3. argue
4. crumb
5. crew
6. tune
7. juice
8. refuse
9. truth
10. young
11. clue
12. trunk
13. amuse
14. suit
15. rude
16. trust
17. dew
18. stuck
19. rescue
20. brush

Challenge

computer
mustard
tissue
customer
attitude

Name ______________________ Date ____________

Once Upon a Cool Motorcycle Dude
Spelling: Vowel Sounds /ŭ/, /yo͞o/, and /o͞o/

Proofreading for Spelling

Find the misspelled words and circle them. Write them correctly on the lines below.

Outside the palace, the steep hillsides are covered with early morning duw. Princess Daisy gets up and picks up a bruish and ribbons to fix her hair. Suddenly, she hears someone singing outside her window.

"Hmmm," says the princess. "The tun sounds familiar, but I don't recognize the voice." When she tries to open the window, the latch is stuk. Princess Daisy goes out on the balcony and says, "I trest you will accept my invitation to come in and join me for a meal." The singer does not refews the princess' kind invitation. They enjoy juise, bread, froot and a cup of tea for breakfast.

But the troth is Princess Daisy is bored. And to amuze herself, she wants the singer to open an old trunck with a bunsh of music. The singer does, and when he begins to sing, the furniture comes alive! Now they all can have breakfast!

1. ______________ 7. ______________
2. ______________ 8. ______________
3. ______________ 9. ______________
4. ______________ 10. ______________
5. ______________ 11. ______________
6. ______________ 12. ______________

Spelling Words

1. bunch
2. fruit
3. argue
4. crumb
5. crew
6. tune
7. juice
8. refuse
9. truth
10. young
11. clue
12. trunk
13. amuse
14. suit
15. rude
16. trust
17. dew
18. stuck
19. rescue
20. brush

Challenge

computer
mustard
tissue
customer
attitude

Name ______________________ Date ____________

Action Verbs

An **action verb** tells what a person or thing does, did in the past, or will do.

action verb
Everyone likes pretty, shiny things.
The giant lost his favorite ring.

Thinking Question
Which word shows what a person or thing does?

1–10. Write the action verb in each sentence.

1. The giant searched everywhere for the ring. ______________
2. He jumped over a mountain. ______________
3. He swam across the ocean. ______________
4. Now the giant stands in the forest. ______________
5. He looks down. ______________
6. The giant sees his ring. ______________
7. A dragon wears the ring around her neck. ______________
8. The giant smiles at his friend the dragon. ______________
9. He gives the ring to the dragon. ______________
10. The happy dragon wags her tail. ______________

Name _______________ Date __________

Main Verbs and Helping Verbs

Some verbs are more than one word. The **main verb** is the most important verb. The **helping verb** comes before the main verb.

helping verb **main verb**
Maya is writing a fairy tale.

Thinking Question
Which is the most important verb? Which verb comes before it?

1–10. Write *HV* above each helping verb. Write *MV* above each main verb.

1. Maya and Charlie are making a book.
2. They have talked about their plan.
3. Maya will type the story.
4. She has thought about the main character.
5. The main character will ride a purple horse.
6. The horse will leap over the castle gate.
7. Charlie has drawn pictures for the story.
8. He was drawing with pencils.
9. Now he is coloring with markers.
10. Maya and Charlie will show the book to their friends.

Name _______________________ Date ___________

Linking Verbs

A **linking verb** tells what someone or something is, or what someone or something is like. Most linking verbs are forms of the verb be.

linking verb
The motorcycle is fast.

Thinking Question
Which word shows what a person or thing is? Which word shows what a person or thing is like?

1–10. Underline the linking verb in each sentence.

1. The story is a fairy tale.
2. At first the princess in the fairy tale appeared fragile.
3. The dude on the motorcycle was there to save the ponies.
4. The princess is willing to sit and spin gold thread.
5. In time, the princess became quite strong.
6. Her situation was no longer hopeless.
7. The giant, who stole the princess's ponies, now seemed weak in comparison to her.
8. The princess was able to beat the giant all on her own.

Name ______________________ Date ____________

Complete Sentences

A complete sentence expresses a complete thought. To change a sentence fragment to a complete sentence, first identify what information is missing. Then write a new sentence.

fragment	complete sentence
Gemma is	Gemma is writing a story.
Went to see wizard	Then Louisa went to see the wizard.

1–7. Change each fragment to a complete sentence.

1. Writing a fairy tale

____

2. In her fairy tale, the main character Louisa

____

____

3. Louisa heard that the wizard

____

____

4. wandered in the valley

____

____

5. The wizard

____

6. Louisa proved

____

7. have written stories

____

Name ______________________ Date ____________

Word Choice

Less Exact Verbs	More Exact Verbs
A tiny elf happily went through the forest.	A tiny elf sang and danced through the forest.

1–6. Replace each underlined verb with a more exact verb. Write the new sentence on the line.

1. The elf fell over a pebble and ended up on the ground.

____

2. A young woman saw the tiny elf and took him up in her hand.

____

3. The elf wiped dirt from his knees and thanked the young woman.

____

4. The young woman laughed and asked the elf his name.

____

5. The elf removed his hat and gave his name with a bow.

____

6. Then the elf jumped down and hid behind a mushroom.

____

Name ______________________ Date ____________

Focus Trait: Organization

Comparison and Contrast Paragraphs

Poorly Organized Comparison Paragraph	Logically Organized Comparison Paragraph
Folktales and fairy tales have many things in common. Folktales have animal characters, while fairy tales usually don't. Both often have magical elements. They are both set in a long-ago time and place.	Folktales and fairy tales have many things in common. Both often have magical elements. They are both set in a long-ago time and place.

A. Read the contrast paragraph. Cross out sentences that do not belong.

1. Folktales are different from fairy tales in some ways. Folktales often have animal characters, while fairy tales usually don't. Sometimes fairy tales do have animal characters, though. Folktales do not have royal characters, while fairy tales often do. Both have magical events.

B. Read the topic sentence below. Write sentences that support the topic sentence with details. Write a complete paragraph.

Pair/Share **Work with a partner to choose sentences that add details to the main idea.**

2. Fairy tales and realistic stories are very different.

____

____

____

____

____

Name ______________________ Date ____________

Fact and Opinion

Read the selection below.

Bringing Cartoons to Life

Everyone likes cartoons! The action, the funny voices, and sounds combine to entertain and thrill us. But how do these elements come together to form a movie?

The first step in making any movie is coming up with a story idea. Then someone presents this idea to a movie studio. If the studio likes it, the script is written. Then artists draw pictures to go with the script, and actors record the voices of the characters. The characters are the best part of cartoons. Artists make sure characters are believable and fun. Then the art department uses computers to bring together words and sounds to make the characters come alive onscreen.

Once the characters are created, artists work on the backgrounds in the scenes. A computer is used again to add lighting and effects. Then, the whole movie is reviewed to make sure everything works together.

It takes a lot of time, hard work, and creativity to make a good cartoon. The final result is worth the effort. Once the cartoon is finished, people can enjoy it for years to come.

Complete the T-Map to show facts and opinions about making cartoons. Write complete sentences.

Fact	Opinion

Name ______________________ Date ____________

Fact and Opinion

Read the selection below.

The Screenplay's Importance

What's the most important part of a movie? I think it is the screenplay! The screenplay is the script where all the action and dialogue is written. Without the screenplay, there is no story to be filmed. Without the screenplay, actors and actresses have no words to say in front of the camera!

Unfortunately, there are many bad screenplays because good screenplays are hard to write. So what makes a good screenplay?

First, you need a great idea. If the story is boring, no one will want to see the movie. If the story is not original enough, people will not want to see it either because they want to see something new.

Characters are also important. Are the characters in the screenplay intriguing?

Then there's the dialogue, which is the words the characters say. Is the dialogue compelling or dull? An entire screenplay about two people talking about the weather will put a lot of people to sleep.

Finally, a screenplay with good pacing will keep the audience interested from the beginning until the end.

If you ever write a screenplay, keep these elements in mind!

Use a T-Map like the one shown to record facts and opinions in the selection about screenplays. Then answer the questions below.

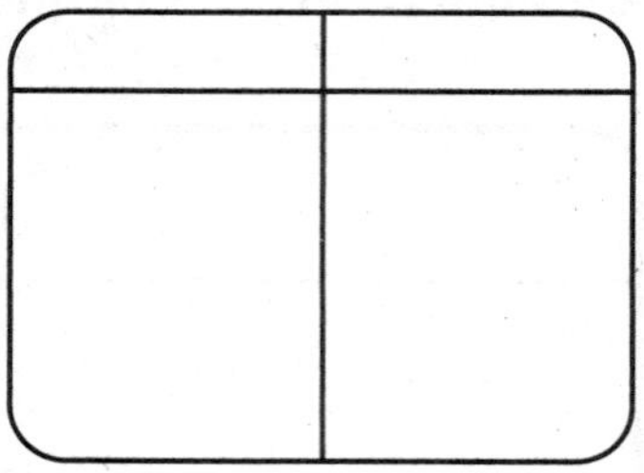

1. Why does the writer of the selection think that screenplays are important?

____

____

____

2. Write one fact from the selection. Where could you verify the fact?

____

Name ______________________ Date __________

Greek and Latin Word Parts *phon, photo, graph, auto, tele*

autograph	autobiography	automobile	symphony
photograph	telephone	photocopy	cinematographer

Activity Read the words in the box above. Look for Greek and Latin word parts to help you understand the meaning of each word. Then use a word from the box to complete each sentence below.

1. The movie actress signed an ______________ for her fan.
2. I used the ______________ to call the theater for the movie schedule.
3. My mom drove the ______________ to the movie theater.
4. At the movie premiere, I used a camera to take a ______________ of the actors.
5. The movie director wrote an ______________ about his life.
6. The ______________ won an award for his filming technique.
7. The movie soundtrack features a ______________ by a famous composer.
8. I will ______________ this movie article from the library to share with the class tomorrow.

Name ______________________________ Date ____________

Coming Distractions: Questioning Movies
Spelling: Vowel Sounds /o͞o/ and /o͝o/

Vowel Sounds /o͞o/ and /o͝o/

Basic **Complete the puzzle by writing the Basic Word for each clue.**

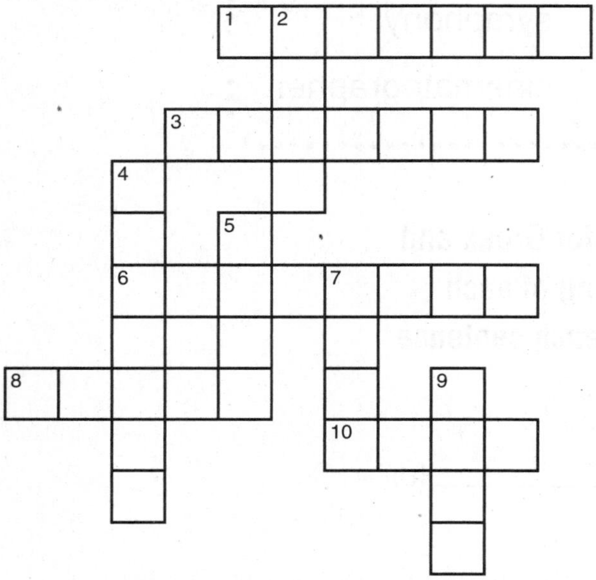

Across

1. bent or twisted
3. not sensible
6. a collection of recipes
8. a seat with legs but no arms
10. a bent object used to hold something

Down

2. the cover on a house
4. mammal with masklike face markings
5. thick hair from sheep
7. low, woody plant; a shrub
9. instrument used for work

Challenge 11–14. **You've just finished your homework assignment. Before putting it in your backpack, you check it over for errors. Tell what you might find. Use four Challenge Words. Write on a separate sheet of paper.**

Spelling Words

1. bloom
2. cookbook
3. tool
4. shampoo
5. put
6. wool
7. stool
8. proof
9. prove
10. group
11. brook
12. foolish
13. bush
14. crooked
15. booth
16. raccoon
17. hook
18. groom
19. roof
20. soup

Challenge

bulletin
cocoon
cushion
proofread
marooned

Spelling Word Sort

Write each Basic Word beside the correct heading.

/o͞o/ spelled *oo*	**Basic Words:** **Challenge Words:** **Possible Selection Words:**
Other spellings for /o͞o/	**Basic Words:**
/o͝o/ spelled *oo*	**Basic Words:** **Possible Selection Words:**
/o͝o/ spelled *u* followed by a consonant	**Basic Words:** **Challenge Words:**

Spelling Words

1. bloom
2. cookbook
3. tool
4. shampoo
5. put
6. wool
7. stool
8. proof
9. prove
10. group
11. brook
12. foolish
13. bush
14. crooked
15. booth
16. raccoon
17. hook
18. groom
19. roof
20. soup

Challenge

bulletin
cocoon
cushion
proofread
marooned

Challenge Add the Challenge Words to your Word Sort.

Connect to Reading Look through *Coming Distractions: Questioning Movies*. Find words in the selection that have the /o͞o/ and /o͝o/ spelling patterns on this page. Add them to your Word Sort.

Name ______________________ Date ____________

Coming Distractions: Questioning Movies
Spelling: Vowel Sounds /o͞o/ and /o͝o/

Proofreading for Spelling

Find the misspelled words and circle them. Write them correctly on the lines below.

The next time you go to a movie, be sure to stay putt until the end to watch the credits. Some people think it's fullish, but the credits list the people involved in the movie. They are also prouf of the work the groop did.

I now invite you to take a moment to picture some of the following scenes that might be created on the set: flowers in blewm, a family in a restaurant buth enjoying bowls of hot sewp, a bottle of shampo on a rock by a brock, and a veterinarian showing a young girl how to properly groum her puppy. It takes many people to create these simple scenes.

I recently visited a movie studio and went behind the scenes. I met some of the people who make movie scenes scary, exciting, or magical. I can proov it, too. I was camera happy and took a zillion pictures!

1. ______________ 7. ______________
2. ______________ 8. ______________
3. ______________ 9. ______________
4. ______________ 10. ______________
5. ______________ 11. ______________
6. ______________

Spelling Words

1. bloom
2. cookbook
3. tool
4. shampoo
5. put
6. wool
7. stool
8. proof
9. prove
10. group
11. brook
12. foolish
13. bush
14. crooked
15. booth
16. raccoon
17. hook
18. groom
19. roof
20. soup

Challenge

bulletin
cocoon
cushion
proofread
marooned

Name ______________________ Date ____________

Coming Distractions: Questioning Movies
Grammar: Simple Verb Tenses

Present and Past Tenses

The **present tense** shows action that is happening now. The **past tense** shows that an action already happened. Form the past tense by adding *–ed* to the end of a regular verb.

present tense
I watch a movie with my family.

past tense
I watched a movie with my family.

Thinking Question
When does the action take place?

1–8. Write the verb given in parentheses in the past tense.

1. (looks) The new movie ______________ like fun!
2. (walk) I ______________ to the movie theater with my dad.
3. (amaze) The special effects in the movie ______________ us!
4. (dance) The actors and actresses ______________ in the movie.
5. (impresses) The actress ______________ the critics with her moving performance.
6. (love) I ______________ the cute animals in the movie.
7. (dislikes) My brother ______________ the dancing scenes.
8. (talks) At the theater, the person next to me ______________ too loud.

Name ______________________ Date ____________

Future Verb Tense

The **future tense** shows action that has not happened yet. The future tense is formed by using the helping verb *will* plus a verb.

future tense
I will watch the movie with my friends.

Thinking Question
What verb tense should I use to show when the action takes place?

1–8. Write the verb given in parentheses in the future tense.

1. (talk) We ______________ about the movie tomorrow.
2. (love) You ______________ the animation in that movie!
3. (discuss) The teacher ______________ the film tomorrow.
4. (take) My parents ______________ me to see the movie.
5. (like) Everyone ______________ the action scenes.
6. (see) You ______________ an adorable parrot in the movie.
7. (laugh) You ______________ at the dog scene.
8. (write) I ______________ a movie review tomorrow.

Name ______________________ Date ____________

Consistent Use of Tenses

Choose a verb tense to write in and continue to write in that tense. Usually, all of the verbs in a paragraph or sentence should be in the same tense. Change tenses when you want to show a change in time.

past tense: I watched a movie with a friend. After the movie, we discussed it.

present tense: We still remember and laugh at the funny parts.

future tense: Next time, we will watch a scary movie.

Thinking Question
Are the verbs telling about a particular time? Are they all in the same tense?

1–6. Choose the correct verb tense for the sentences. Write the correct verb on the line.

1. (go/will go) Tomorrow I will see a movie with my family. Then we ______________ out to dinner.
2. (will like/liked) The scenery amazed me! I especially ______________ the scene at the beach.
3. (steal/stole) Some actors dislike filming with animals because the animals ______________ the scene.
4. (will buy/buy) First, we will buy movie tickets, and then we ______________ some popcorn and drinks.
5. (liked/like) I love movies about cats! I also ______________ movies about dogs.
6. (decide/decided) Yesterday it rained all day, so we ______________ to go to the movie theater.

Name ______________________ Date ____________

Simple Subjects and Predicates

Simple Subject	Simple Predicate
The students	will watch a movie about horses. (future tense)
The students	watch a movie about horses. (present tense)
The students	watched a movie about horses. (past tense)

1–3. Underline the simple subject in the sentences below. Write whether the sentence is in the future tense, present tense, or past tense.

1. My mother loves old movies! ____________
2. The talented actor danced in the movie. ____________
3. The boy will wear his eyeglasses at the theater.

   ____

4–6. Underline the simple predicate in the sentences below. Write whether the sentence is in the future tense, present tense, or past tense.

4. My cousin dislikes scary movies. ____________
5. The director will be at the theater. ____________
6. My classmates talked about the beautiful scenes.

   ____

Name ______________________ Date ____________

Sentence Fluency

Mixed Tenses	Same Tense
My cousin Susan takes acting lessons. She will want to be an actress.	My cousin Susan takes acting lessons. She wants to be an actress.

Rewrite each pair of sentences by changing the underlined verbs to the tense shown in parentheses.

1. Last year, Susan got a small role in a comedy. She will play a waitress. (past)

____

____

2. My entire family will go to opening night. We clapped loudly at the end! (past)

____

____

3. Now I own the DVD. I kept it on my bookshelf. (present)

____

4. I always laugh at the part about the messy spaghetti. Susan will drop spaghetti on a grumpy customer. (present)

____

____

5. Maybe someday I will act in the movies. Maybe I design costumes. (future)

____

____

Name ______________________ Date ____________

Focus Trait: Voice

Using Different Kinds Of Sentences

Statement	Command
In a movie, there might be ordinary people with real problems.	Think about all the movies that feature ordinary people with real problems.

A. Read each statement. Rewrite it as a question, an exclamation, or a command.

Statements	Rewritten
1. The family might have trouble affording their lifestyle.	Question:
2. You might write a screenplay about your life.	Exclamation:
3. Studios have to get the word out about their movies.	Command:

B. Read each statement. Use a different sentence type to express a positive or negative opinion in response.

Pair/Share **Work with a partner to brainstorm words for a positive and a negative response.**

Statement	Rewritten
4. Panning the camera can create a scary effect.	Positive:
5. Half light and half shadow can make a character seem evil.	Negative:

Name ____________________ Date __________

Understanding Characters

Read the selection below.

Moving On

On moving day, Juan woke up excited, nervous, and ready to go. Living in a tiny apartment for so long, he was sure he'd love his new house. He would have a yard, a basement, and his own bedroom!

But Juan was also a little sad. He wasn't sure if he'd make new friends and like his new neighborhood as much as he liked Harbor Woods.

After breakfast, Juan looked at the room he had shared with his sister Lily since she was a baby. He would miss this place.

"Goodbye, old home!" he said.

As the car pulled onto the street, Juan had tears in his eyes. His mom saw he was sad and reminded him, "There will be many things to love in our new home." Juan smiled and agreed.

As they got closer to the new house, Juan started to plan how he would decorate his room and how he and his new friends could play catch in the backyard.

He knew that even though he'd miss his old friends and home, he would enjoy living here. It was a new start.

They unlocked the door and walked in. Immediately, Juan smiled.

"Welcome home!" he said to his family. And he really meant it!

Complete the Column Chart to understand Juan's character by his thoughts, actions, and words. Write in complete sentences.

Thoughts	Actions	Words

Name ____________________ Date __________

Understanding Characters

Read the selection below.

Living a Dream

Crack!

The ball sailed into the air. Every eye in the park was on it, watching and waiting. Did it have what it needed to carry beyond the fence? The centerfielder didn't think so. He went back, back, back . . . and then jumped into the air.

The crowd stood silent.

The centerfielder came down to earth and opened his glove. The ball wasn't there! It had landed just in front of the fence. The crowd roared! The centerfielder kicked the ground in disgust.

Toby wasn't watching the ball. He carried his 75-pound frame around the bases. Baseball had been his passion for all of his ten long years. This is why he had trained all those hours. He was living his dream.

As he rounded third base, Toby could tell the ball was close behind him. He had to beat it. He slid into home. Then all eyes fell on the umpire.

"Safe!" was the call.

Toby's teammates lifted him onto their shoulders and paraded him around the park. Toby was on top of the world!

Analyze the characters' thoughts, feelings, and actions to answer the questions about character traits. Use a Column Chart like the one shown here to organize your thoughts. Then write your answers to the questions below.

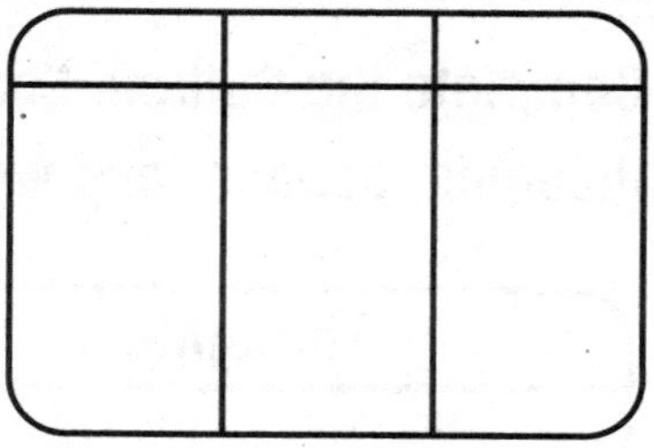

1. How does Toby feel about baseball? How do you know?

____

____

2. What can you tell about the centerfielder?

____

____

Name ______________________ Date __________

Figurative Language (Idioms)

chow down	head over heels	good as gold
heart of gold	feast or famine	safe and sound

Rewrite each sentence using one of the idioms above.

1. My mother helps others because she is so kind and loving.

   ____

2. The quiet children were very well behaved during the long car trip.

   ____

   ____

3. When I finally sat down for lunch, I ate quickly without talking.

   ____

   ____

4. My best friend really loves the movie we watched.

   ____

5. The mother couldn't rest until all her children were tucked in their beds at home.

   ____

   ____

6. When I go to the library, I either see many books I want to read or none at all. It's always too many or too few.

   ____

   ____

Name ________________________ Date ____________

Vowel Sounds /ou/ and /ô/

Basic Read the paragraph. Write the Basic Words that best complete the sentences.

I am a (1) __________ member of my school's bird-watching club. Every Saturday we leave at (2) __________ to go to the national park. Today, we looked for a (3) __________. It was sunny at first, but then it got (4) __________. Our adviser reminded us not to speak (5) __________ as we scanned the skies. Megan thought she saw something, but it was a (6) __________ alarm. Then we saw a bird fly from the (7) __________. We watched it (8) __________ a field mouse. The bird spread its wings wide, and it seemed to (9) __________ in the air. Suddenly, the bird dived and grabbed its meal with a sharp (10) __________!

Challenge 11–14. Write an e-mail message to your friend telling about a sporting event you have seen. Use four Challenge Words. Write on a separate sheet of paper.

Spelling Words

1. aloud
2. bald
3. hawk
4. south
5. faucet
6. proud
7. claw
8. tower
9. stalk
10. couple
11. howl
12. false
13. dawn
14. allow
15. drown
16. pause
17. fault
18. cause
19. amount
20. cloudier

Challenge

applaud
foul
browse
gnaw
doubt

Name ______________________ Date ____________

Me and Uncle Romie
Spelling:
Vowel Sounds /ou/ and /ô/

Spelling Word Sort

Write each Basic Word beside the correct heading.

/ou/ spelled *ou*	Basic Words: Challenge Words: Possible Section Words:
/ou/ spelled *ow*	Basic Words: Challenge Words: Possible Section Words:
Other sounds for *ou*	Basic Words:
/ô/ spelled *aw*	Basic Words: Challenge Words:
/ô/ spelled *au*	Basic Words: Challenge Words: Possible Section Words:
/ô/ spelled *a* before *l*	Basic Words: Possible Selection Words:

Spelling Words

1. aloud
2. bald
3. hawk
4. south
5. faucet
6. proud
7. claw
8. tower
9. stalk
10. couple
11. howl
12. false
13. dawn
14. allow
15. drown
16. pause
17. fault
18. cause
19. amount
20. cloudier

Challenge

applaud
foul
browse
gnaw
doubt

Challenge Add the Challenge Words to your Word Sort.

Connect to Reading Look through *Me and Uncle Romie*. Find more words that have the /ou/ and /ô/ spelling patterns on this page. Add them to your Word Sort.

Name ______________________ Date ____________

Proofreading for Spelling

Me and Uncle Romie
Spelling: Vowel Sounds /ou/ and /ô/

Find the misspelled words and circle them. Write them correctly on the lines below.

Mr. Rico's students are planning to paint a mural on the wall outside their classroom. Mr. Rico turns on the fawcet and rinses the brushes off. He checks the amont of paint available for the project while the students think alowd.

Everyone has a different idea. Rosa wants to paint a cuple of bawld eagles sitting high up on a towor. Jason thinks the mural should show a coyote letting out a houl at the silvery moon. Aidan says he wants to paint a box of matches with the words "Do Not Play With Matches." Matches are the cauze of many fires due to human falt. And Victoria wants to know if Mr. Rico will alow her to paint a race car. Mr. Rico likes everyone's ideas.

Before the students get started, Mr. Rico says, "Don't droun your brush with too much paint."

1. ______________
2. ______________
3. ______________
4. ______________
5. ______________
6. ______________
7. ______________
8. ______________
9. ______________
10. ______________
11. ______________

Spelling Words

1. aloud
2. bald
3. hawk
4. south
5. faucet
6. proud
7. claw
8. tower
9. stalk
10. couple
11. howl
12. false
13. dawn
14. allow
15. drown
16. pause
17. fault
18. cause
19. amount
20. cloudier

Challenge

applaud
foul
browse
gnaw
doubt

Name ______________________ Date __________

Conjunctions *and, but,* and *or*

The words *and*, *but*, and *or* are conjunctions. A **coordinating conjunction** is a word that connects other words or groups of words in a sentence. *And* joins together. *But* shows contrast. *Or* shows choice.

conjunction

Workers and tourists fill the subway station each day.

Thinking Question
What word joins other words or groups of words in the sentence?

1–4. Write the coordinating conjunction in each sentence.

1. They can take the subway or the bus into town.

____

2. The boys ride the subway, but their friends take the bus.

____

3. The subway car sways and shakes. __________

4. The train speeds down the track and rumbles through the tunnel. __________

5–8. Complete each sentence. Write the coordinating conjunction that has the meaning shown in parentheses.

5. Steve sat in his seat, __________ Barry stood in the aisle. (shows contrast)

6. The tunnel lights flicker __________ flash. (joins together)

7. We can get off here, __________ we can get off at the next stop. (shows choice)

8. They stepped off the train __________ walked through the turnstile. (joins together)

Name ______________________ Date ____________

Subordinating Conjunctions

A **conjunction** is a word that connects two words, groups of words, or sentences. Words such as *if*, *because*, *although*, *after*, *when*, and *where* are called **subordinating conjunctions.** They connect ideas to form a complex sentence.

if	If I lived in New York City, I'd play in a park a lot.
because	I liked visiting New York City because I went to the Statue of Liberty!
after	After I blew out my birthday candles, we ate some cake.

Thinking Question
Does one part of the sentence depend on the other part to make sense? What word shows this?

1–6. Find the subordinating conjunction in each sentence. Write it on the line.

1. If I lived in New York City, I would go to museums often. __________
2. My uncle took me to the art gallery, where he will show his work. __________
3. After we took a walk in Central Park, we got ice cream sundaes! __________
4. Although my uncle grew up in New York City, he was born in North Carolina. __________
5. When I grow up, I want to live in New York City. __________
6. I want to live in a big city because there will be so many things to see and do there. __________

Name ______________________ Date ____________

Correlative Conjunctions

Correlative conjunctions are pairs of words that connect ideas in a sentence. The words do not appear next to each other in a sentence. One of the words is always a conjunction.

both...and	Both my uncle and I like jelly.
either...or	I like either pepper jelly or strawberry jam on toast.
neither...nor	Neither the heat nor the humidity bothered me.
not only...but	Not only was the train late, but it was also crowded.

Thinking Question
What two words help make a strong connection between two ideas in the sentence?

1–5. Underline the two correlative conjunctions in each sentence. Circle the conjunction in each word pair.

1. I can either take the train from North Carolina to New York City or fly there.
2. I don't know whether I'd prefer to go sightseeing or shopping this morning!
3. Both my uncle and aunt like eggs for breakfast.
4. Neither the problem with the subway nor the traffic on the road stopped us from getting to the museum at opening time.
5. Not only was there a crowd in the museum to view my uncle's art, but there was also a line of people waiting to see the show.

Name ______________________ Date ____________

Kinds of Sentences

Kind of Sentence	End Mark	Example
Statement	period (.)	Tomoko is waiting at the bus stop.
Question	question mark (?)	Does this bus go by the aquarium?
Command	period (.)	Get in line to buy a ticket.
Exclamation	exclamation mark (!)	That line is so long!

1–6. Write the correct end mark for each sentence. Then label each sentence *statement, question, command,* or *exclamation*.

1. The city streets are very busy ______________________
2. That bus is going so fast ______________________
3. Can you give me directions ______________________
4. Look both ways ______________________
5. I've never seen such a big crowd

   ____
6. I am headed uptown ______________________

7–12. Correct six errors in this ad. There are two missing capital letters and four incorrect or missing end marks.

Are you visiting our beautiful city soon! do you wonder how you'll ever find your way around town? Jonny's Guided Walking Tour is here to help. let one of our cheerful tour guides show you around, or use one of our easy-to-read maps? Either way, you'll learn about our city's rich history and see all of its important landmarks Everyone agrees. Jonny's Guided Walking Tours are totally cool

Name ______________________________ Date ____________

Ideas

Both...and	Both my parents and I like to visit new places.
Either...or	Either I can visit my aunt, or I can stay home.
Neither...nor	Neither my aunt nor my uncle could find their keys.
Whether...or	I can't decide whether to go to a movie or a museum.

Activity Rewrite each pair of sentences. Use the correlative conjunctions given in parentheses to connect the ideas in one sentence.

1. (Either, or) I can ride my bike across the park to get to the other side of town. I can walk across the park.

____

____

2. (Whether, or) I don't know if it would be easier to take the train to the museum. I don't know if it would be easier to take the bus to the museum.

____

____

3. (Neither, nor) The eggs are not cooked yet. The bacon is not cooked yet.

____

4. (Both, and) I'd like to tour New York City's Little Italy. I'd like to tour New York City's Chinatown.

____

Name ______________________ Date ____________

Focus Trait: Word Choice
Using Sensory Words

Without Sensory Words	With Sensory Words
The smell of barbecue and roasting corn led us straight to the picnic area.	The sweet, smoky smell of sizzling barbecue and roasting corn led us straight to the crowded picnic area.

A. Rewrite each sentence using sensory words to add details.

Without Sensory Words	With Sensory Words
1. Some children sold fresh lemonade in plastic cups.	Some children sold fresh, ____________ lemonade in ____________ plastic cups.
2. We all played a game of tag on the grass.	We all played a ____________ game of tag on the ____________ grass.

B. Sensory words can help you to create an image. Rewrite the sentence below using sensory and other words to create an image for the reader.

Pair/Share **Work with a partner to brainstorm new words for your sentences.**

Without Sensory Words	With Sensory Words
3. When it began to get dark, families laid their blankets down on the grass to watch the fireworks show.	____________ ____________ ____________ ____________ ____________

Name ______________________ Date ____________

Conclusions and Generalizations

Read the selection below.

On the Trail

May 28, 1849
Independence, Missouri

Dear Jack,

My family leaves for the Oregon Trail in a few days to start a new life out west. Since you are my best friend, I decided to write you a letter describing the trip so far. First, we took a boat from St. Louis to Independence, Missouri. While we were in town, we gathered food and water that we believe will last the entire journey.

There are many other families traveling with us. Some, like our family, want to buy land in Oregon. Others are headed for the California gold fields. We are glad that we aren't alone because we must protect ourselves from wild animals and other dangers.

It is spring now. The journey west is over 2,000 miles by wagon train. We worry because we might have to travel over the winter months. We have packed plenty of warm clothes, blankets, and coats for the trip. Hopefully, we'll be fine.

Your friend,
Nate

Complete the Idea-Support Map with text details from the letter. Draw a conclusion about travel on the Oregon Trail. Write complete sentences.

Conclusion:

Text Detail:

Text Detail:

Name ____________________ Date __________

Conclusions and Generalizations

Dear Mr. Winston
Comprehension: Conclusions and Generalizations

Read the selection below.

A New Friend?

"Want to come over?" Sam asked Madi.

"Okay," Madi said. She didn't want to seem too excited, but she was amazed that Sam was asking her over. She had wanted this since September.

They walked to Sam's house. It took them ten minutes to walk around the greenhouse and the stable. When Madi saw the house, her mouth dropped open.

"Let's go to my room," said Sam. "You have to see all my great stuff." All afternoon, Sam showed Madi her MP3 player, her laptop computer, her robotic dog, her widescreen TV, and all her video games.

"Let's play one," said Madi.

"Oh no," said Sam. "I can't let just anyone play with my stuff."

"I should call my mom," said Madi.

"Here," said Sam, "I guess you can use my cell phone. Just say the number and it will dial it for you!"

Madi looked at Sam. And then she hit each number on the phone with her finger.

Analyze the characters' words and actions to identify their true thoughts and feelings. Use an Idea-Support Map like the one shown to organize your thoughts. Answer the questions below.

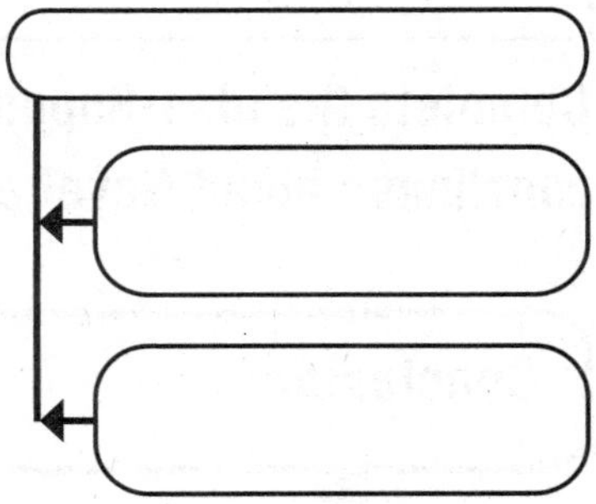

1. When Madi saw Sam's house, her mouth dropped open. What conclusion can you draw about Sam's house?

____

____

2. At first, Madi is excited to be going to Sam's house. How does she feel at the end of the story?

____

____

____

Name ______________________ Date ____________

Antonyms

honest	thoughtful	borrow	healthy
genuine	ashamed	guilty	local

Read each sentence. Rewrite each using one of the antonyms above.

1. My wallet is made from fake leather.

   ____

2. I was proud when I threw the baseball through my neighbor's window.

   ____

   ____

3. We went shopping at a distant mall.

   ____

4. Monica asked if I could lend her my book.

   ____

5. My sister was sick.

   ____

6. I was lying when I said I liked to eat liver and onions.

   ____

7. She is a very thoughtless person.

   ____

8. My brother thinks that I am innocent of taking his baseball glove.

   ____

   ____

Name ______________________________ Date ____________

Vowel + /r/ Sounds

Basic Complete the puzzle by writing the Basic Word for each clue.

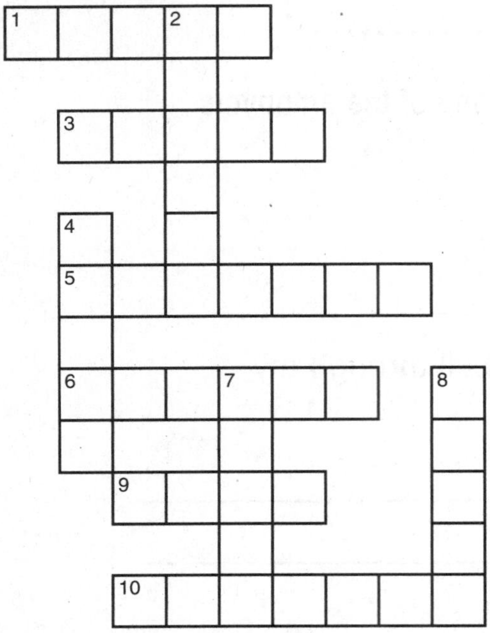

Across

1. unkind
3. a piece of cloth worn around neck or head
5. to make something ready
6. to mend
9. back
10. to discover differences and similarities

Down

2. not enough
4. a flash of light
7. a warning signal
8. to frighten

Challenge 11–14. You have watched a movie about taking a submarine trip deep in the ocean. Write a story about it. Use four Challenge Words. Write on a separate sheet of paper.

Spelling Words

1. spark
2. prepare
3. cheer
4. tear
5. scarf
6. scare
7. repair
8. earring
9. scarce
10. weird
11. sharp
12. rear
13. spare
14. gear
15. hairy
16. compare
17. alarm
18. harsh
19. upstairs
20. square

Challenge

weary
startle
appear
barnacle
awareness

Name ______________________________ Date ______________

Spelling Word Sort

Write each Basic Word beside the correct heading.

/îr/ spelled *ear*	Basic Words: Challenge Words:
/îr/ spelled *eer*	Basic Words:
Other spellings for /îr/	Basic Words:
/är/ spelled *ar*	Basic Words: Challenge Words: Possible Selection Words:
/âr/ spelled *are*	Basic Words: Challenge Words:
/âr/ spelled *air*	Basic Words:
Other spellings for /âr/	Basic Words: Possible Section Words:

Spelling Words

1. spark
2. prepare
3. cheer
4. tear
5. scarf
6. scare
7. repair
8. earring
9. scarce
10. weird
11. sharp
12. rear
13. spare
14. gear
15. hairy
16. compare
17. alarm
18. harsh
19. upstairs
20. square

Challenge

weary
startle
appear
barnacle
awareness

Challenge Add the Challenge Words to your Word Sort.

Connect to Reading Look through *Dear Mr. Winston*. Find words that have the vowel + /r/ spelling patterns on this page. Add them to your Word Sort.

Name ______________________ Date ____________

Dear Mr. Winston
Spelling:
Vowel + /r/ Sounds

Proofreading for Spelling

Find the misspelled words and circle them. Write them correctly on the lines below.

I'm so jazzed! On our way to visit my grandparents, we saw a Grizzly Giant. You're probably thinking we saw a huge black, heiry bear with sharpp teeth. Or, that maybe we saw a very tall, weard person wearing a teer-shaped diamond earing. Nope. The Grizzly Giant is at least 200 feet tall and 30 feet around. It's a Sequoia tree!

Dad shifted into first geer, pulled over, and stopped the car. We went for a walk to look at these giant trees and discovered that you can even walk through some of them!

We heard clapping and a loud cher coming from the visitors center. Since we were on vacation and had lots of spar time, we decided to explore. Inside, the park ranger told us the upsteirs theater had a short movie about the park. She looked at her squar-shaped watch and said the next show started in five minutes.

1. ______________ 6. ______________
2. ______________ 7. ______________
3. ______________ 8. ______________
4. ______________ 9. ______________
5. ______________ 10. ______________

Spelling Words

1. spark
2. prepare
3. cheer
4. tear
5. scarf
6. scare
7. repair
8. earring
9. scarce
10. weird
11. sharp
12. rear
13. spare
14. gear
15. hairy
16. compare
17. alarm
18. harsh
19. upstairs
20. square

Challenge
weary
startle
appear
barnacle
awareness

Name ______________________ Date ____________

Commas with Introductory Words and Names

Sometimes a sentence begins with an introductory word or words. Use a **comma** after any introductory words. When addressing a person, use one or two commas to set off the person's name from the rest of the sentence.

Okay, that sounds like fun!
When are we leaving, Mom?
What should I do, Cindy, if you're late?

Thinking Question
Does the sentence have an introductory word? Does it include the name of the person being addressed?

1–5. Rewrite each sentence and add commas where they are needed.

1. David did you bring an extra sweater?

____

2. No that's not my sweater Mr. Park.

____

3. Well someone left a sweater here on the chair.

____

4. Ask the girl Nancy if the sweater is hers.

____

5. Last week I lost a red sweater.

____

Name ______________________ Date ____________

Commas with Dates and Places

Use a comma to separate the day and the year in a date. You should also use a comma to separate the city and the state in a place name.

My sister was born on January 17, 2009.
We moved from Chicago, Illinois, to Houston, Texas.

Thinking Question
Do the commas remind you to pause?

1–5. Rewrite each sentence and add commas where they are needed.

1. On January 18 2009 we brought my sister home.

____

2. The hospital was in Pasadena Texas.

____

3. She has a checkup on January 25 2009.

____

4. Her checkup will be in Houston Texas with our family doctor.

____

____

5. On February 1 2009 we will have a party in Bellaire Texas at my aunt's house.

____

____

Name ______________________ Date ____________

Commas in a Series

Use commas to separate items in a series. You do not need to use a comma after the last word in a series.

She is going to the drugstore, bank, and library.
I like to read about space, other cities, famous people, and animals.

Thinking Question
Did you notice that a comma is placed after the last item before and*? That helps keep the meaning clear.*

1–5. Rewrite each sentence and add commas where they are needed.

1. Alex Ginger Mark and I study together at the library.

   ____

2. Ginger is really good at math social studies and science.

   ____

3. We looked up new recipes for salsa guacamole tacos and bean dip.

   ____

   ____

4. To make salsa, we need to buy tomatoes onions limes and peppers.

   ____

   ____

5. We will make enough salsa for a snack now lunch tomorrow and the party this weekend.

   ____

   ____

Name ______________________ Date ____________

Kinds of Nouns

Common Nouns	Proper Nouns	Singular Nouns	Plural Nouns
girl city day month	Ann Orlando Thanksgiving June	apple day class fox	apples days classes foxes

1–3. Write each noun and tell if it is *common* or *proper*.

1. Joe and Sal each snuck a box into their classroom.

____

____

2. Several holes had been poked into the lids with a pencil.

____

____

3. That morning, Ms. Li heard a strange noise under her desk.

____

____

4–6. Write the plural form of the noun in parentheses.

4. (sandwich) The children were eating their ______________.
5. (box) Then, the lids popped off the two ______________.
6. (frog) Suddenly, ______________ were jumping all over the room.

Name ______________________________ Date ____________

Conventions

Incorrect Use of Commas	Correct Use of Commas
Katie, bought a pet snake from a shop, in Austin Texas. She needs to feed the snake mice frogs fish, and lizards! Her mom said, "Katie you must be kidding." The date on the store receipt is August 7 2010. So Katie, has just three days left to get her money back.	Katie bought a pet snake from a shop in Austin, Texas. She needs to feed it mice, frogs, fish, and lizards! Her mom said, "Katie, you must be kidding." The date on the store receipt is August 7, 2010. So, Katie has just three days left to get her money back.

Activity Read the paragraph below. Add commas where they are needed for introductory words, addressing a person, dates, places, and series of words.

I want a pet snake, but I don't know how to ask my dad for permission. What should I say? I can already hear him telling me, "Richard you know better than to bring another animal into the house." You see I already have a dog a cat two hamsters a gecko and a frog. In fact I bought Moose, one of my hamsters, on April 1 2010 – just one month ago! However a snake would really make my animal family complete. The pet store has gopher snakes python snakes and corn snakes from San Diego California. One of them could be mine!

Focus Trait: Organization

Opinions, Reasons, and Details

Good writers support their opinions with details and reasons. When you write your thoughts about a story, support your opinion with details from the text. List the opinion first. Then give the details that helped you form that idea or opinion.

Opinion	Cara in "Dear Mr. Winston" is a likeable character.
Supporting Detail	She tells Mr. Winston about her favorite TV show.
Supporting Detail	She makes an honest mistake when she accidentally tells him who sold her the snake.

Read the opinions about *Dear Mr. Winston*. Write three different details to support each opinion.

1. **Opinion:** Cara truly wants to know more about her snake.

   Detail ____

   ____

   Detail ____

   ____

   Detail ____

   ____

2. **Opinion:** It's interesting that Cara's father is more upset than her mother is.

   Detail ____

   ____

   Detail ____

   ____

   Detail ____

   ____

Name ______________________________ Date ______________

Author's Purpose

Read the selection below.

Dancing with the Swans

My grandmother, Nana, took me to see my first ballet when I was eleven years old. She told me we would see *Swan Lake*, her favorite ballet. I had never seen a ballet before, so I worried that I wouldn't understand the story. Nana said she would explain everything to me.

While we were driving, Nana told me that *Swan Lake* is a fairy tale brought to life by dancers and music. It is the story of a prince who must marry someone he doesn't love. He runs away to hide by a lake. There, he sees a swan turn into a beautiful woman, named Odette. Odette explains that she is bewitched. A spell turns her into a swan at night. To break this spell, Odette must find true love. The prince promises Odette his love and rescues her.

When we arrived at the theater, we had front row seats! Soon, the lights dimmed and the music started. The dancers were graceful. Since Nana had explained the story, I understood the ballet without any words. After the ballet, I told my grandmother how much I enjoyed the show. I told her that I would like to see another ballet the next time one came to town.

Complete the Inference Map with details that explain the author's purpose.

Detail:

Detail:

Detail:

Author's Purpose:

Name ______________________________ Date ______________

Author's Purpose

Read the selection below.

Painter Paul Klee

As a child, painter Paul Klee (KLAY) was a very good violinist. Both of his parents were musicians. It seemed likely that their son would follow in their footsteps. But Paul was also a gifted artist. He drew landscapes and sketches.

Paul decided to study art, not music. When he was nineteen, he went to a private art school. A teacher encouraged him to use his imagination, and Paul never forgot it.

In 1906, Paul married a pianist named Lily Stumpf. They lived in Munich, Germany. For several years, Paul had trouble painting. But then he traveled to Tunisia, Africa. The landscapes there inspired Paul, and the trip was the turning point in Paul's career. He began to explore color and mosaics in his art. He exhibited his works for the first time after this trip.

Paul Klee became a successful artist. In 1935, Paul became very sick and could not paint. A few years later, he started to feel better. He painted several new artworks before becoming ill again. He died on June 29, 1940.

Use an Inference Map like the one shown here to figure out the author's purpose. Then answer the questions below.

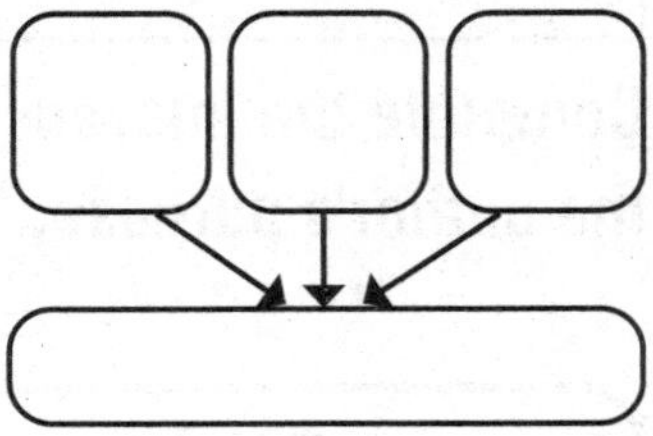

1. Why do you think the author discusses Paul's family?

____

____

2. How does the author view Paul's ability to overcome obstacles? Support your answer with text details.

____

____

____

Name ______________________ Date ______________

Analogies

An analogy is a comparison that shows how things are related. Read each set of words. Think about the relationship between the first pair of words. Add another word to complete the analogy.

1. rise:drop as above: ______________
2. fall:plunge as nice: ______________
3. disheartened:positive as hungry: ______________
4. escaped:got away as loyal: ______________
5. returned:went away as together: ______________
6. discouraged: saddened as high: ______________
7. border:frame as cover: ______________
8. entrance:exit as beginning: ______________

Name ______________________ Date ____________

More Vowel + /r/ Sounds

Basic Write the Basic Word that best replaces the underlined word or words in each sentence.

1. My older sister Pam gets up at the beginning of the day to run cross-country. ____________
2. Running is her favorite competition. ____________
3. There are a little more than a dozen students on her team. ____________
4. Their updated uniforms are red and gold. ____________
5. The race path goes through the woods near the creek. ____________
6. Pam's teammates fight hunger and dryness as they train. ____________
7. They often get grubby as they run through mud and under tree branches. ____________
8. Their shoes get old and used up very quickly. ____________
9. Muscles get painful and ache from all the activity. ____________
10. The good feeling running gives Pam is well deserving of the effort. ____________

Spelling Words

1. learn
2. dirty
3. worn
4. sore
5. thirst
6. burn
7. record
8. cure
9. board
10. course
11. worth
12. early
13. return
14. pure
15. world
16. search
17. worse
18. thirteen
19. sport
20. current

Challenge

curious
thorough
earnest
portion
foreign

Challenge 11–14. A friend of yours is planning a trip to another country. Write a letter wishing your friend a good trip. Use four Challenge Words. Write on a separate sheet of paper.

Name ________________________ Date ____________

Spelling Word Sort

Write each Basic Word beside the correct heading.

/ôr/ spelled *or*	**Basic Words:** **Challenge Words:** **Possible Selection Words:**
/ôr/ spelled *ore*	**Basic Words:** **Possible Selection Words:**
Other spellings for /ôr/	**Basic Words:** **Possible Selection Words:**
/ûr/ spelled *ir* or *ur*	**Basic Words:** **Possible Selection Words:**
/ûr/ spelled *ear* or *or*	**Basic Words:** **Challenge Words:**
/yo͝or/ spelled *ure*	**Basic Words:**
Other spellings for /yo͝or/	**Challenge Words:**

Spelling Words

1. learn
2. dirty
3. worn
4. sore
5. thirst
6. burn
7. record
8. cure
9. board
10. course
11. worth
12. early
13. return
14. pure
15. world
16. search
17. worse
18. thirteen
19. sport
20. current

Challenge

curious
thorough
earnest
portion
foreign

Challenge Add the Challenge Words to your Word Sort.

Connect to Reading Look through *José! Born to Dance*. Find more words that have the vowel + /r/ spelling patterns on this page. Add them to your Word Sort.

Name ______________________ Date ____________

José! Born to Dance
Spelling:
More Vowel + /r/ Sounds

Proofreading for Spelling

Find the misspelled words and circle them. Write them correctly on the lines below.

Doris Humphrey was born in 1895 in Oak Park, Illinois. It was pur joy for her as a young child to lirn new dance routines. At first, she was stiff like a bord. Doris soon opened her own dance studio. In 1928 Doris and Charles Weidman left to form their own group in New York. They would go on to rekord their choreographic works and produce some of the outstanding performers in the wurld.

Her career ended due to arthritis, for which there was no kure. Not being able to dance hurt Doris werse than her ailment itself. Dance would always bern in her like a fire. However, she did not retern to California in serch of other work. Instead, she became José's mentor and the artistic director of his dance company. Doris was one of the founders of American modern dance.

1. ______________ 6. ______________
2. ______________ 7. ______________
3. ______________ 8. ______________
4. ______________ 9. ______________
5. ______________ 10. ______________

Spelling Words

1. learn
2. dirty
3. worn
4. sore
5. thirst
6. burn
7. record
8. cure
9. board
10. course
11. worth
12. early
13. return
14. pure
15. world
16. search
17. worse
18. thirteen
19. sport
20. current

Challenge
curious
thorough
earnest
portion
foreign

Name ______________________ Date __________

Subject and Object Pronouns

A **subject pronoun** is a pronoun that tells who or what does the action of a sentence. An **object pronoun** is a pronoun that tells who or what receives the action of the verb.

subject pronoun

He studied dance for many years.

object pronoun

Grandmother made breakfast for him every morning.

Thinking Question

What pronoun tells who or what does the action of the sentence? What pronoun tells who or what receives the action of the verb?

1–4. Underline the subject pronoun in each sentence.

1. We watched José dance in the show.
2. I couldn't wait to see the performance.
3. Have you ever seen a dance recital?
4. He should dance in all of the shows.

5–8. Write the pronoun in parentheses that can take the place of the underlined word or words.

5. (him, you) The birds sang to José during breakfast. ______
6. (them, us) Mama drank hot chocolate with José and Grandmother. ______
7. (him, me) José said to Grandmother, "Please give José more!" ______
8. (you, us) "Can you save some for Mama and me?" Grandmother asked, with a smile. ______

Name ______________________ Date ____________

Reflexive Pronouns

Reflexive pronouns can be used to show that a subject is performing an action on itself. Reflexive pronouns may also be used to bring attention to an action. Reflexive pronouns must agree with the subject.

reflexive pronouns
myself, yourself, himself, herself, itself, ourselves, yourselves, themselves

Emily laced up the ballet slippers herself.

1–8. Write the correct reflexive pronoun on the line in the sentences below.

1. (herself, himself) Henry injured ____________ while practicing a dance routine.
2. (myself, ourselves) I made the dance costumes ____________ !
3. (yourself, itself) Help ____________ to some juice after you've mastered the dance steps.
4. (themselves, herself) She rewarded ____________ with a new pair of ballet shoes.
5. (ourselves, yourselves) We dressed ____________ before the dance recital.
6. (itself, themselves) The students picked out the dance songs ____________ .
7. (itself, herself) Jenny practiced the dance moves by ____________ .
8. (myself, ourselves) Before the dance recital, we looked at ____________ in the mirror.

Name ______________________________ Date ____________

Pronoun-Antecedent Agreement

An **antecedent** is a word or phrase that a following word refers back to. Pronouns often have antecedents.

antecedent **pronoun**
Musicals are popular, and (they) feature singing and dancing.

In the above sentence, musicals is the antecedent. The word they is the pronoun that is used instead of repeating the word musicals. The pronoun agrees with its antecedent in number.

1–4. Write the correct pronoun to complete each sentence.

1. (she, he) Fred Astaire was a famous actor, and __________ was well-known for his dancing.
2. (They, You) Ginger Rogers danced with Fred Astaire. ________ moved gracefully together.
3. (They, He) Gene Kelly danced in many movies. __________ are worth watching!
4. (They, It) Gene Kelly and Leslie Caron danced in *An American in Paris*. ______ was a great movie.

5–8. Circle the pronoun in each sentence. Underline the antecedent.

5. Shirley Temple was a child star, and she could tap dance, too.
6. Musicals are fun, but they can be long.
7. Dancers need to be careful when they perform.
8. When my sister and I took tap dance lessons, we wore special shoes.

Name ______________________ Date ____________

Plural Nouns

Singular	Plural
one **valley**	several **valleys**
a **bunny**	some **bunnies**
this **tooth**	these **teeth**
one **moose**	both **moose**

1–6. Write the plural form of the noun in parentheses to complete each sentence.

1. (hobby) Ballroom dancing is one of my aunt's __________.
2. (country) This type of dance is performed in many __________.
3. (man) Women and __________ wear fancy costumes.
4. (foot) Dancers kick their __________ and glide across the floor.
5. (city) Some __________ host ballroom dancing contests.
6. (key) One of the __________ to winning is practice, practice, practice!

7–12. Correct six errors in this paragraph. There are six plural nouns written incorrectly. Use proofreading marks.

My brother takes dance lessons on Fridayes. There are girls and boyes in his class. Last week, my parents and I watched his dance recital with many other families. I sat in the front row with several childs I knew. Some dancers wore tap shoes on their foots. Other dancers acted out stories. In one dance, the performers were dressed as sheeps! After the show, we went to two partys for the dancers.

Name ______________________ Date __________

Sentence Fluency

You can combine sentences with pronouns and subordinating conjunctions.

Choppy Sentences	Combined Sentences
José and his family stayed in Nogales. José and his family waited for permission to enter the United States.	José and his family stayed in Nogales while they waited for permission to enter the United States.

1–5. Combine each pair of sentences. Replace the underlined subject with a pronoun. Use the subordinating conjunction in parentheses. Write the new sentence on the line.

1. Papa decided to leave Mexico. Papa was worried about the war. (because)

____

____

2. José drew such beautiful pictures of trains. Everyone thought José would become an artist. (since)

____

____

3. José studied for three years. José learned English. (before)

____

____

4. José felt lonely. José walked around on a cold day. (when)

____

____

Name ______________________________ Date ______________

Focus Trait: Organization

Writing a Strong Opening

Question: Why was José's trip to New York important to him?

Weak Opening	Strong Opening
José went to New York to find out what he should do with his life.	I think José's trip to New York was important in helping him learn what he wanted to do with his life.

Read each question. Use words from the question to write a strong opening statement for a response essay.

Question	Opening Statement
1. Do you think José's early struggles learning English helped him in other ways?	
2. Do you believe that seeing famous paintings in New York had a positive or a negative effect on José?	
3. Do you think José gave a gift to the world?	

Name ______________________________ Date ______________

Fact and Opinion

Read the selection below.

The Barn Owl

Every summer, I went to stay on my grandfather's farm. I liked getting away from the noisy city and being in the quiet countryside, breathing fresh air. There were so many places to explore.

During one visit when I was 11, I was in the barn getting some hay for my grandfather's horse when I heard a rustling noise from above. I looked up and saw an animal. At first I wasn't sure what it was. Then I realized it was a small owl. I knew there were many types of owls. What type of owl had I found?

After I fed the horse, I told my grandfather about the owl. He came back with me to look at it. When he saw it, he said it was a barn owl. He pointed out its beautiful white feathers with some yellow and orange marks. A barn owl's face is funny-looking and shaped like a heart. Like all owls, they sleep in the daytime and hunt at night. My grandfather told me he was happy to have owls on the farm because they hunt mice.

Use the T-Map to list facts and opinions about barn owls. Write complete sentences.

Fact	Opinion

Name ________________________ Date ______________

Fact and Opinion

Read the selection below.

A Cute Predator

Screech owls are so cute that it is hard to imagine one as a vicious hunter. But like all animals, owls need to eat. And as birds of prey, they hunt and kill for food. Screech owls favor any of a variety of small animals—songbirds, insects, fish, and small mammals such as mice and moles.

Screech owls hunt all night long, from dusk until dawn. But they do most of their work during the first four hours of darkness. During this time, the screech owl perches in a tree, waiting until a prey animal comes scurrying along. Once the owl eyes a tasty mouse, it dives quickly and gracefully, seizing the rodent in its sharp talons.

Once caught, there is no hope for the prey's escape. Like all owls, screech owls usually swallow small prey whole, right on the spot. If the owl catches larger prey, it may carry the animal to a perch in a nearby tree to gobble it up in bite-sized pieces.

Analyze the selection to identify facts and opinions presented by the author. Use a T-Map like the one shown here to organize your findings. Then answer the questions below.

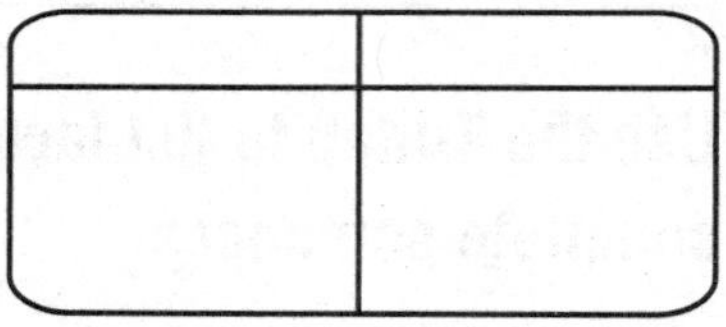

1. Is the first sentence a fact or an opinion? ______________
   Explain your response. ______________________
   ____

2. How could you verify if the statements in the last paragraph are facts or opinions? ______________
   ____
   ____

Name ______________________ Date ____________

Suffixes –*ful*, –*less*, –*ness*, –*ment*

cheer	use	assign	still
success	dark	entertain	

To complete each sentence below, select a word from the box and add the suffix *–ful, –less, –ness,* or *–ment.* Read the completed sentence to be sure it makes sense.

1. My teacher gave the class a homework ____________ over the weekend.
2. The tool was ____________ after I dropped it and it broke.
3. The coach thought practice was ____________ when we each made three goals.
4. The ____________ look on her face told me that she was in a great mood.
5. Spotted owls hunt their prey at night in the ____________.
6. I could see my reflection in the calm ____________ of the water.
7. The ____________ for the party included two talented musical acts.

Name ______________________ Date ____________

Compound Words

Basic **Write the Basic Word that best replaces the underlined word or words.**

My parents asked me to (1) look after my little sister. As soon as their car left the (2) lane from our garage, Amelia decided to be naughty. She found the scissors and gave her doll a (3) short trim. Now you can see the doll's whole (4) part of the face above her eyes. Then she ran into my room and broke my (5) instrument for telling time. I know there were (6) more than twenty pieces of it on the floor. I scolded Amelia, and she seemed to cry (7) for all time. She was so upset that she even refused to play Tinkerbell, who is her favorite (8) pretend character. But I grabbed a (9) not far away (10) small lamp powered by batteries and waved it around. She stopped crying and was fine. Watching Amelia is a hard job!

1. ______________ 6. ______________
2. ______________ 7. ______________
3. ______________ 8. ______________
4. ______________ 9. ______________
5. ______________ 10. ______________

Challenge 11–14. **Write a journal entry about a school trip your class took to a big city. Use four Challenge Words. Write on a separate sheet of paper.**

Spelling Words

1. somebody
2. fireplace
3. nearby
4. toothbrush
5. homesick
6. make-believe
7. anything
8. all right
9. goodbye
10. forehead
11. classmate
12. flashlight
13. haircut
14. twenty-two
15. driveway
16. alarm clock
17. baby-sit
18. airport
19. forever
20. mailbox

Challenge

field trip
absent-minded
life jacket
skyscraper
nevertheless

Name ______________________________ Date ____________

Spelling Word Sort

Write each Basic Word beside the correct heading.

One word	**Basic Words:** **Challenge Words:** **Possible Selection Words:**
With a hyphen	**Basic Words:** **Challenge Words:**
Two separate words	**Basic Words:** **Challenge Words:** **Possible Selection Words:**

Spelling Words

1. somebody
2. fireplace
3. nearby
4. toothbrush
5. homesick
6. make-believe
7. anything
8. all right
9. goodbye
10. forehead
11. classmate
12. flashlight
13. haircut
14. twenty-two
15. driveway
16. alarm clock
17. baby-sit
18. airport
19. forever
20. mailbox

Challenge

field trip
absent-minded
life jacket
skyscraper
nevertheless

Challenge Add the Challenge Words to your Word Sort.

Connect to Reading Look through *The Screech Owl Who Liked Television*. Find compound words. Add them to your Word Sort.

Name ____________________ Date __________

Proofreading for Spelling

Find the misspelled words and circle them. Write them correctly on the lines below.

Anyone who has ever had a pet knows how much joy it can provide. Whether the pet is a puppy curled up in its owner's lap sniffing at a brand new doggy tothbrush, a chatty parrot asking for a snack as it sits on a toy mailboxx in its cage, or a cute playful kitten retrieving a toy mouse by the fireplase, the bond between pets and their owners is a strong one.

Kiko is a great pet! She looks like a dog and walks like a dog. But she doesn't need to have sombody take her for a walk, nor would she get homesik if she were boarded at the kennel. In addition, she never needs a harecut. Kiko is a well-behaved pet. She doesn't bark at anythink, or cry when her owner says goodbie when leaving to meet a clasmate at the airpert. Sometimes Kiko sits in the drivway. Kiko is a good pet, all reght! Kiko is a robot dog!

1. ____________ 7. ____________
2. ____________ 8. ____________
3. ____________ 9. ____________
4. ____________ 10. ____________
5. ____________ 11. ____________
6. ____________ 12. ____________

Spelling Words

1. somebody
2. fireplace
3. nearby
4. toothbrush
5. homesick
6. make-believe
7. anything
8. all right
9. goodbye
10. forehead
11. classmate
12. flashlight
13. haircut
14. twenty-two
15. driveway
16. alarm clock
17. baby-sit
18. airport
19. forever
20. mailbox

Challenge

field trip
absent-minded
life jacket
skyscraper
nevertheless

Name ______________________ Date ____________

Capitalizing Historical Events and Documents

Proper nouns are always capitalized. The names of important historical events and documents are also proper nouns and should be capitalized.

Thinking Question
What word names a particular event or document?

a war, the Civil War
the amendment, the Thirteenth Amendment

Remember, do not capitalize small words like *and*, *of*, and *the*.

1–4. Write these sentences correctly. Add capital letters when they are needed.

1. The american revolution began in 1776.

____

____

2. The declaration of independence was written the next year.

____

____

3. President Lincoln delivered his gettysburg address in 1863.

____

____

4. The battle of bataan occurred during world war II.

____

____

Name ______________________ Date ____________

Capitalizing the Titles of Books, Stories, and Essays

The titles of books, stories, and essays are **proper nouns** and should always be capitalized. Do not capitalize small words such as *and*, *of*, and *the* unless they begin the title.

book *There's a Tarantula in My Purse*
story "The Screech Owl Who Liked Television"

Remember, put the titles of book chapters, stories, and essays inside quotation marks.

Thinking Question
Which words are part of a title?

1–4. Write these sentences correctly. Add capital letters where they are needed. Be sure to underline book titles.

1. I like Jean Craighead George's book *how to talk to your dog.*

____

____

2. Have you read Mark Twain's short story, "the celebrated jumping frog of calaveras county"?

____

____

3. A book by Jean Craighead George that I want to read is *julie of the wolves.*

____

____

4. Two of Ralph Waldo Emerson's famous essays are "the poet" and "experience."

____

____

Name _______________________ Date ____________

Capitalizing Languages, Races, and Nationalities

The names of languages, races, and nationalities are **proper nouns.** They should always be capitalized.

languages: English, Spanish, Quechua, Arabic, Swahili
races: African American, Pacific Islander
nationalities: Canadian, Spanish, Chilean, Saudi Arabian

Thinking Question
What word names a language, race, or nationality?

1–4. Write these sentences correctly. Add capital letters where they are needed.

1. In middle school, chinese and russian language classes are offered.

____

____

2. I am part latino and part italian.

____

____

3. swedish, danish, and norwegian people live in northern Europe.

____

____

4. moroccans and south africans live in opposite ends of Africa.

____

____

Name ______________________ Date __________

The Screech Owl Who Liked Television
Grammar: Spiral Review

Kinds of Verbs

Action Verb	Helping Verb and Main Verb
The three puppies barked all night long.	The puppies are chewing Mr. Arnold's slippers.

1–4. Underline the action verb in each sentence.

1. Mom got the puppies at a shelter.
2. The whole family loved the puppies at first sight.
3. Francis and I take the puppies for a walk every day.
4. The puppies climbed into their basket for a nap.

5–8. Underline the helping verb once and the main verb twice.

5. Jamie is reading an article about screech owls.
6. A small gray owl had built a nest in a tree outside his window.
7. The owl has flown to another part of the yard.
8. The owl will return to the nest with food for its babies.

9–10. Combine each pair of sentences to make one sentence with a compound predicate. Write the sentence on the line.

9. Our new dog Rough sits. He waits for the school bus to arrive.

____

____

10. Rough's old owners moved. They could not take Rough with them to their new apartment.

____

____

Name ______________________ Date ____________

Conventions

Capitalize all proper nouns. Capitalize:

- historical events and documents
- titles of books, stories, and essays
- names of languages, races, and nationalities

Do not capitalize small words like *and*, *of*, and *the*. Put the titles of book chapters, stories, and essays inside quotation marks.

1–4. Write these sentences correctly. Add capital letters where they are needed.

1. In canada, many people speak both english and french.

____

____

2. The hebrew word *shalom* and the arabic word *salaam* both mean "peace."

____

____

3. The ancient greeks and romans both controlled huge empires.

____

____

4. Books by walter jones include *play ball!* and *the swinging step.*

____

____

Name ______________________ Date ____________

Focus Trait: Ideas

Vivid Details

Vivid supporting details help readers remember your point and make your writing more specific and persuasive.

No Vivid Detail	Vivid Detail
You shouldn't eat junk food. It is bad for you.	You shouldn't eat junk food. The high sugar content can cause cavities. Eating too much junk food can also lead to weight problems.

A. Fill in the blank with the title of your favorite book. Then write two vivid supporting details that would help persuade others that the book is good.

My favorite book is ______________________________

Vivid supporting detail: ______________________________

____

Vivid supporting detail: ______________________________

____

B. Work with a partner. Select something such as a sports team, movie, or food that you both agree is the best. Work together to write a paragraph to persuade others to agree. Start with a statement of what you think is the best. Then include at least two vivid details that support your point.

____

____

____

____

____

____

____

Name ______________________________ Date ____________

Sequence of Events

Read the selection below.

Flood!

On the morning of April 13, 1992, there was a massive flood in downtown Chicago. Thousands of people fled, terrified of being trapped. Later, they heard what had happened.

First, a hole about 20 feet wide had broken in an underwater tunnel in the Chicago River. Over 250 million gallons of water flowed into the tunnel. The water surged quickly through a large network of old tunnels. Many tunnels couldn't hold the surge and cracked. Water gushed into basements across the area.

By noon, over a million people had been removed safely from downtown. Electricity and gas were shut off. Buses and trains were rerouted, affecting the whole city.

Emergency workers from up to 100 miles away came to help. It took three days to plug the holes and stop the flooding. More than six weeks passed before things went back to normal. When it was all over, the flood had cost over a billion dollars.

Use the Flow Chart to show the sequence of events that took place during the 1992 Chicago Flood. Write complete sentences.

Event:

↓

Event:

↓

Event:

↓

Event:

Name ______________________ Date __________

Sequence of Events

Read the selection below.

The Blizzard of 1888

When too much snow falls all at once, it can be deadly. That's what happened on January 12, 1888, the day the Great Blizzard struck the Great Plains of the United States.

When Tom Anders and his sister Winnie left for school that morning, large snowflakes fell thickly from the sky. After walking the two miles to school, they looked like snowmen!

All that day, the snow fell. By the afternoon, more than two feet of fresh, fluffy snow covered the ground. Because the storm was worsening the teacher dismissed school early.

Tom and Winnie started the walk home. The snow fell so heavily they could barely see their way. They held hands tightly as they plunged through the drifts. Finally they saw a faint gleam of light, and then they were home! Their feet were so numb they sat before the large kitchen fire for an hour before they had any feeling in their toes.

Many people never reached their homes that day. When the temperature dropped that night, people and farm animals who were outdoors froze to death within minutes. The Blizzard of 1888 was the worst this country has ever seen.

Use a Flow Chart like this one to organize the events of the selection. Then answer the questions.

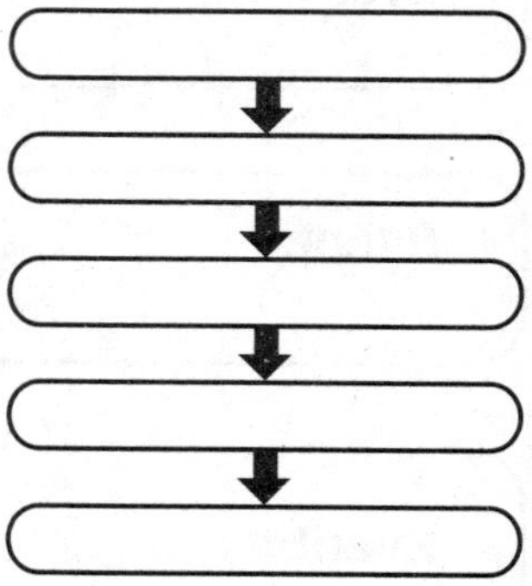

1. What clues does the author give you to help you understand the sequence of events?

____

____

____

2. Explain an event in the selection that influences future events.

____

____

Name ______________________ Date ____________

Synonyms

damaged	dangerous	flee	protective
daring	wobbles	frightened	

Read each sentence. Rewrite each sentence by using one of the synonyms above in place of the underlined word or words.

1. The brave warrior led his troops in battle.

____

2. We practiced how to escape if there was a fire in the school.

____

3. Some parts of the world experience harmful earthquakes.

____

4. The vase was broken during the move.

____

5. My older brother is very caring toward me.

____

6. During a storm, my dog is scared of the thunder.

____

7. During an earthquake, the ground shakes.

____

Name ____________________ Date __________

Words with *-ed* or *-ing*

Basic Complete the puzzle by writing the Basic Word for each clue.

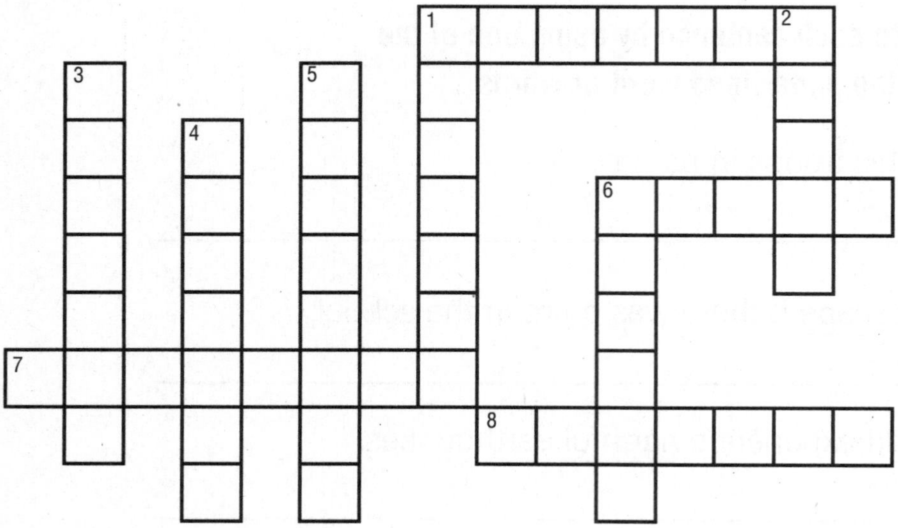

Across

1. fell in drops
6. to rush at top speed
7. shutting with a click
8. gaining a victory

Down

1. moving to music
2. challenged
3. punching or slapping
4. a lined pattern
5. boasting
6. going up

Spelling Words

1. rising
2. traced
3. stripped
4. slammed
5. dancing
6. striped
7. winning
8. snapping
9. bragging
10. handled
11. dripped
12. begged
13. dared
14. skipped
15. hitting
16. spotted
17. raced
18. dimmed
19. spinning
20. escaped

Challenge

urged
striving
whipped
breathing
quizzed

Challenge 11–14. Your class had a spelling bee yesterday. Write a short paragraph about it for your school paper. Use four of the Challenge Words. Write on a separate sheet of paper.

Name ______________________ Date ____________

Spelling Word Sort

Write each Basic Word beside the correct heading.

Adding *-ed*: final *e* dropped	**Basic Words:** **Challenge Words:**
Adding *-ing*: final *e* dropped	**Basic Words:** **Challenge Words:** **Possible Selection Words:**
Adding *-ed*: final consonant doubled	**Basic Words:** **Challenge Words:** **Possible Selection Words:**
Adding *-ing*: final consonant doubled	**Basic Words:** **Possible Selection Words:**

Challenge Add the Challenge Words to your Word Sort.

Connect to Reading Look through *The Earth Dragon Awakes.* Find words that have *-ed* or *-ing*. Add them to your Word Sort.

Spelling Words

1. rising
2. traced
3. stripped
4. slammed
5. dancing
6. striped
7. winning
8. snapping
9. bragging
10. handled
11. dripped
12. begged
13. dared
14. skipped
15. hitting
16. spotted
17. raced
18. dimmed
19. spinning
20. escaped

Challenge

urged
striving
whipped
breathing
quizzed

Name ______________________ Date ____________

Proofreading for Spelling

The Earth Dragon Awakes
Spelling: Words with *-ed* or *-ing*

Find the misspelled words and circle them. Write them correctly on the lines below.

My grandfather beged his parents to let him leave home to see the world. When they finally agreed, my grandfather began danceing and spining across the spoted rug in the living room. He escapt disaster as he nearly slamed into the wall. But with excitement in the air, he skiped dinner and racd upstairs to get his suitcase. He packed some pants and his favorite stiped shirts.

He was a young man when he left his home in Peru, South America. My grandfather handld all his own travel arrangements, and before he left, he tracid a map for his parents, showing the route the steamship would be traveling. For twenty-one days he did not see land. When the lights on the steamship dimed, my grandfather sat and thought about his future. The steamship arrived in San Francisco on April 18, 1906, the day of the big earthquake.

1. ____________ 7. ____________
2. ____________ 8. ____________
3. ____________ 9. ____________
4. ____________ 10. ____________
5. ____________ 11. ____________
6. ____________ 12. ____________

Spelling Words

1. rising
2. traced
3. stripped
4. slammed
5. dancing
6. striped
7. winning
8. snapping
9. bragging
10. handled
11. dripped
12. begged
13. dared
14. skipped
15. hitting
16. spotted
17. raced
18. dimmed
19. spinning
20. escaped

Challenge

urged
striving
whipped
breathing
quizzed

Name ______________________ Date ____________

Singular Possessive Nouns

A **singular possessive noun** shows ownership by one person or thing. Add *-'s* to a singular noun to make it possessive.

singular possessive noun
the Earth Dragon's anger

Thinking Question
What word shows ownership by one person or thing?

1–8. Write each phrase another way. Use the possessive form of the underlined noun.

1. the father <u>of Chin</u> ____________ father
2. the son of <u>Ah Sing</u> ____________ son
3. the rumble <u>of an earthquake</u> an ____________ rumble
4. the shout <u>of a person</u> a ____________ shout
5. the courage <u>of a father</u> a ____________ courage
6. the fear <u>of the boy</u> the ____________ fear
7. the help <u>of a friend</u> a ____________ help
8. the smile <u>of the rescuer</u> the ____________ smile

Name ____________________ Date __________

Plural Possessive Nouns

A **plural possessive noun** shows ownership by more than one person or thing. When a plural noun ends with *-s*, add only an apostrophe to make it possessive. When a plural noun does not end in *-s*, add an apostrophe and *-s* to make it possessive.

plural possessive noun

the dragons' caves the men's stories

Thinking Question
What word shows ownership by more than one person or thing?

Write each phrase another way. Use the possessive form of the underlined noun.

1. legends <u>of different countries</u>
   different ____________________ legends
2. the long necks <u>of the sea serpents</u>
   the ____________________ long necks
3. the footprints <u>of the children</u>
   the ____________________ footprints
4. the huge wings <u>of the dragons</u>
   the ____________________ huge wings
5. the brave actions <u>of the young women</u>
   the ____________________ brave actions
6. the towers <u>of the castles</u>
   the ____________________ towers

Name ______________________ Date ____________

Apostrophes in Possessive Nouns

Some plural nouns do not end in *-s*. To make these plural nouns possessive, add *-'s*.

plural possessive nouns
her feet's soles his teeth's braces

1–8. Write each phrase another way. Use the possessive form of the underlined noun.

1. the choice of the people ____________________
2. the soft wool belonging to the sheep ____________________
3. the nests belonging to the mice ____________________
4. the tracks of the deer ____________________
5. the annoying honks of the geese ____________________
6. the stubbornness of the oxen ____________________
7. the colored fins belonging to fish ____________________
8. the safety of the children ____________________

Name ______________________ Date ____________

Simple Verb Tenses

Present Tense	That volcano **erupts** about every hundred years.
Past Tense	It last **erupted** in 1945.
Future Tense	I wonder if it **will erupt** in my lifetime.

1–6. Underline the verb in each sentence. Write *present, past,* or *future* for each verb.

1. Kate's uncle Alan moved to Los Angeles last year. ______________
2. The area experiences several earthquakes every year. ______________
3. Alan got a job at an earthquake research laboratory. ______________
4. He will study earthquake activity there for two years. ______________
5. His research will provide scientists with new information. ______________
6. Kate misses her uncle and his silly jokes. ______________

7–10. Correct this journal entry. There are four mistakes in verb tense. Write the correct verbs on the lines below.

Yesterday morning I woke up with a jolt. Books fall off my shelf. Then the pictures on my walls will crash to the floor. It takes me a few seconds, but finally I understood. It was an earthquake! All day, we will wait for aftershocks. Luckily, there were none.

7. ______________ 9. ______________

8. ______________ 10. ______________

Name ______________________ Date ____________

Ideas

You can use possessive nouns to make details clearer by showing ownership.

Unclear Detail	Clear Detail
The siren was louder than the cries.	The siren was louder than my baby brother's cries.

1–6. Rewrite each sentence to show ownership of the underlined word or words. Use possessive nouns. Write the new sentence on the line.

1. The tornado siren frightened our visitors.

____

2. The loud, shrill sound made the windows rattle.

____

3. Jacob said we should hurry to the shelter.

____

4. The shelter is a basement room with emergency supplies.

____

____

5. My uncle entertained us with songs while we waited for the all-clear signal.

____

____

6. The music helped everyone to relax, even the dog.

____

Name ______________________ Date ____________

Lesson 12
PRACTICE BOOK

The Earth Dragon Awakes
Writing: Write to Persuade

Focus Trait: Ideas

Giving Facts and Examples

When you write a problem-solution paragraph, follow these steps:

1. State the problem clearly.
2. Explain why you think it is a problem.
3. Give one or more possible solutions.
4. Use facts and examples to support the possible solutions.
5. Tell which solution you think is best, and explain why.

Think of a problem that you can help to fix. Complete the outline for a problem-solution paragraph.

1. Problem: ______________________

____

2. Reason: ______________________

____

3. Possible solution: ______________________

____

a. Fact/example: ______________________

____

b. Fact/example: ______________________

____

4. My solution: ______________________

____

Name ______________________ Date ____________

Cause and Effect

Read the selection below.

Protecting Coral Reefs

Tourism brings many visitors to areas where beautiful coral reefs grow. As a result, the coral reefs suffer. People come to snorkel, dive, and boat. These activities are bad for the reefs because people and their boats break the fragile coral. They also stir up sediment, which creates stress on corals.

Large numbers of tourists increase the demand for fish and shellfish at local restaurants. Because of this, some of the world's most popular coral reefs are overfished. Today people are working to balance the important tourist industry with the need to protect the coral reefs.

Complete the Flow Chart with cause-and-effect relationships in the selection. Write in complete sentences.

Cause:

↓

Effect:

↓

Effect:

↓

Effect:

Name ______________________ Date ____________

Antarctic Journal
Comprehension:
Cause and Effect

Cause and Effect

Read the selection below.

Antarctic Fur Seals

A kind of seal that lives in the Antarctic is the fur seal. Fur seals get their name from their thick, silky fur. Their fur is so beautiful that people want it for coats and for hats. In the nineteenth century, the fur seals were hunted so much that they almost died out. As a result, fur seals seem not to trust humans, even today.

Today, these marvelous marine mammals have made quite a comeback. They live in great numbers on the rocky islands west of the Antarctic continent. Why did the seals come back? One reason is that people stopped hunting them as much.

Another reason is stranger. People also hunted whales in great numbers. Whales eat krill, a small shrimp-like sea animal. Fur seals also eat krill. Because there were fewer whales, there was more krill for the fur seals to eat. So their numbers grew.

Fur seals are not as threatened today as they once were. However, they still need our attention and protection.

Use a Flow Chart like the one shown to identify cause-and-effect relationships in the selection. Then answer the questions below.

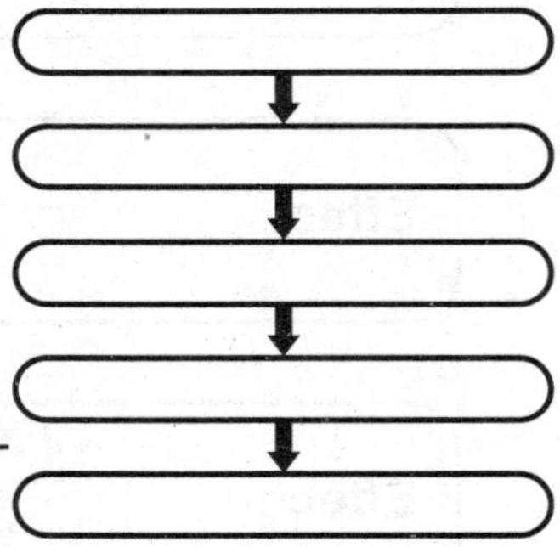

1. What caused the fur seals to almost become extinct?

____

____

2. What was the result of too much hunting of whales?

____

____

Name ____________________________ Date ____________

Greek and Latin Word Parts *spect*, *struct*, *tele*, and *vis*

Each word in the box comes from a Greek or Latin word. *Spect* means "look." *Vis* means "see." *Struct* means "build," and *tele* means "far away." Use the meanings of the Greek and Latin word parts to help you understand the meanings of the words.

respect	instruct	telescope	vision
inspected	visible	television	construction

Complete each sentence using one of the words from the box above. Write the correct word on the line.

1. We used a ____________ to see the planet Jupiter.
2. The class watched an interesting program on ____________ .
3. The teacher will ____________ us on what to do in a fire drill.
4. Be polite and show ____________ to all people.
5. Germs are small and only ____________ with a microscope.
6. I need glasses to correct my ____________ .
7. Get your car ____________ to make sure it is safe.
8. Wear a hard hat at the building ____________ site.

Name ____________________ Date ____________

More Words with *-ed* or *-ing*

Basic **Write the Basic Word that best replaces the underlined word or words.**

1. My family likes to go walking for exercise on summer vacation. ____________
2. We are placing together a plan for our next trip. ____________
3. We are looking for information about what to do. ____________
4. Last summer, we journeyed to a national park. ____________
5. My brother and I planned our route. ____________
6. Our mother volunteered to help us. ____________
7. My brother had a habit of rambling off on his own. ____________
8. Mom was starting to get worried, but he returned. ____________
9. We may try going to the lake! ____________
10. My dad is calling ahead for cabin reservations. ____________
11. I am inspecting our raft for leaks. ____________

Challenge 12–14. **Write a short paragraph about having dinner and then playing a game with your family or friends. Use three of the Challenge Words. Write on a separate sheet of paper.**

Spelling Words

1. wiped
2. covered
3. mapped
4. pleasing
5. slipped
6. putting
7. traveled
8. seeking
9. visiting
10. mixed
11. shipped
12. phoning
13. offered
14. smelling
15. hiking
16. checking
17. fainted
18. landed
19. becoming
20. wandering

Challenge

amusing
entertained
admitted
stunning
starving

Name ______________________ Date ____________

Spelling Word Sort

Antarctic Journal
Spelling: More Words with *-ed or -ing*

Write each Basic Word beside the correct heading.

***-ed*: no spelling change**	**Basic Words:** **Challenge Words:** **Possible Selection Words:**
***-ing*: no spelling change**	**Basic Words:**
***-ed*: final *e* dropped**	**Basic Words:** **Possible Selection Words:**
***-ing*: final *e* dropped**	**Basic Words:** **Challenge Words:** **Possible Selection Words:**
***-ed*: final consonant doubled**	**Basic Words:** **Challenge Words:** **Possible Selection Words:**
***-ing*: final consonant doubled**	**Basic Words:** **Challenge Words:** **Possible Selection Words:**

Spelling Words

1. wiped
2. covered
3. mapped
4. pleasing
5. slipped
6. putting
7. traveled
8. seeking
9. visiting
10. mixed
11. shipped
12. phoning
13. offered
14. smelling
15. hiking
16. checking
17. fainted
18. landed
19. becoming
20. wandering

Challenge

amusing
entertained
admitted
stunning
starving

Challenge Add the Challenge Words to your Word Sort.

Connect to Reading Look through *Antarctic Journal*. Find words that have *-ed* or *-ing*. Add them to your Word Sort.

Name ______________________ Date __________

Proofreading for Spelling

Antarctic Journal
Spelling: More Words with *-ed* or *-ing*

Find the misspelled words and circle them. Write them correctly on the lines below.

I liked smeling the fresh coffee while I miksed pancake batter and the blueberries that were shiped to Palmer Station. As I was mixing one day, I heard a loud rumbling noise. Before I could go outside to investigate, I had to put on my parka, a wool hat, and boots. I also coverd my face with sunscreen and grabbed my sunglasses because I didn't want to risk a bad sunburn or snow blindness. My sunglasses were dirty and needed to be wipet. They landded on the snow when I was out wandereng around and sliped on the ice last night. My friends thought I'd fainttted, but that was not the case. I am new here and hikeing on open ground is a bit tricky.

When I got outside, I saw a big blue whale and a newborn calf exhaling a blast of hot wet air. It was such a pleaseing site! I really enjoy visitting new places!

1. ______________ 7. ______________
2. ______________ 8. ______________
3. ______________ 9. ______________
4. ______________ 10. ______________
5. ______________ 11. ______________
6. ______________ 12. ______________

Spelling Words

1. wiped
2. covered
3. mapped
4. pleasing
5. slipped
6. putting
7. traveled
8. seeking
9. visiting
10. mixed
11. shipped
12. phoning
13. offered
14. smelling
15. hiking
16. checking
17. fainted
18. landed
19. becoming
20. wandering

Challenge

amusing
entertained
admitted
stunning
starving

Name ______________________ Date ____________

Regular and Helping Verbs

You form the past tense of **regular verbs** by adding *-ed*: He walked. If the verb ends in *e*, drop the *e* before adding *-ed*: They moved.

A **helping verb** such as *have*, *has*, or *had* comes before the main regular verb and tells more about what happened in the past. Helping verbs must agree with the subject of the sentence.

Thinking Question
Which verb ends with -ed? Which verb comes before the regular verb and tells more about the action?

1–8. Write the past-tense form of the verb in parentheses. Underline the helping verb, if there is one.

1. She has (walk) __________ home every day for a week.
2. Chantal (watch) __________ the snow fall from her window.
3. The ranger has (save) __________ the injured fur seal.
4. The guide (instruct) __________ us how to walk in the snow.
5. Our class has (learn) __________ how to help protect animals.
6. Armando (wish) __________ he could see a live whale.
7. She (wipe) __________ the lens of the telescope.
8. Lee has (follow) __________ the marathon with interest.

Name ______________________________ Date ____________

Past Participles

Form the past tense of regular verbs by adding *–ed* to its present-tense form. The **past participle** of regular verbs is the same as the past-tense form.

past participle
Dennis had lifted the heavy box.
He has strained to get it up the stairs.

Thinking Question
Does the main verb end with -ed?

1–8. Underline the past participle in each sentence.

1. NASA has launched a new space probe to Jupiter.
2. I have wanted to travel in space.
3. The first man has walked on the Moon.
4. Neil Armstrong had trained for his trip to the moon for many years.
5. The Italian astronomer Galileo Galilei had observed the moons of Jupiter.
6. We have waited until after dark to look for shooting stars.
7. The Hubble telescope has photographed many distant galaxies.
8. Astronomers had considered Pluto a planet until 2006.

Name ______________________ Date ____________

Using Helping Verbs

Antarctic Journal
Grammar: Regular Verbs

Helping verbs such as *have*, *has*, or *had* are often used with **past participles**. This is another way to show that something happened in the past. The helping verb must agree with the subject of the sentence.

Correct: Angela has watched the seals this week.

Incorrect: We has watched wildlife the whole time.

Thinking Question
Does the helping verb agree with the subject of the sentence?

1–8. Write the correct form of the verb *have* and the past participle for the regular verb in parentheses.

1. Arturo (want) ______________________ a new sled for months.
2. She (wait) ______________________ for the polar bears to appear all afternoon.
3. The birds (live) ______________________ on that rocky island for years.
4. People (hunt) ______________________ fur seals too much.
5. The first lesson (cover) ______________________ the wildlife of Antarctica.
6. The snow (thicken) ______________________ over the cold ground.
7. She (fix) ______________________ the car already.
8. We (worry) ______________________ about this dinner all day.

Name ______________________ Date ___________

Conjunctions

Use the conjunction *and* to join words or groups of words together. Use *or* to show a choice between items and *but* to show contrast.

The man and his dog arrived at the cabin.
It could snow or rain before the day ends.
The sun shined brightly yesterday, but the skies are gray today.

1–5. Write the conjunction that has the meaning shown in parentheses. If the sentence is compound, add a comma (,) before the conjunction and write *compound* next to the sentence.

1. (joins together) Clouds are forming __________ snow will fall soon.
2. (shows contrast) The temperature rises __________ the wind blows harder.
3. (joins together) The professor __________ his dog Milo prepare for the blizzard.
4. (joins together) The professor puts on a sweater __________ stokes the fire.
5. (shows choice) Will Milo __________ the professor fall asleep first?

6–8. Write a verb to complete each sentence.

6. Would you rather drive or __________ to the store?
7. The weather reporter has predicted a storm and I __________ to stay inside.
8. She has predicted storms before, but she __________ always been correct.

Name ______________________________ Date ____________

Conventions

When you revise your writing, be sure that the form of the helping verb *have* used with a past participle agrees with the subject of the sentence. Also make sure that you have used the past-tense form of a regular verb correctly.

1–8. Write a correct helping verb and the correct past participle of the regular verb in parentheses on the line.

1. Sheila (look) ____________________ after the garden.

2. The icicles (form) ____________________ on the roof.

3. Rolling hills (stretch) ____________________ in front of them.

4. A red-tailed hawk (soar) ____________________ overhead.

5. A bright star (twinkle) ____________________ above.

6. The noise (scare) ____________________ the boys.

7. You really (cook) ____________________ a good stew!

8. The girls (switch) ____________________ on the lantern.

Name ______________________ Date __________

Focus Trait: Voice

Persuasive Letter

Formal Tone	*Friendly Tone*
I'd like to invite you to see the snowmen and the ice sculptures.	Let's go see the snowmen and the ice sculptures together!

A. Read the parts of a letter below. Change some words to sound more friendly and sincere. Write your new words on the line.

Formal Tone	*Friendly Tone*
1. Dear Maria Martinez,	Dear __________
2. I hope you will join my family and me at the museum.	____________________ to the museum with ______________
3. There will be an exhibit on Antarctica.	We'll see an exhibit on ______________ ____________________

B. Rewrite each sentence using a friendly voice. Add or take out words, use synonyms, or change the sentence structure.

Pair/Share **Work with a partner to come up with reasons to go to the museum.**

Formal Tone	*Friendly Tone*
4. Since you like penguins so much, you should know that there will be live penguins.	
5. I have read that the museum will also have a penguin slide set up on the first day.	

Name ______________________ Date ____________

Text and Graphic Features

Read the selection below.

An Insider's Guide to Fish Care

Owning tropical fish can be fun, but it's also work. Follow these simple rules and your fish will lead happy, healthy lives.

- **Don't touch or hit the tank.** It disturbs the fish and their watery home.
- **Feed your fish every day.** Different types of fish eat different foods. It is also very important that they are not overfed. Ask the pet shop employees what to feed your fish and how much to feed them.
- **Make sure your fish are compatible.** You might enjoy having a lot of fish and watching them all swim together. However, certain types of fish just can't be in the same tank. Before you buy a fish, always ask whether it can live with the ones you already have.
- **Don't overstock your tank.** Having too many fish in the same tank can be harmful. They may fight for space or food or even try to eat each other if they feel threatened.
- **Maintain and clean the tank.** This must be done so that fish aren't harmed by algae and fungi. A clean tank also lets people see the fish better and enjoy their company.

Owning fish has many rewards and can give you a lot of happiness. Just make sure you take care of them properly!

This special message is brought to you by Fish Fans of America.

Complete the Column Chart to identify the purpose of text features used in the selection.

Text Feature	Location	Purpose

Name ______________________ Date ____________

Text and Graphic Features

Read the selection and examine the graph below.

Water in Nectar and Honey

How to read this chart

The bar graph below compares how much water is in nectar and honey. A thick bar represents each substance. Thin vertical lines, labeled 0 to 100, show percentage of water. Follow a thick bar from left to right. The line it ends near tells the percentage of water in the substance.

Who can use this chart

A beekeeper who wants to know what the hive needs might find this information useful. A dietitian, or a person studying the food value of honey, might find it interesting, too.

Water in Nectar and Honey

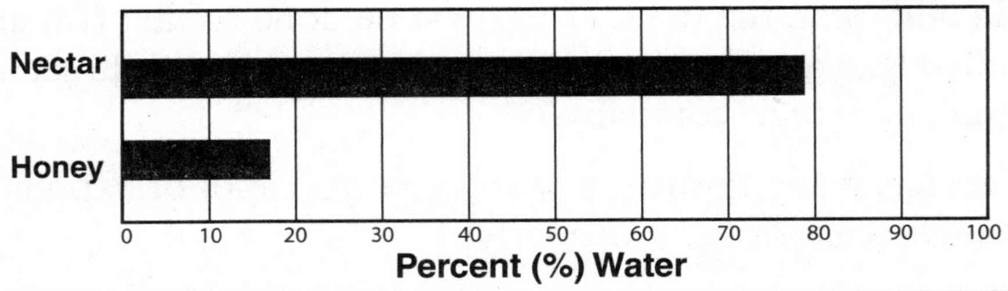

Analyze the selection's text and graphic features. Use a Column Chart to organize your thoughts. Then write your answers to the questions below.

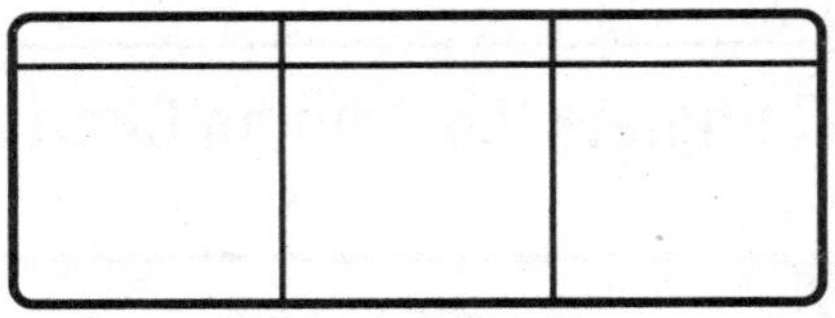

1. Why is information presented in a graph?

____

____

2. What kind of information is given in the bold headings?

____

____

Name ______________________ Date ____________

Suffixes *-able* and *-ible*

edible	changeable	collapsible
agreeable	visible	breakable

Each sentence below includes a word with the suffix *-ible* or *-able*. Complete each sentence.

1. A plastic apple is not edible because
   ____
2. One thing that can be described as collapsible is
   ____
3. The most agreeable people are the ones who
   ____
4. One example of changeable weather is snow on one day and
   ____
5. Something that is visible in the night sky is
   ____
6. One thing that is breakable is
   ____

Name ______________________ Date __________

Final Long *e*

Basic **Complete the puzzle by writing the Basic Word for each clue.**

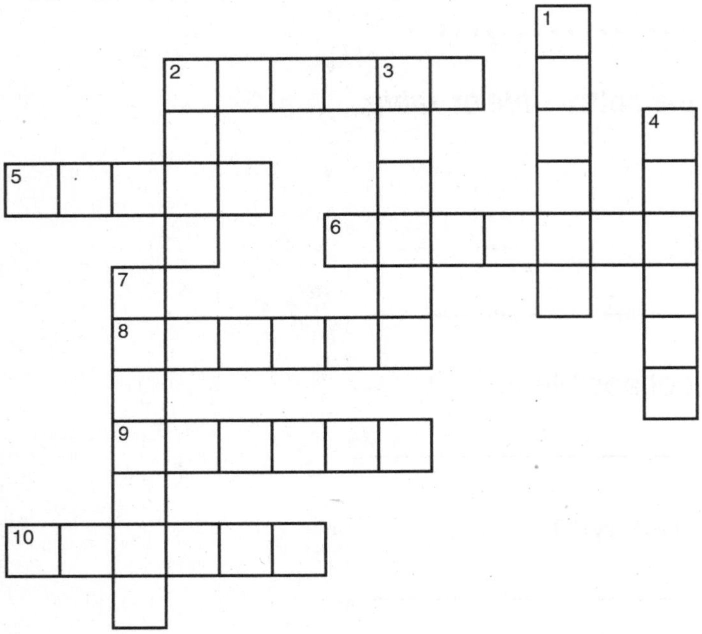

Across

2. sleepy
5. unoccupied
6. grassland
8. starving
9. music
10. constant

Down

1. hurt or wound
2. responsibility
3. full of stars
4. a lot of
7. smokestack

Challenge 11–14. **Write a story about a detective working on a case. Use three of the Challenge Words. Write on a separate sheet of paper.**

Spelling Words

1. turkey
2. lonely
3. colony
4. steady
5. hungry
6. valley
7. hockey
8. starry
9. melody
10. movie
11. duty
12. drowsy
13. chimney
14. plenty
15. daily
16. alley
17. fifty
18. empty
19. injury
20. prairie

Challenge

envy
fiery
mercy
discovery
mystery

Name ______________________ Date ____________

Spelling Word Sort

Write each Basic Word beside the correct heading.

Final /ē/ spelled *y*	**Basic Words:** **Challenge Words:** **Possible Selection Words:**
Final /ē/ spelled *ey*	**Basic Words:**
Other spellings for final /ē/	**Basic Words:**

Challenge Add the Challenge Words to your Word Sort.

Connect to Reading Look through ***The Life and Times of the Ant***. Find words that have the final /ē/ spelling patterns on this page. Add them to your Word Sort.

Spelling Words

1. turkey
2. lonely
3. colony
4. steady
5. hungry
6. valley
7. hockey
8. starry
9. melody
10. movie
11. duty
12. drowsy
13. chimney
14. plenty
15. daily
16. alley
17. fifty
18. empty
19. injury
20. prairie

Challenge

envy
fiery
mercy
discovery
mystery

Name ____________________ Date __________

Proofreading for Spelling

Find the misspelled words and circle them. Write them correctly on the lines below.

How would you like to share your bedroom with not one but fiftie or more of your closest friends? It might be crowded, but one thing is for sure—you wouldn't be lonelie. The underground nest of some ants can house up to 10 million ants. A colonie of ants can be found in many places—in an allie or in a valey. Ants love to feed on dead termites, caterpillars, and insects. They will eat the crumbs from your turky sandwich. These are some of the useful functions in the environment that hungery ants perform dayily. The next time you have some free time, instead of watching football or hocky on TV, try watching a movey about ants to learn more about these fascinating creatures!

1. ____________________ 6. ____________________
2. ____________________ 7. ____________________
3. ____________________ 8. ____________________
4. ____________________ 9. ____________________
5. ____________________ 10. ____________________

Spelling Words

1. turkey
2. lonely
3. colony
4. steady
5. hungry
6. valley
7. hockey
8. starry
9. melody
10. movie
11. duty
12. drowsy
13. chimney
14. plenty
15. daily
16. alley
17. fifty
18. empty
19. injury
20. prairie

Challenge

envy
fiery
mercy
discovery
mystery

Name ______________________ Date ____________

Present Participles

The **present participle** of regular verbs is formed by adding *-ing* to the verb. If the verb ends in *e*, drop the *e* before adding *-ing*.

walk + ing = walking

move + ing = moving

The **participle** form of a verb can be used as an adjective.

The crawling ants look very busy.

Their scurrying bodies are all over the grass.

Thinking Question
Which verb form ending in -ing *describes a noun?*

1–8. Write the correct form of the present participle in parentheses on the lines.

1. The (forage) ______________ ants ran for cover from the rain.
2. Their (shelter) ______________ nest keeps the rain out.
3. The (tower) ______________ anthill is really something to see!
4. The (shift) ______________ walls of the nest are not sturdy.
5. Last week, a (feast) ______________ armadillo ate many ants.
6. Its (project) ______________ nose dug them out.
7. Today, (harvest) ______________ ants are gathering leaves.
8. Their (slice) ______________ jaws cut leaves.

Name ______________________ Date ____________

Past Participles

Form the **past participle** of regular verbs by adding *-ed* to the verb. If the verb ends in *e*, drop the *e* before adding *-ed*. If the verb ends in *y*, drop the *y* and add *-ied*.

present	**past participle**
mix	mixed
store	stored
study	studied

Remember that the **participle** form of a verb can be used as an adjective.

Workers move stored eggs each day.
The ants must move to an expanded nest.

Thinking Question
Which verb form that tells about a past action modifies a noun?

1–8. On the line, write the correct form of the past participle for the regular verb shown in parentheses.

1. (chew) ____________ dirt and saliva form little bricks for ant tunnels.
2. (pack) ____________ dirt outside the tunnels forms an anthill.
3. Its (curve) ____________ roof traps heat from the sun.
4. (exchange) ____________ food bonds the ants of the colony.
5. A (damage) ____________ nest calls for extra work.
6. The (tire) ____________ ants keep working.
7. A totally (ruin) ____________ nest means starting over.
8. Workers can put any (rescue) ____________ larvae in the new nest.

Name ______________________________ Date ____________

Participial Phrases

A **participial phrase** begins with a **participle** and describes a noun.

Participial phrases are formed using past and present participles.

The children playing with the puppy leaped for joy.
Mariella returned to find her picnic lunch covered with ants.

Thinking Question
Which phrase contains a participle that tells about a subject?

1–5. Underline the participial phrase in each sentence.

1. Ants scurrying through the grass are in search of food.
2. Ants chewing on dirt are expanding their nest.
3. Ants working on their nest are ignored by the people above them.
4. Leafcutter ants have jaws adapted for cutting leaves.
5. Leaf parts carried in their jaws arrive back at the nest.

6–8. Write a participle based on the word in the parentheses to complete each participial phrase.

6. Ants (nest) ____________ beneath the rocks were left alone.
7. Ants often do not escape alive from a nest (disturb) ____________ by an anteater.
8. A picnic (invade) ____________ by ants is an unhappy scene.

Name ______________________ Date ____________

Writing Correct Sentences

The table shows different ways you can write sentences correctly.

Correct	I need a project partner. Will you be my partner?
Statement	I need a project partner.
Question	Have you found a project partner yet?
Command	Find a partner to complete your science project.
Exclamation	How very interesting their project is!
Using a participle	Working together, we can easily complete a science project.

1–3. Write these sentences correctly. Add capital letters and end marks. Write each run-on sentence as two sentences.

1. our science project will be about ants let's get to work

____

2. first we should make a poster will you draw some pictures

____

3. how many kinds of ants should we show on our poster

____

4–6. Combine the sentences correctly using a participle.

4. We will finish our report on time. We are working an hour a day.

____

5. We can take turns reading. It will be fun to share our work.

____

6. The poster is already finished. It is ready to hang up in the classroom.

____

Name ______________________ Date ____________

Sentence Fluency

You can combine sentences with participles to make them more varied and interesting.

People were watching the ants. They were curious.
People <u>watching</u> the ants were curious.

Rosa stood up. Her arm was covered with ants.
Her arm <u>covered</u> with ants, Rosa stood up.

1–5. Combine the sentences using participles. Use correct punctuation and capitalization. Write the sentence on the line.

1. We are learning about ants. We find them interesting.

   ____

2. The ant is one of the strongest creatures on Earth. It can lift five times its weight.

   ____

   ____

3. We created a proposal. We hope to buy an ant farm for our class.

   ____

4. We will become keen observers. We will improve our science skills.

   ____

5. We will properly care for our ant farm. It will be a great addition to our class.

   ____

Name ______________________ Date ____________

Focus Trait: Organization

Ordering Important Details

Unordered Details	Ordered Details
A honeybee's legs carry pollen to the plants that the bee visits. The legs of a honeybee allow it to do much more than walk. Like all insects, a honeybee has six legs.	Like all insects, a honeybee has six legs. The legs of a honeybee, however, allow it to do much more than walk. Its legs also carry pollen to the plants that the bee visits.

Read each main idea. Number the details below to show the order that best supports the main idea. Write the number on the line.

Main idea: It is easy to identify a honeybee.

_____ A honeybee's body is about half an inch long.

_____ A honeybee's body has three parts.

_____ Its body is hairy, and it is yellow and black in color.

_____ Like many insects, honeybees have four wings.

Main idea: Honeybees are important insects.

_____ Pollen must move from plant to plant so new plants can grow.

_____ Honeybees help farmers produce billions of dollars worth of crops.

_____ Honeybees help plants grow by carrying pollen from one plant to another.

_____ Honeybees pollinate many food crops, such as apples, nuts, cucumbers, and cherries.

Name ______________________ Date ____________

Main Ideas and Details

Read the selection below.

Winter Wonderland

Each year the approaching winter brings a sense of excitement to people who like snow.

Snow is great because you can have so much fun outside. Making snow angels, sledding, and building a snowman are great ways to spend time outside with family and friends.

If the snow is light and fluffy and packs well, you can even build a snow fort to hide from your "enemies" during snowball fights! You can catch snowflakes on your tongue and jump in snowdrifts three feet high.

And when the weather gets really cold, you can go inside your warm house and watch the snow outside fall quietly to the ground. Sipping cocoa under a cozy blanket, you can tell stories and talk about winter adventures to come.

Winter is a season to celebrate for its joy and beauty. It only lasts a few months each year, but it creates memories that last a lifetime!

Complete the Web below to identify the main idea and details about winter. Write your answers in complete sentences.

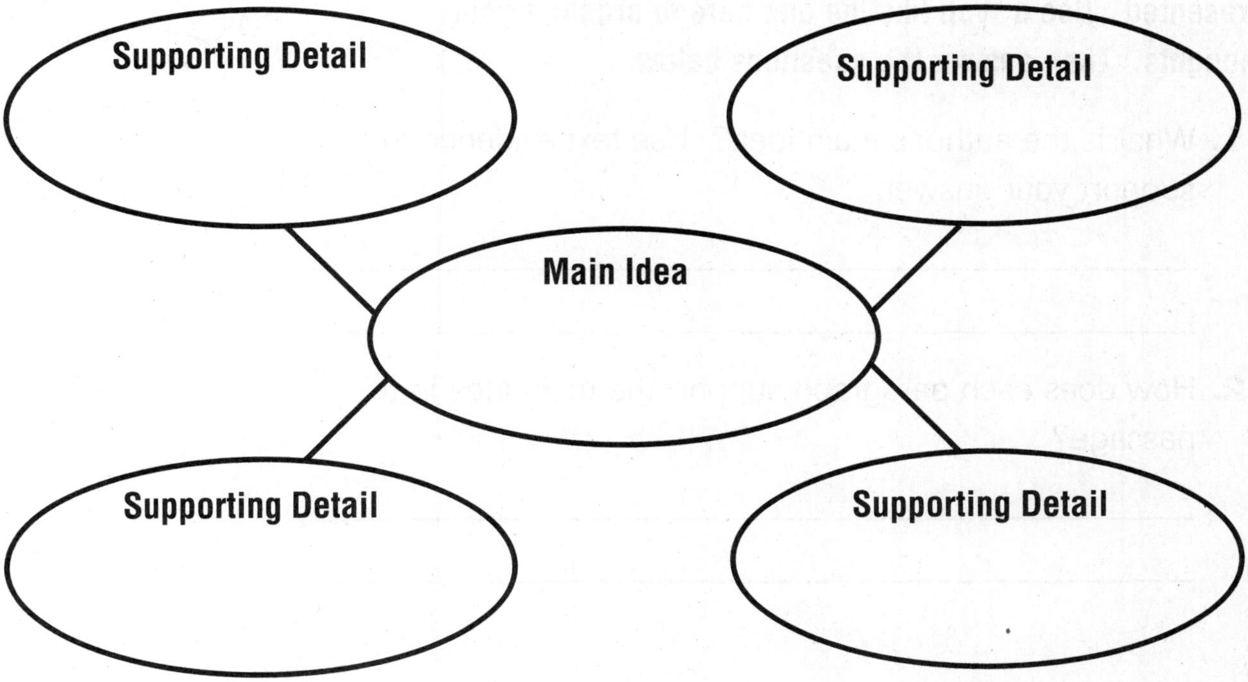

Name ______________________ Date __________

Main Ideas and Details

Read the selection below.

It's "Just" a Thunderstorm

Everyone fears tornadoes and earthquakes. But we rarely worry about thunderstorms. They seem so common that they're just annoying, right?

Wrong. Thunderstorms can be dangerous. About 10,000 severe thunderstorms strike the United States each year, bringing high winds that break tree limbs and uproot trees. These winds can down power lines. Some turn into tornadoes.

Severe thunderstorms may produce hail and flooding. Hail can damage cars and injure animals and people. Floods damage property and trap people and animals.

Lightning can be a very dangerous part of a severe storm. It can cause fires or other damage. It also can strike people directly and kill them.

The U.S. Weather Service provides early warnings about severe storms. When you hear these, remember that even though we see them more often than tornadoes, thunderstorms are no less dangerous.

Analyze the selection to evaluate the main idea and details presented. Use a Web like the one here to organize your thoughts. Then answer the questions below.

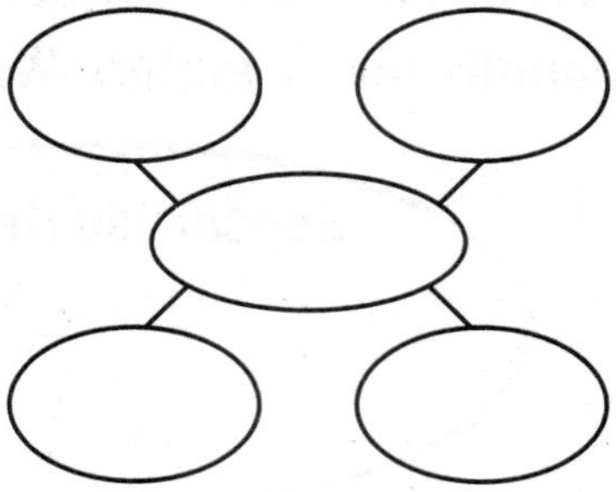

1. What is the author's main idea? Use text evidence to support your answer.

____

____

2. How does each paragraph support the main idea in the passage?

____

____

Name ______________________ Date ____________

Ecology for Kids
Vocabulary Strategies:
Multiple-Meaning Words

Multiple-Meaning Words

crash	channel	shape	tire
track	place	thunder	

Read each sentence. Write the number of the correct definition for the underlined word on the blank.

1. The glass fell off the table with a crash. ____________
1. a loud noise **2.** a collision, a wreck

2. Everyone cheered as he ran around the track. ____________
1. a mark, as a footprint **2.** a course set up for racing

3. The boat sailed down the channel. ____________
1. a waterway **2.** a means of communicating

4. She didn't want anyone to take her place. ____________
1. an area or region **2.** a position in line

5. The football player was in great shape. ____________
1. the outline of something **2.** physical condition

6. After we saw the lightning, we heard some thunder. ____________
1. to speak loudly **2.** a loud noise from the sky

7. I could not ride my bike because there was a hole in the tire. ____________
1. rubber covering a wheel **2.** to run out of energy

Name ______________________ Date ____________

Changing Final *y* to *i*

Basic **Write the Basic Word to complete each analogy.**

1. *Trees* are to *forests* as *cities* are to _____ .
2. *Biggest* is to *largest* as *smallest* is to _____ .
3. *Weakest* is to *strongest* as *liveliest* is to _____ .
4. *Seeds* are to *plants* as *caterpillars* are to _____ .
5. *Smoother* is to *rougher* as *tougher* is to _____ .
6. *Happier* is to *merrier* as *windier* is to _____ .
7. *Better* is to *best* as _____ is to *noisiest.*
8. *Lightest* is to *darkest* as *ugliest* is to _____ .
9. *Cleaning* is to *chores* as *photography* is to _____ .
10. *Cold* is to *colder* as *busy* is to _____ .

1. ____________________ 6. ____________________
2. ____________________ 7. ____________________
3. ____________________ 8. ____________________
4. ____________________ 9. ____________________
5. ____________________ 10. ____________________

Challenge 11–14. **You helped out at the community garage sale. Tell how you sorted items for sale. Use four of the Challenge Words. Write on a separate sheet of paper.**

Spelling Words

1. tiniest
2. hobbies
3. copied
4. countries
5. pitied
6. easier
7. laziest
8. families
9. spied
10. happiest
11. ladies
12. friendlier
13. studied
14. busier
15. breezier
16. prettiest
17. noisier
18. healthier
19. butterflies
20. funniest

Challenge

heaviest
categories
communities
multiplied
qualities

Name ______________________ Date ____________

Spelling Word Sort

Ecology for Kids
Spelling: Changing Final *y* to *i*

Write each Basic Word beside the correct heading.

Adding *-es* to a consonant + *y* word	**Basic Words:** **Challenge Words:** **Possible Selection Words:**
Adding *-ed* to a consonant + *y* word	**Basic Words:** **Challenge Words:**
Adding *-er* to a consonant + *y* word	**Basic Words:**
Adding *-est* to a consonant + *y* word	**Basic Words:** **Challenge Words:**

Challenge Add the Challenge Words to your Word Sort.

Connect to Reading Look through ***Ecology for Kids***. Find words that change the final *y* to *i* before adding *-es, -ed, -er,* or *-est*. Add them to your Word Sort.

Spelling Words

1. tiniest
2. hobbies
3. copied
4. countries
5. pitied
6. easier
7. laziest
8. families
9. spied
10. happiest
11. ladies
12. friendlier
13. studied
14. busier
15. breezier
16. prettiest
17. noisier
18. healthier
19. butterflies
20. funniest

Challenge

heaviest
categories
communities
multiplied
qualities

Name ______________________ Date ____________

Proofreading for Spelling

Ecology for Kids
Spelling: Changing Final *y* to *i*

Find the misspelled words and circle them. Write them correctly on the lines below.

Observing nature can be entertaining and informative. Nature has been speid upon and studyed through the ages and has taught ladys, gentlemen, and familes many lessons. We have coiped things we see happening in nature to make us healthyer and friendlyer. We have pityd people who take no notice of nature. Some of the prettyiest and funnieste things can be found in nature—look at a sunset, or look at baby birds, each noiser than the other, opening their mouths wide to be fed. Many people have found that some of their happist times have been spent observing nature.

1. ____________ 7. ____________
2. ____________ 8. ____________
3. ____________ 9. ____________
4. ____________ 10. ____________
5. ____________ 11. ____________
6. ____________ 12. ____________

Spelling Words

1. tiniest
2. hobbies
3. copied
4. countries
5. pitied
6. easier
7. laziest
8. families
9. spied
10. happiest
11. ladies
12. friendlier
13. studied
14. busier
15. breezier
16. prettiest
17. noisier
18. healthier
19. butterflies
20. funniest

Challenge

heaviest
categories
communities
multiplied
qualities

Name ______________________________ Date ____________

Using Irregular Verbs

Verbs that do not add *-ed* to show past action are called **irregular verbs**. You must remember the spellings of irregular verbs.

present tense verb: give
irregular past tense verb: gave

Thinking Question
What verb does not add -ed *to show past action?*

1–8. Write the correct form of the verb in parentheses to show past action.

1. The scientist (know) how to protect the environment.
   ____
2. Our science teacher (brings) photographs of various ecosystems to class. ________________
3. She (tells) us that one way to protect the environment is to stop pollution. ________________
4. It would also help the environment if we (grow) our own vegetables. ________________
5. We (take) very long showers. ________________
6. We (leave) the lights on in empty rooms.
   ____
7. We (drive) everywhere instead of walking or riding bikes.
   ____
8. My family and I (make) a plan for how to save water, electricity, and gasoline. ________________

Name ______________________ Date ____________

The Special Verb *be*

The verb *be* tells what someone or something is or is like. It does not show action. It can be used as a main verb or a helping verb. The verb *be* has special forms for different tenses and different subjects.

forms of the verb *be*

subject	**present tense**	**past tense**
I	am	was
he, she, it	is	was
we, you, they	are	were

past participle with form of helping verb *have*

I, we, you, they	have been
he, she, it	has been

Thinking Question
What is the subject? What is the tense? What form of be *is correct?*

1–6. Write the form of the verb *be* in parentheses that correctly completes each sentence.

1. Last week, the students (are, were) learning about ecosystems. ________
2. An ecosystem (is, are) a place where groups of living and nonliving things interact with their environment. ________
3. Forests, lakes, and deserts (is, are) examples of ecosystems. ________
4. Yesterday, I (am, was) working on a project about the ocean. ________
5. Today, I (am, was) presenting my project about the ocean to my classmates. ________
6. I (been, have been) enjoying learning about the ocean. ________

Name ______________________ Date ____________

Helping Verbs

Many **irregular verbs** change spelling when they are used with **helping verbs**. Often the new spelling uses *n* or *en* to show past tense.

Irregular verb: grow
Past tense: grew
Past tense form with helping verb: had grown

1–5. On the line, write the correct form of the verb in parentheses.

1. My class had (drive) ____________ all morning to get to the seashore.
2. Then we had (ride) ____________ in a boat to get to a mangrove swamp.
3. It was the first time I had (see) ____________ such a unique ecosystem.
4. When it heard us coming, a heron had (hide) ____________ among the trees.
5. Afterwards, a scientist had (speak) ____________ to us about preserving mangrove swamps.

Name ____________________ Date __________

Kinds of Pronouns

Ecology for Kids
Grammar: Spiral Review

Subject Pronouns	**He** and **she** read books about lightning.
Object Pronouns	Rachel introduced **him** to **us**.

1–4. Write a subject pronoun or an object pronoun to replace the underlined word or words in each sentence.

1. Dr. Frank Josephs gathered data from an experiment. __________
2. The experiments were performed by him and his assistant Lydia. __________
3. Dr. Josephs showed Lydia the data. __________
4. These scientists are studying the relationship between ice in clouds and lightning storms. __________

5–7. Combine the sentences by using the connecting word in parentheses. Change one of the subjects to a pronoun.

5. The light is hard to see. The light flashes in a fraction of a second. (because)

   ____

   ____

6. The scientists collect all the data. The scientists write a detailed report. (after)

   ____

   ____

7. Ms. Blaine was busy. Ms. Blaine answered all our questions about thunder and lightning. (although)

   ____

   ____

Name ______________________ Date ____________

Conventions

Incorrect Form of Verb
They dove into the bay and <u>taked</u> a look at its ecosystem.
Correct Form of Verb
They dove into the bay and <u>took</u> a look at its ecosystem.

1–5. Choose the correct form for the verb in the parentheses. Rewrite the sentences to make the author's meaning clear.

1. Yesterday, the scientists (find, found) an unfamiliar creature in the bay.

____

____

2. When they returned to shore, they (brung, brought) it to the laboratory.

____

____

3. They now (know, knew) some of the changes that happened as a result of pollution in the bay.

____

____

4. The scientists (writed, wrote) a report about their findings.

____

____

5. They (gived, gave) a talk about their discoveries.

____

____

Name ______________________ Date ____________

Focus Trait: Ideas

Focusing on the Main Idea

Good writers keep readers interested by keeping the details in each paragraph focused on its main idea. This writer deleted a sentence that did not support the main idea.

Lightning is caused by electric charges. Ice and raindrops move quickly in a storm cloud and create a charge at the bottom of the cloud. At the same time, an opposite charge is created on the ground. When sparks from the cloud meet sparks from the ground, they create a bolt of lightning. ~~A tree hit by a bolt of lightning can sometimes survive.~~

Main idea: *Lightning is caused by electric charges.*

Read the paragraph and write the main idea. Then cross out the sentence that does not support the main idea.

1. A fulgarite is a long tube in the ground created by lightning. First, lightning hits the ground and goes deep into the soil. A bolt of lightning has as much power as all the power plants in the United States can make in the same amount of time! The heat from the lightning melts sand in the ground, forming a fulgarite. This crusty tube shows the shape of the lightning bolt.

Main idea: ____

2. Benjamin Franklin performed an experiment that is now famous. He flew a kite in a big storm. A key was tied to the bottom of the kite string. Lightning struck, and sparks flew from the key! You can estimate how far lightning is by listening to thunder. A silk ribbon on the string kept Franklin's hand from getting hurt.

Main idea: ____

Name ______________________ Date ____________

Compare and Contrast

Read the selection below.

Horsing Around

Peanut, a golden colored horse, woke in the barn. She peered out the window to find fat snowflakes falling from the sky. The earth was covered in a thick blanket of snow!

"Look, it's snowing outside!" Peanut said to a brown horse named Chestnut.

"So?" Chestnut mumbled. He was eating his breakfast of hay.

"Let's go out and play in the snow," Peanut said.

Chestnut shook his head. "I don't like the cold."

"Wear your horse blanket, and you will be warm," Peanut said.

"I don't want to get my hooves and shiny coat wet or dirty," he said.

"But you will have fun!" Peanut said.

"I don't like to have fun. I want to stay inside where it's warm and dry."

Peanut shrugged, put on her warm blanket, and stepped outside onto the fresh snow. She trotted to the maple tree and stopped to examine the hoof prints she made in the snow. When Peanut looked back at the barn, she saw Chestnut wearing his blanket. He placed one hoof in the snow and shivered.

"Too cold!" Chestnut said and ran back into the barn.

Use the Venn Diagram to show how Peanut and Chestnut are similar and different. Try to use complete sentences.

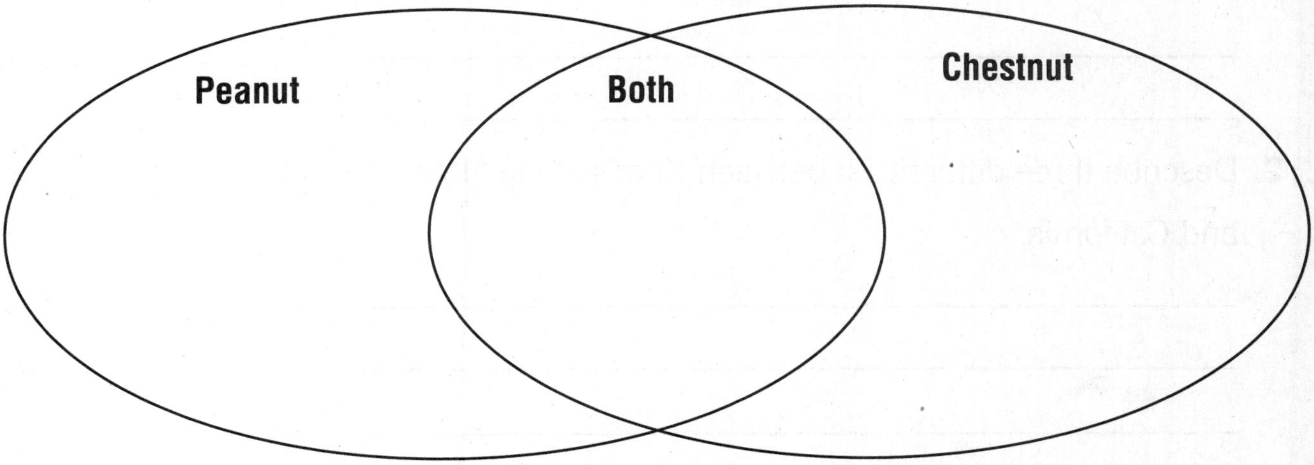

Name ______________________ Date ____________

Compare and Contrast

Read the selection below.

Hard Times

Dear Aunt Teresa,

Guess what? I got the job at Chez Pierre! I'll be working with the famous Chef Pierre himself! It wasn't easy getting the job. Besides my training at culinary school, I had to prepare some of Pierre's most popular dishes.

I love New York, but I miss California, the beach, and family and friends. But I've made lots of friends. The people in New York are as friendly as they are in California.

The weather here in New York is a lot different. I can't wear light clothing all year like in California. In the winter, I have to bundle up in layers of clothes. Summers in New York can be as hot as Los Angeles, though. But the great thing about New York is the changing seasons. We don't have that in California. You should see the colorful leaves in the autumn! And the New York snow is magnificent! I've never seen snow in Los Angeles!

Please visit soon!

Love,
Kerri

Use a Venn Diagram to compare Kerri's life in New York with her life in California. Then answer the questions.

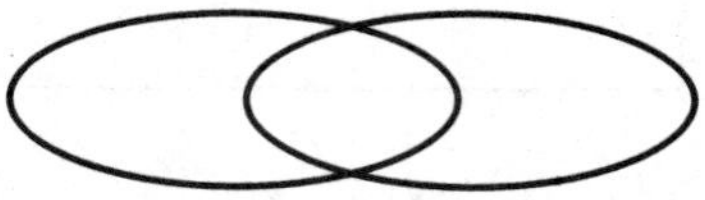

1. Explain whether Kerri prefers life in New York or California.

____

____

2. Describe three differences between Kerri's life in New York and California.

____

____

____

Name ______________________________ Date ____________

Using Context

Read each sentence or pair of sentences. Then circle the answer that best explains the meaning of the underlined word.

1. Don't shove so hard on the wagon. Just give it a nudge.
   a. kick **b.** gentle push **c.** flower

2. There were no factories or businesses on the street–only the dwellings of people who lived there.
   a. houses **b.** cars **c.** barns

3. After several mechanics failed to fix the car, we found a person who was capable of making the repair.
   a. has the ability to **b.** does not understand **c.** wants to

4. They did a thorough job picking up the bedroom. Not one thing remained on the floor.
   a. fast **b.** sloppy **c.** complete

5. The class didn't shout in protest when they got the big assignment, but several students grumbled about how hard it was.
   a. muttered **b.** hummed **c.** yelled

6. Bill thought he was safe at first, but the umpire thought he was out. Bill was angry about the call and started to quarrel with the umpire.
   a. discuss quietly **b.** argue **c.** dance

7. The trees sway in heavy winds, but they don't fall over.
   a. swing back and forth **b.** march **c.** circle

Name ______________________ Date ____________

Spelling /k/, /ng/, and /kw/

Basic **Write the Basic Word that best replaces the underlined word or words in each sentence.**

1. Some students love the subject of gymnastics.
2. We avoid dangerous gymnastic exercises.
3. Some fear making a blunder while performing.
4. A gymnast hit her feet on the balance beam.
5. Her feet will hurt until they're iced.
6. She will present a query to her coach about safety.
7. These two gymnasts have the same ability on the parallel bars.
8. Young gymnasts perform for the community audience.
9. Soon the empty scoreboard will show our score.
10. The scoreboard is flashing now in charged lights!
11. Let's have our outdoor party after practice.

1. ____________ 7. ____________
2. ____________ 8. ____________
3. ____________ 9. ____________
4. ____________ 10. ____________
5. ____________ 11. ____________
6. ____________

Challenge 12–14. **Write about the headline below. Use three Challenge Words. Write on a separate sheet of paper.**

IMPORTANT ARCHAEOLOGICAL DISCOVERY MADE

Spelling Words

1. risky
2. track
3. topic
4. blank
5. question
6. pocket
7. monkey
8. junk
9. equal
10. ache
11. public
12. attack
13. struck
14. earthquake
15. picnic
16. banker
17. electric
18. blanket
19. mistake
20. stomach

Challenge

request
skeleton
peculiar
attic
reckless

Name ________________________ Date ____________

Riding Freedom
Spelling: /k/, /ng/, and /kw/

Spelling Word Sort

Write each Basic Word beside the correct heading.

/k/ spelled *ck*	**Basic Words:** **Challenge Words:** **Possible Selection Words:**
/k/ spelled *k* or *c*	**Basic Words:** **Challenge Words:** **Possible Selection Words:**
Other spellings for /k/	**Basic Words:**
Spellings for /kw/	**Basic Words:** **Challenge Words:**
/ng/ before *k*	**Basic Words:**

Spelling Words

1. risky
2. track
3. topic
4. blank
5. question
6. pocket
7. monkey
8. junk
9. equal
10. ache
11. public
12. attack
13. struck
14. earthquake
15. picnic
16. banker
17. electric
18. blanket
19. mistake
20. stomach

Challenge

request
skeleton
peculiar
attic
reckless

Challenge Add the Challenge Words to your Word Sort.

Connect to Reading Look through *Riding Freedom*. Find words that have the /k/, /ng/, and /kw/ spelling patterns on this page. Add them to your Word Sort.

Name ______________________ Date ____________

Lesson 16
PRACTICE BOOK

Riding Freedom
Spelling: /k/, /ng/, and /kw/

Proofreading for Spelling

Find the misspelled words and circle them. Write them correctly on the lines below.

The stagecoach driver was glad to pull into the station yard. It had been a riskey ride. There was always the threat that outlaws would attak them. There was an eqal threat of the area being struk by an earthkwake. The driver had to leave her seat to remove some junck that obstructed the trak. She thought it might be an ambush—but all was well.

She was carrying a special passenger—a bankar, who carried a lot of money in his pockit. This passenger was very demanding—he even asked for an extra blankit. It all was enough to make the driver's stomak acke!

1. ______	7. ______
2. ______	8. ______
3. ______	9. ______
4. ______	10. ______
5. ______	11. ______
6. ______	12. ______

Spelling Words

1. risky
2. track
3. topic
4. blank
5. question
6. pocket
7. monkey
8. junk
9. equal
10. ache
11. public
12. attack
13. struck
14. earthquake
15. picnic
16. banker
17. electric
18. blanket
19. mistake
20. stomach

Challenge

request
skeleton
peculiar
attic
reckless

Name ______________________________ Date ____________

Adjectives

An **adjective** is a word that gives information about a noun. An adjective can tell *what kind* or *how many*.

A sudden boom of thunder scared the six horses.
drinking fountain (fountain for drinking)

Thinking Question
What words describe a noun? What noun does each word describe?

1–3. Write the adjectives that describe the underlined nouns. Then write *what kind* or *how many* for each adjective.

1. We saw several flashes of bright lightning across the sky.

____

2. The frightened horses bolted down the steep hill.

____

3. The cold, hard rain soaked the driver.

____

4–6. Write each adjective and the noun that it describes.

4. Today, heavy traffic often clogs the streets of big cities.

____

5. Drivers tied their horses to hitching posts while they ate their noon meal.

____

6. The rough, dirt roads of the past have been replaced by smooth highways.

____

Name ______________________ Date ______________

Adjectives After *be*

Adjectives describe nouns and words like *I*, *it*, and *we*. An adjective can follow the word it describes. This usually happens when an adjective follows a form of the verb *be*.

She was proud.

Thinking Question
What adjective follows a form of be*? What word does it describe?*

1–8. Underline each adjective. Then write the word that it describes on the line.

1. The river was deep. ______________
2. I am warm under the blanket. ______________
3. The driver is calm. ______________
4. It is foggy along the way. ______________
5. We were tired from the journey. ______________
6. The horses are strong. ______________
7. The coach was confident. ______________
8. The ride is bumpy. ______________

Name ______________________ Date ____________

Articles

An **article** is a kind of adjective. There are three articles: *a*, *an*, and *the*. *The* is used before a specific noun. *A* and *an* are used before a general noun. *A* is used before words that begin with a consonant sound. *An* is used before words that begin with a vowel sound.

one of a kind: the book I told you about
the right answer

any of a kind: a book, an artist, an honor

Thinking Question
What is the article in the sentence? What noun does it refer to?

Activity Write the correct article on each line.

We set out from ________ house early in ________ morning. Our horse went along at ________ steady pace. After ________ hour, I began to get tired. Then I heard ________ noise that made me sit up straight. It sounded like ________ bird. If so, it was ________ loudest bird I had ever heard. I kept ________ eye out, but I didn't see it. I did keep hearing ________ sound all through our ride, however. It was ________ interesting sound, even if it was also rather disturbing. What it was, I'll never know.

Name ______________________ Date ____________

Writing Proper Nouns

Proper Nouns			
People	**Pets**	**Places**	**Things**
Charlotte Parkhurst	Sparky	California	Monday
E. B. Stuart	Fluffy	Pikes Peak	January
Dr. Richard Cohen	Miss Bobo	Redwood Forest	Valentine's Day
Uncle Harry	Flicker	San Diego Museum of Art	Gold Rush

1–3. Write the proper noun or nouns in each sentence correctly on the line. Add capital letters and periods where they are needed.

1. Our driver, mr j d jones, helped us with our luggage.

____

2. On thursday, we hiked through the rocky mountains.

____

3. We spent the fourth of july with mr and mrs shaw.

____

4–6. Rewrite the sentences, replacing the underlined pronouns with proper nouns.

Dear Grandma,

We arrived safely at Concord Station in Culver City. We spotted Aunt Julie and her cute little puppies. She was waving to us. Patty and Rosie climbed into the back of the wagon with the dogs. They were so tired. They fell asleep before we reached the ranch.

Love, Addie

4. ______________________________

____

5. ______________________________

6. ______________________________

Name ______________________ Date ____________

Sentence Fluency

Short, Choppy Sentences	Combined Sentences with Adjective
The stagecoach pulled up to the inn. The stagecoach was crowded.	The crowded stagecoach pulled up to the inn.

1–2. Combine each pair of sentences by moving an adjective before a noun.

1. The seats inside the coach softened the bumpy ride. The seats were leather.

____

____

2. The door rattled the entire ride. The door was creaky.

____

____

Short, Choppy Sentences	Combined Sentences with Adjectives
The travelers were tired. They were hungry.	The travelers were tired and hungry.

3–4. Combine each pair of sentences by joining adjectives with the word *and*.

3. The old stagecoach was leaky. It was damp.

____

____

4. The scenery was beautiful on their journey west. The scenery was wild.

____

____

Name ______________________ Date ______________

Focus Trait: Ideas

Describing with Similes

Description	Description with Simile
The passengers huddled together.	The passengers huddled together like a bunch of grapes.

A. Read each description. Make it more vivid by adding a simile using *like* or *as*.

Description	Description with Simile
1. The river water was cold.	The river water was ______________________
2. The dark clouds moved quickly.	The dark clouds moved ______________________

B. Read each sentence. Add a simile to each sentence to make the description more vivid. Write your new sentences.

Pair/Share **Work with a partner to brainstorm similes to add.**

Description	Simile Added
3. The river had risen.	
4. The wood of the bridge moaned.	
5. The bridge timbers swayed.	

Name ______________________ Date ____________

Sequence of Events

Read the selection below.

Raising a Puppy to Be a Service Dog

Did you know that you can raise a puppy that will one day become a service dog? You could help change the life of someone with a disability.

Most organizations that train service dogs ask that you first fill out an application. Only the best candidates are chosen for the program.

To raise a successful service dog, you will then need to spend lots of time with it. These puppies need lots of love and cuddling and daily walks.

Next, your puppy will need to ride in the car with you whenever possible. This will get the dog used to traveling with its future owner. Taking the puppy to crowded parks and playgrounds will also help it get used to being around a lot of people.

Finally, you will probably have to attend special puppy training classes. All these things will prepare your puppy for its service dog training.

Complete the Flow Chart to show the sequence of events in raising a service dog puppy. Write in complete sentences.

Name ______________________ Date __________

Sequence of Events

Read the selection below.

A Life of Service

I wasn't always a service dog. In fact, I didn't know what was happening the day I first felt Max's big, warm hands pick me up and take me out of my cage. I was only a puppy, and I was frightened. The big hands simply petted me and gave me a treat.

After I gathered the courage to look up and see what belonged to the hands, I met Max. He looked so tall! Max came every day to pet me and give me treats. He seemed to want to be friends.

When I grew up a little, Max brought me to his house. We played lots of games! First, he taught me his favorite game: I opened a door, and I would win a treat. Now I play a difficult game. I hear a certain combination of sounds and do a task. If I get it right, I win more treats. I love playing with Max. I've become an expert!

Use a Flow Chart like the one here to help you explain the sequence of events. Then answer the questions below.

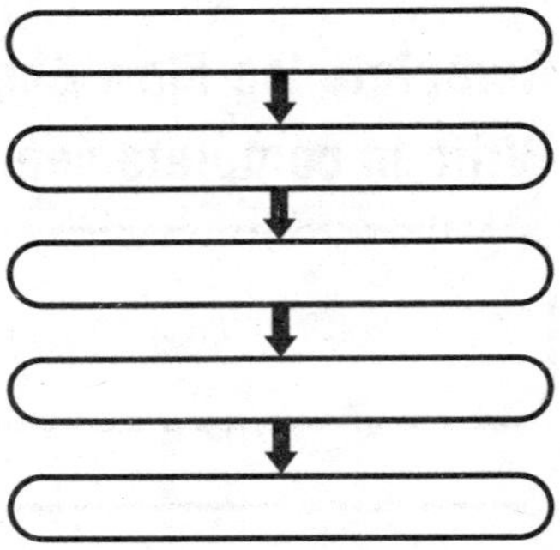

1. When did the narrator's service training begin? Support your answer with details from the selection.

____

____

____

2. How did the narrator become an "expert"? Support your answer with details from the selection.

____

____

____

Name ______________________ Date ____________

Suffixes *-ion*, *-ation*, *-ition*

information	exhibition	attention	graduation
competition	combination	cooperation	

Each sentence shows a word in parentheses that uses the suffix *–ion*, *–ation*, *or –ition*. Complete the sentence using the word in parentheses.

1. (information) When I read a newspaper ______________
____
2. (competition) She was excited about being ______________
____
3. (exhibition) He wanted to go see the paintings at ______________
____
4. (combination) I think that ice cream and cake is ______________
____
5. (attention) Yelling very loud will get you ______________
____
6. (cooperation) When you're working in a group at school
____
7. (graduation) After you finish school, ______________
____

Name ____________________ Date __________

Final /j/ and /s/

Basic Write the Basic Word that best completes each group.

1. preparation, training, ____________
2. workplace, department, ____________
3. buggy, coach, ____________
4. destruction, wreckage, ____________
5. observe, see, ____________
6. twofold, double, ____________
7. possibility, likelihood, ____________
8. bundle, carton, ____________
9. wedlock, matrimony, ____________
10. supervise, guide, ____________
11. look, peep, ____________

Challenge 12–14. Describe a garment you are designing for a school play. Use three Challenge Words. Write on a separate sheet of paper.

Spelling Words

1. glance
2. judge
3. damage
4. package
5. twice
6. stage
7. carriage
8. since
9. practice
10. marriage
11. baggage
12. office
13. message
14. bridge
15. chance
16. notice
17. ridge
18. manage
19. palace
20. bandage

Challenge

fringe
average
fleece
fragrance
excellence

Name ______________________ Date __________

Lesson 17
PRACTICE BOOK

The Right Dog for the Job
Spelling: Final /j/ and /s/

Spelling Word Sort

Write each Basic Word beside the correct heading.

/j/ in one-syllable words	**Basic Words:** **Challenge Words:**
/ĭj/ in two-syllable words	**Basic Words:**
/ĭj/ in words with more than two syllables	**Challenge Words:** **Possible Selection Words:**
Final /s/ spelled *ce*	**Basic Words:** **Challenge Words:** **Possible Selection Words:**

Spelling Words

1. glance
2. judge
3. damage
4. package
5. twice
6. stage
7. carriage
8. since
9. practice
10. marriage
11. baggage
12. office
13. message
14. bridge
15. chance
16. notice
17. ridge
18. manage
19. palace
20. bandage

Challenge

fringe
average
fleece
fragrance
excellence

Challenge Add the Challenge Words to your Word Sort.

Connect to Reading Look through ***The Right Dog for the Job.*** Find words that have the final /j/ and /s/ spelling patterns on this page. Add them to your Word Sort.

Name ______________________ Date ____________

Proofreading for Spelling

Find the misspelled words and circle them. Write them correctly on the lines below.

My sister Jenny's new guide dog, Goldie, is now a welcome member of our household. She came with very little bagage, just one squeaky toy. We've been to the pet store tweice sinse then, so now Goldie has a big basket of dog toys in Jenny's offise.

Goldie's a hero, too! A few weeks ago, she and Jenny walked along the rige behind our house. Jenny tripped and sprained her ankle. Goldie barked for help, and a police officer on a nearby brige heard her. He came, put a bandag on Jenny's ankle, and helped her home.

Last week there was a guide-dog award ceremony. The judje called Goldie and Jenny up on staje. He read a mesage Jenny had sent describing Goldie's actions. Then he gave Goldie a medal and Jenny a pakage with dog treats. Goldie looked like the queen of the palase.

1. ______________ 7. ______________
2. ______________ 8. ______________
3. ______________ 9. ______________
4. ______________ 10. ______________
5. ______________ 11. ______________
6. ______________ 12. ______________

Spelling Words

1. glance
2. judge
3. damage
4. package
5. twice
6. stage
7. carriage
8. since
9. practice
10. marriage
11. baggage
12. office
13. message
14. bridge
15. chance
16. notice
17. ridge
18. manage
19. palace
20. bandage

Challenge

fringe
average
fleece
fragrance
excellence

Name ______________________________ Date ____________

Adverbs That Tell How, When, and Where

An **adverb** is a word that tells something about a verb. Some adverbs tell *how*, *when*, or *where*. An adverb can come before or after the verb. Most adverbs that tell *how* end in *-ly*.

The adverbs in this sentence tell about the verb *played:*

when — Yesterday; **how** — happily; **where** — outside

Yesterday, our puppy played happily outside.

Thinking Question
What is the verb? What word tells how *about the verb?*

1–5. The verb in each sentence is underlined. Write the adverb. Then write whether it tells *when*, *how*, or *where*.

1. Leon talked softly to the new puppy. ____________________
2. Robo licked Leon's face excitedly. ____________________
3. Suddenly, Leon hugged Robo. ____________________
4. Now the family plays with Robo. ____________________
5. Leon taught Robo to sit there. ____________________

6–10. Underline each adverb. Write the verb it describes.

6. Someday Robo will learn how to behave. ____________________
7. He secretly chewed Dad's new slippers. ____________________
8. Mom put the puppy outside. ____________________
9. Robo wagged his tail innocently. ____________________
10. Everyone immediately laughed at the dog's expression.
____

Name _______________ Date _______________

Adverbs of Frequency and Intensity

An **adverb** is a word that tells something about a verb. Some adverbs tell how often something happens.

We usually walk in the park.
Ralph sometimes barks at birds.

Some adverbs tell how much of something is done.

He ate enough, but he hardly slept.
She almost won the race.

Thinking Question
Which word is the verb? Which word tells how often or how much?

1–5. The verb in each sentence is underlined. Write the adverb that tells *how often*.

1. I always take my dog, Pal, for a walk. _______________
2. Pal and I visit the dog park often. _______________
3. I usually make him wear his leash in the park.
   ____
4. One little black dog seldom barks. _______________
5. Pal never barks or bites. _______________

6–10. Underline each adverb. Write the verb it describes.

6. We sometimes swim with our dogs. _______________
7. Pal scarcely stopped at the water's edge. _______________
8. I almost won a race with Pal. _______________
9. My good dog, Pal, nearly lost that race! _______________
10. Pal follows me a lot. _______________

Name ______________________ Date ____________

Adverbs in Different Parts of Sentences

An **adverb** is a word that tells something about a verb. Adverbs often follow the verb. Some adverbs can be used at the beginning, middle, or end of a sentence.

adverb: carefully
Carefully, Mrs. Marsh trained her service dog.
Mrs. Marsh carefully trained her service dog.
Mrs. Marsh trained her service dog carefully.

Thinking Question
What is the adverb that tells about the verb? In what part of the sentence is the adverb?

1–5 The verb in each sentence is underlined. Write the adverb.

1. Often a dog trainer makes careless mistakes. ____________
2. Puppies in their first year of life learn best. ____________
3. A trainer repeats the commands again. ____________
4. Our teacher usually knows every dog. ____________
5. I think about my dog a lot. ____________

6–10 Underline each adverb. Write the verb it describes.

6. Once, five of the guide dogs got an award. ____________
7. Three of the dogs had won before. ____________
8. He quickly drank all the water in his bowl. ____________
9. The best guide dog works for Mrs. Hatcher now. ____________
10. Spot, please come here. ____________

Name ____________________ Date __________

Possessive Nouns

Compare how singular and plural possessive nouns are formed.

Singular Noun	This is the guide dog owned by Tim.
Singular Possessive Noun	This is Tim's guide dog.
Plural Noun (ending in *-s*)	The blankets of the puppies are red.
Plural Possessive Noun	The puppies' blankets are red.
Plural Noun (not ending in *-s*)	The dogs owned by the women are gentle.
Plural Possessive Noun	The women's dogs are gentle.

1–6. Write each phrase another way. Use the possessive form of each noun.

1. the bark of the dog — the ____________ bark
2. the squeaks of the mice — the ____________ squeaks
3. the honks made by the geese — the ____________ honks
4. the shouts of the men — the ____________ shouts
5. a giggle made by a child — a ____________ giggle
6. a cry belonging to a puppy — a ____________ cry

Name ______________________________ Date ____________

Word Choice

Good writers choose precise **adverbs**. An adverb can change the meaning of a sentence.

She walked painfully across the street.

She walked lazily across the street.

She walked proudly across the street.

Activity **Read the story. Then fill in the blanks with precise adverbs. Create a story that makes sense.**

My aunt Remedios is ninety years old. ________________ we visited her in Arizona. Her canine companion, Charles, whined ________________ when we arrived. Aunt Remy sat ________________ in her wheelchair. My mother told us that she could ________________ walk.

During our visit, we saw that Charles helped Remy ________________ . That good dog ________________ left my aunt's side. When Remy accidentally dropped something, Charles ________________ picked it up in his mouth. When she rolled her chair ________________ , Charles followed.

I know that Aunt Remy would be lonely without her dog. I ________________ miss Charles, too.

Name _______________ Date _______________

Focus Trait: Voice

Writing a Friendly Letter

A friendly letter is something you write to a person that you know well.

Heading	450 Bond Street Lakeside, OH 12345 June 1, 2009
Greeting	Dear Grandmother,
Message	I just opened the birthday gift you sent to me. I love the necklace and matching bracelet. Blue gemstones are my favorite! I will think of you whenever I wear the pretty jewelry. Thank you very much.
Closing	Your loving granddaughter,
Signature	Alyssa

Write a message for a thank-you note on the lines below. State the reason you are writing the letter and connect ideas in an orderly way. Use words you would in regular speech.

Dear _______________

____

____

____

____

____

____

____

Name ____________________ Date ____________

Understanding Characters

Read the selection below.

Coming Home

Abby jumped out of bed as soon as she felt the sun on her face. Today was the Big Day! It had been almost a year since her father left to serve in the military. Today, he was coming home.

"The house looks perfect," Abby thought as she brushed her teeth. The decorations she had made hung in every room. Their mother had been cooking for days to prepare for the big party to welcome Dad home.

Abby put on her new dress in the shade of blue her father loved. Then she ran down to the living room. Ben was already there, picking up the books and games they had left out last night. Abby straightened a few pillows on the couch. Then she helped Ben carry their things upstairs.

Just as she closed her closet door, the downstairs door slammed.

Abby and Ben looked at each other. For a moment, neither seemed to breathe.

Then came the familiar voice. "I'm home!"

Ben and Abby flew down the stairs just in time to see their mother and father hugging. As their father turned to them, they jumped into his arms to give him the hug they had been waiting so long to give.

"Welcome home!" Abby and Ben shouted. "We missed you!"

Complete the Column Chart to record the characters' thoughts, actions, and words. Use complete sentences.

Thoughts	Actions	Words

Name ______________________ Date ____________

Understanding Characters

Read the selection below.

Winners

Jesse was worried. How could he go up against his best friend? It was Eddie who had taught him to wrestle. Now if Eddie lost this match, his team couldn't go to the state finals. And going to state finals had always been Eddie's biggest dream.

Jesse climbed into the ring. From across the mat, Eddie grinned and gave his trademark wink. Jesse felt sick to his stomach. Then he took a deep breath and made a decision.

The match began. Jesse tried a few standard pins on Eddie, who easily freed himself and then quickly put Jesse in a hold. Jesse's fans and coach were screaming at him. What was wrong with him?

As they circled each other, Eddie said, "Don't insult me. Make this match mean something!"

Jesse's eyes widened. Eddie knew Jesse was trying to let him win!

Then Eddie spoke again. "Don't worry. I'll beat you anyway!"

"Oh, yeah?" Jesse grinned, pinning Eddie. The crowd roared.

But Eddie was right. He overturned the pin and won the match. Eddie was the winner! And, standing beside him and cheering, so was Jesse.

Use a Column Chart like this one to help you analyze Jesse's and Eddie's behavior and motives. Then answer the questions below.

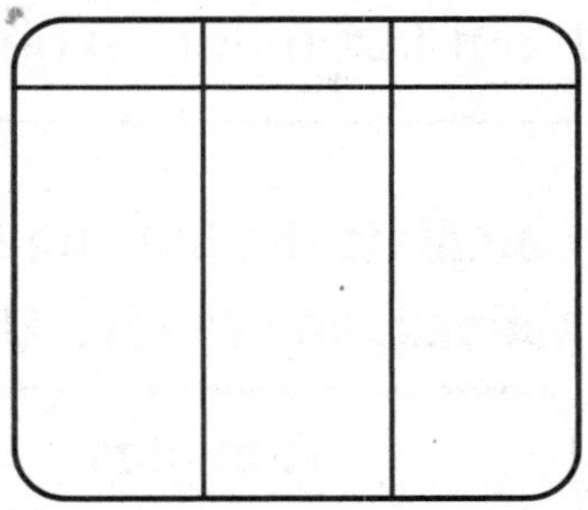

1. What was Jesse's decision in paragraph two? What do you think was his motive?

____

____

____

2. What do Eddie's words "Make this match mean something" tell you about Eddie's character?

____

____

____

Name ______________________ Date __________

Moon Runner
Vocabulary Strategies:
Homophones, Homonyms, and Homographs

Homophones, Homonyms, and Homographs

loan / loan	route / root	packed / pact	tea / tee
sole / soul	heal / heel	morning / mourning	

Each sentence below uses either a homophone, homonym, or homograph. Circle the correct form of the word in parentheses to complete each sentence.

1. He has a hole in the (sole, soul) of his shoe.
2. The bus takes the same (route, root) every day.
3. She injured the (heal, heel) of her foot.
4. The team made a (packed, pact) to follow the rules.
5. Jane hates waking up early in the (morning, mourning).
6. The (loan, lone) tree in the field stood out against the sun.
7. We drank a cup of (tea, tee) in the afternoon.

Name ______________________ Date ____________

Prefixes: *re-*, *un-*, *dis-*

Moon Runner
Spelling:
Prefixes: *re-*, *un-*, *dis-*

Basic Read the paragraphs. Write the Basic Words that best complete the sentences.

"Look how (1) ____________ this room is!" my dad said. I said that I had cleaned it earlier, but he told me that I needed to (2) ____________ the whole thing. I didn't want to (3) ____________ him, so I started to organize some of the (4) ____________. I noticed right away that a shelf of books was sagging and (5) ____________, so I decided that I would try to (6) ____________ the whole bookcase. I started to (7) ____________ all of the books onto the floor and took the bookcase apart. This (8) ____________ task took longer than cleaning the room would have taken.

"George!" exclaimed my father. "I (9) ____________ that I asked you an hour ago to clean your room!"

Now I remember why I (10) ____________ cleaning so much!

Challenge 11–14. Your favorite store is going out of business. Write an e-mail to a friend about your last visit to the store. Use four Challenge Words. Write on a separate sheet of paper.

Spelling Words

1. unused
2. refresh
3. dislike
4. replace
5. unpaid
6. redo
7. disorder
8. unplanned
9. distrust
10. rewind
11. untrue
12. unload
13. recall
14. displease
15. uneven
16. rebuild
17. restart
18. uncover
19. untidy
20. discolor

Challenge

disband
rearrange
discontinue
refund
unusual

Name ______________________ Date ____________

Moon Runner
Spelling:
Prefixes: *re-*, *un-*, *dis-*

Spelling Word Sort

Write each Basic Word beside the correct heading.

***re-* +** **base word**	**Basic Words:** **Challenge Words:**
***dis-* +** **base word**	**Basic Words:** **Challenge Words:**
***un-* +** **base word**	**Basic Words:** **Challenge Words:**

Challenge **Add the Challenge Words to your Word Sort.**

Spelling Words

1. unused
2. refresh
3. dislike
4. replace
5. unpaid
6. redo
7. disorder
8. unplanned
9. distrust
10. rewind
11. untrue
12. unload
13. recall
14. displease
15. uneven
16. rebuild
17. restart
18. uncover
19. untidy
20. discolor

Challenge

disband
rearrange
discontinue
refund
unusual

Name ______________________ Date ______________

Proofreading for Spelling

Moon Runner
Spelling:
Prefixes: *re-*, *un-*, *dis-*

Find the misspelled words and circle them. Write them correctly on the lines below.

Everyone in town thought Max had won the race, but Ginny knew that was untru. She was one of the unpayed volunteers at the finish line handing out water and towels to the athletes. As she gathered the unussed towels, Ginny said that the track coach would uncovr who should replaise Max as the winner.

Even though I knew I'd won, I was sure that changing the outcome would be difficult. They'd have to redue the race results in the paper, too.

The next day, the coach said, "I dislik and destrust rumors. Rumors discoler the reputation of this race. Since I don't recal seeing who won, I want to rifresh my memory. I am going to rewinde and restaart the race tape." When he realized that I'd won instead of Max, I was relieved.

1. ______________ 8. ______________
2. ______________ 9. ______________
3. ______________ 10. ______________
4. ______________ 11. ______________
5. ______________ 12. ______________
6. ______________ 13. ______________
7. ______________

Spelling Words

1. unused
2. refresh
3. dislike
4. replace
5. unpaid
6. redo
7. disorder
8. unplanned
9. distrust
10. rewind
11. untrue
12. unload
13. recall
14. displease
15. uneven
16. rebuild
17. restart
18. uncover
19. untidy
20. discolor

Challenge
disband
rearrange
discontinue
refund
unusual

Name ______________________ Date ____________

Moon Runner
Grammar: Prepositions and Prepositional Phrases

Prepositions

A **preposition** shows the connection between words in a sentence. Some prepositions describe time, such as *before*, *after*, or *during*. Others describe place, such as *over*, *in*, *on*, *above*, or *below*.

preposition
The runners raced on the track.

Thinking Question
What word shows a connection between other words in the sentence?

1–10. Find the preposition in each underlined phrase. Write the preposition on the line.

1. The track team will practice inside the gym. ____________
2. We use the outdoor track during warm weather. ____________
3. Jack and Liam arrange the hurdles on the track. ____________
4. Pedro easily leaps over every hurdle. ____________
5. Then I bang my knee into the third hurdle. ____________
6. I stumble a bit before I fall. ____________
7. Then I tumble to the ground. ____________
8. The coach kneels beside me. ____________
9. She wraps a bandage around my knee. ____________
10. After a long, hard practice, everyone is tired. ____________

Name ______________________ Date ____________

Prepositional Phrases

A **prepositional phrase** begins with a preposition and ends with a noun or a pronoun. All of the words in between are part of the prepositional phrase.

prepositional phrase
The girls have been best friends for a long time.

At school, they join many of the same clubs.

Thinking Question
What phrase begins with a preposition and ends with a noun or pronoun?

1–6. In each sentence below, underline the preposition. Write the prepositional phrase.

1. The soccer team's field is behind our school.
____

2. Jenna was the team goalie until this week.
____

3. The coach made Rosie the new goalie during yesterday's game.
____

4. Rosie wondered why Jenna ignored her after the game.
____

5. Before going home, Rosie and Jenna talked.
____

6. They seemed friendly at today's game.
____

Name ______________________ Date ____________

Using Prepositions and Prepositional Phrases to Provide Details

A prepositional phrase can also provide details to help describe a noun. The noun it helps describe is not part of the prepositional phrase.

noun described **preposition**
Our school (play) this year is <u>about</u> a female athlete.

Thinking Question
What is the prepositional phrase in the sentence? What details does it give about the sentence?

1–6. Look at the underlined preposition. Write a detail on the lines below to complete each sentence. Then circle the noun being described.

1. My book report is <u>about</u> ________________.
2. I did research and read a book <u>by</u> ________________.
3. I wrote my report <u>on</u> ________________.
4. I was excited to see how everyone <u>at</u> ________________ liked it.
5. The next day, I accidentally left my report on the table <u>in</u> ________________.
6. The topic <u>of</u> ________________ will be how to improve my memory!

Name ______________________ Date ____________

Verbs in the Present

Subject-Verb Agreement	
Singular subjects	Mira **signs** up for the race. She **studies** the race route. Her dad **fixes** the camera before the big race.
Plural subjects	The two friends **wish** each other luck. Then they **take** their places at the starting line.

1–6. Write the verb that correctly completes each sentence.

1. (wait, waits) The runners __________ for the start of the race.
2. (fall, falls) Selma __________ far behind the other runners.
3. (catch, catches) She __________ up to them near the finish line.
4. (fly, flies) Suddenly, Selma __________ past everyone.
5. (hug, hugs) Her parents __________ her after the race.
6. (rush, rushes) The judge __________ over with the first place ribbon.

Name ______________________ Date __________

Ideas

Prepositional phrases tell when, where, or how. You can use prepositional phrases in your writing to add descriptive detail to sentences.

1–6. Add a prepositional phrase that adds descriptive detail to complete the sentences below.

1. The marathon route ran

____.

2. Volunteers passed out water

____.

3. The winner is crowned

____.

4. My father finished his first marathon

____.

5. Rain began to fall

____.

6. We hugged Dad

____.

Name ________________________ Date ____________

Focus Trait: Word Choice

You can vary your choice of descriptive words and details to make your writing more interesting.

Without Descriptive Words	With Descriptive Words
He lay down on the couch.	He flopped down on the living room couch and sighed in exhaustion.

Rewrite the sentences to include descriptive adjectives, verbs, or phrases that add detail.

1. The bull came toward us.

____

____

____

____

2. The visiting team won the game.

____

____

____

____

3. I wanted a new bicycle.

____

____

____

____

Name ____________________ Date __________

Persuasion

Read the selection below.

Birth of the Special Olympics

Eunice Kennedy Shriver believed individuals with learning disabilities enjoy and benefit from sports. She felt they should have the same chance to participate in sports as people without such disabilities. Eunice had organized Camp Shriver in 1962. She invited children with learning disabilities to take part in sports and activities at her home in Maryland.

In 1967, Ann Burke, a teacher in Chicago, and the Chicago Park District asked Eunice to help them hold a track meet modeled after the Olympic Games. Through this program, 1,000 disabled athletes from around the United States and Canada traveled to Chicago for the Chicago Special Olympics on July 20, 1968. They competed in water sports and other events such as floor hockey.

Eunice helped disabled people through the Special Olympics. Thanks to her, people with learning disabilities can play, compete in sports, and grow. They can be successful at activities that before were not open to them.

Today, the Special Olympics has grown. Participants include more than 2.5 million athletes from countries all over the world. Eunice's dream has made the world a better place.

Analyze the selection to identify and evaluate its persuasive arguments. Use the Idea-Support Map below to organize your thoughts.

Goal:

Reason:

Reason:

Name ______________________ Date ____________

Persuasion

Read the selection below.

Buy Organic Food!

Food quality is an important issue for many consumers. Shoppers look for fruits and vegetables that are fresh, ripe, and unbruised. Shoppers who want the best food should look for food that is labeled as organic.

Organic crops are raised without chemical pesticides. The farmers do not spray poisons on the plants or the soil to get rid of pests. Organic crops are also raised without herbicides. The farmers do not put poisons in the soil to get rid of weeds. The plants and the people who care for them are also protected from these poisons.

Organic foods do not contain growth hormones or genes from other kinds of plants. They are never treated with radiation. Organic foods are pure foods.

For their own health and the health of farmers and farmworkers, people should seek out and pay the higher price charged for these healthier, organic foods.

Analyze the selection to evaluate its persuasive arguments. Use an Idea-Support Map like the one shown here to organize your thoughts. Then answer the questions below.

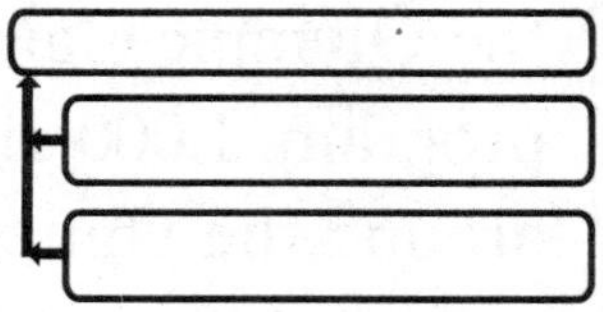

1. What is the author's main argument? Support your answer with details from the selection.

____

____

2. Why does the author think these foods are better? Support your answer with details from the selection.

____

____

Name ______________________ Date ____________

Using a Dictionary

blur	strike	belief
suspicious	harvest	right

Each sentence shows a word in *italics*. Use a dictionary to answer questions about the words or to help you use them in a sentence.

1. The word *blur* can be used as what parts of speech?

____

2. How many syllables does the word *suspicious* have?

____

3. Use the word *strike* with a different meaning in two sentences.

____

____

4. What guide words are found at the top of the page on which *harvest* appears?

____

5. According to your dictionary, which syllable of *belief* is the stressed syllable? How can you tell?

____

____

6. Use the word *right* with a different meaning in two sentences.

____

____

Suffixes: *-ful*, *-less*, *-ness*, *-ment*

Basic **Write the Basic Word that best fits each clue.**

1. full of happiness ____________________
2. without end ____________________
3. a state of tidiness ____________________
4. concrete surface ____________________
5. without sleep ____________________
6. the act of moving ____________________
7. a state of having no strength ____________________
8. using more than is needed ____________________
9. sickness ____________________
10. having bright colors ____________________
11. affection ____________________

Challenge 12–15. Your school newspaper is featuring a health article. Your job is to submit some first-aid tips. Use four of the Challenge Words. Write on a separate sheet of paper.

Spelling Words

1. colorful
2. weakness
3. movement
4. endless
5. truthful
6. illness
7. cheerful
8. useless
9. beautiful
10. restless
11. clumsiness
12. pavement
13. peaceful
14. fondness
15. neatness
16. speechless
17. statement
18. wasteful
19. penniless
20. treatment

Challenge

numbness
ailment
resourceful
cleanliness
appointment

Name ______________________ Date ____________

Harvesting Hope: The Story of Cesar Chavez
Spelling: Suffixes: *-ful*, *-less*, *-ness*, *-ment*

Spelling Word Sort

Write each Basic Word beside the correct heading.

base word + *-ful*	Basic Words: Challenge Words: Possible Selection Words:
base word + *-less*	Basic Words:
base word + *-ness*	Basic Words: Challenge Words:
base word + *-ment*	Basic Words: Challenge Words: Possible Selection Words:

Challenge Add the Challenge Words to your Word Sort.

Connect to Reading Look through *Harvesting Hope: The Story of Cesar Chavez*. Find words that have the suffixes *-ful*, *-less*, *-ness*, or *-ment*. Add them to your Word Sort.

Spelling Words

1. colorful
2. weakness
3. movement
4. endless
5. truthful
6. illness
7. cheerful
8. useless
9. beautiful
10. restless
11. clumsiness
12. pavement
13. peaceful
14. fondness
15. neatness
16. speechless
17. statement
18. wasteful
19. penniless
20. treatment

Challenge

numbness
ailment
resourceful
cleanliness
appointment

Name ______________________ Date ____________

Harvesting Hope: The Story of Cesar Chavez
Spelling: Suffixes: *-ful*, *-less*, *-ness*, *-ment*

Proofreading for Spelling

Find the misspelled words and circle them. Write them correctly on the lines below.

In 1948, Helen Fabela married Cesar Chavez, a man known for his endlest work to improve the treatmint of migrant farm workers in the United States. Though the couple endured rather peniles times and poor living conditions, Helen supported Cesar's work. She also made her own statment by starting a teaching program for Mexican farm workers.

Some dishonest people were not truthfil and started rumors about Mexican farm workers. Helen was spechles at the weekness of their values, and she thought it was uzeles to complain.

Helen had a chearful attitude, and she provided an environment for her husband and eight children that was beautyful and peaseful. Today Helen Chavez is an inspiration to her 31 grandchildren.

1. ______________
2. ______________
3. ______________
4. ______________
5. ______________
6. ______________
7. ______________
8. ______________
9. ______________
10. ______________
11. ______________

Spelling Words

1. colorful
2. weakness
3. movement
4. endless
5. truthful
6. illness
7. cheerful
8. useless
9. beautiful
10. restless
11. clumsiness
12. pavement
13. peaceful
14. fondness
15. neatness
16. speechless
17. statement
18. wasteful
19. penniless
20. treatment

Challenge

numbness
ailment
resourceful
cleanliness
appointment

Name ______________________ Date ____________

Transition Words

Transition words connect sentences and paragraphs. They help readers follow the ideas they are reading or hearing. They show how ideas are related. Some transition words are *also*, *but*, *still*, *however*, *therefore*, *so*, *once*, *since*, and *because*.

transition word

I picked all the beets. However, I have to take some to Mrs. Lopez.

Thinking Question
What word or words tell about time or order? What words help keep ideas moving and changing?

1–4. Underline the transition word in the sentences below.

1. A drought destroyed many farms. Farmers went to California because of that.
2. They found life hard in California. However, they could not go back home.
3. Even the children had to work. So, they were not able to get a good education.
4. Things are somewhat different now. Still, the life of a farm worker is far from easy.

5–8. Select the correct transition word to connect the sentences and write it on the line.

5. On the road to California we saw cars left at the side of the road. (But, Also) __________, there were people just sitting there.
6. Some people's money had run out. (Since, However) __________, they could not turn back.
7. The government tried to help. (Still, Also) __________, there were many people it didn't reach.
8. Those times are long gone. (Since, However) __________ then, there are more ways the government tries to help people.

Name ______________________ Date ____________

Time-Order Transition Words

Transition words connect sentences and paragraphs. Some transition words tell you the order in which events happen. Words such as *first*, *next*, *then*, *before*, *later*, and *finally* show **time order**.

First, we researched the problem. Then we wrote our report.

Thinking Question
Which words tell the order of events? How do they signal to the reader that there is a change?

1–4. Underline the transition words in the sentences below.

1. First, we made flyers about the meeting. Then we put them up all over.
2. Next, we organized a protest march. Finally, our cause was heard.
3. One of the workers told us about her aunt. Later, we got to meet her.
4. She told us she had marched forty years ago. Now, many people her age support our cause.

5–8. Write a transition word on the line to connect the sentences.

5. We can now reach people through the Internet. __________, people had only letters, the phone, flyers, and word of mouth.
6. To mount an Internet campaign, __________ you need a good letter. __________, you need a mailing list.
7. __________ you send the e-mail letter, the waiting begins. __________ a few days, you know by the response if your mailing was a success.
8. __________, you can decide if it is worth using e-mail in the future.

Transitional Phrases and Conclusions

Transitional phrases connect the ideas in sentences. Some transitional phrases include *for example* and *in addition*. Other transitional words are used to begin the conclusion of an article, speech, or essay. Some concluding phrases are *as a result*, *at last*, and *to sum up*.

Thinking Question
Which phrase tells you that you are at the end of an idea or discussion?

1–4. Underline the transitional phrases in the sentences below.

1. Rita started planting a vegetable garden three years ago. As a result, she grows a lot of her family's food.
2. She keeps most of her gardening tools in the shed. In addition, there are rakes and weeders in the garage.
3. Harvesting vegetables can be difficult. For example, pulling carrots out of the ground takes a lot of strength.
4. The more you do it, the stronger you get. Besides that, home-grown vegetables taste great!

5–8. Write a concluding transitional phrase on the line to connect the sentences.

5. The world's population is growing rapidly. ________________, we need to figure out new ways of feeding all the people.
6. I have given you my reasons for planning a school garden. ________________________, we will learn about plants, cooking, and teamwork.
7. After my speech, the principal talked with the teachers. ________________________, they agreed to let us have our school garden.
8. We talked about who should get the food we grow. ________________________, our school cafeteria will now have more fresh vegetables and fruit.

Verbs in the Past

Use the **past-tense form** of a verb to show action that has already happened. Most past tense verbs end in *-ed*. However, irregular verbs have different endings or different spellings. You must memorize those forms.

Past tense: He tired easily. She raked the leaves.
Irregular past tense: She felt sleepy. The candle went out.

1–3. Write the past-tense form of the verb in parentheses to complete each sentence.

1. (finish) The farmer __________ plowing late in the afternoon.
2. (store) He __________ his equipment in the barn.
3. (cook) He __________ his dinner after he got home.

4–6. Write the irregular past-tense form of the verb in parentheses to complete each sentence.

4. (go) Last weekend, we __________ to visit my grandparents.
5. (bend) The hurricane __________ the flag pole in half.
6. (bring) The parents __________ supplies for the event.

Name ______________________________ Date ______________

Sentence Fluency

Transition words connect ideas. They show how ideas are related. They help writers organize their writing, put events in time order, and signal conclusions. They make writing clearer and smoother.

Activity Complete the paragraph below by writing transition words or transitional phrases on each line.

Many people lost their farms during the drought. ______________ , they left their homes and traveled west. Farm owners in California saw a chance for cheap labor. ______________ working so long and hard, there was almost no time for learning or fun. ______________ a crop was all harvested, workers needed to move on. ______________ they had to find a new place to work. ______________ , they had to find a new place to live! ______________ life was so uncertain, no one felt secure.

Focus Trait: Organization

Planning a Personal Narrative

A personal narrative is a story about you and something that happened in your life. Make a list of four events you would like to write about.

1. ______________________________
2. ______________________________
3. ______________________________
4. ______________________________

A. For your personal narrative, choose an event that you remember well or that has special meaning and is important to you. Then fill in the blanks below to help you plan your story.

Topic: I will write about ______________________________

What happened first: ______________________________

Next: ______________________________

Next: ______________________________

Last: ______________________________

What I learned: ______________________________

B. Think about the sensory details that could help the reader share your experience. Write your details on the lines below.

Pair/Share **Work with a partner to brainstorm interesting details.**

I saw: ______________________________

____

I heard: ______________________________

____

I felt: ______________________________

Name ______________________ Date ____________

Main Idea and Details

Read the selection below.

The Trail of Tears

In 1838, the Cherokee Nation had to leave their homes. The Cherokee were a group of Native Americans with farms in Georgia and the Carolinas. They had developed a written language, published a newspaper, and had their own constitution. White people wanted their land because gold had been found there. The U.S. passed a law ordering them to leave.

The Cherokee fought the law. They brought their case to the U.S. Supreme Court. The court agreed, but President Jackson refused to follow its decision. The U.S. Army rounded up the Cherokees. They forced them to move to Oklahoma.

The journey west was hard. Some of the Cherokee traveled in boats. Others traveled on foot. The weather was bad. They did not have the right clothing or enough food. More than 4,000 Cherokee died on the trail. It is called the Trail of Tears because their families cried.

Complete the Web to identify the main ideas and details of the selection.

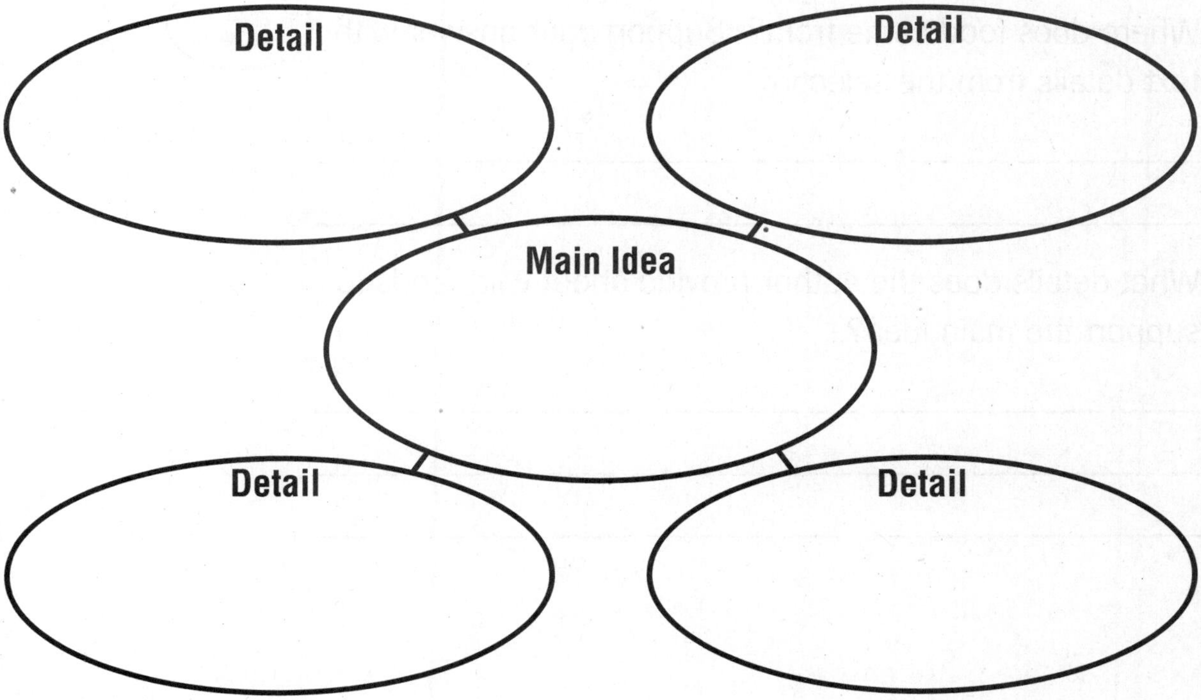

Name ______________________ Date ____________

Main Ideas and Details

Read the selection below.

Wild Foods

These days, most of us get all our food from grocery stores. It's easy to forget that food comes from nature. However, many common plants provide great taste and nutrition.

Dandelions, for example, are more than weeds. They contain Vitamin A, Vitamin C, calcium, and potassium. You can make salad with baby dandelion leaves or cook them like spinach. You can boil the roots or use them to make tea.

Other common plants are safe to eat, too. Chickweed, fiddlehead ferns, and even roses can be food, if they are prepared correctly. Always ask an adult before you prepare or eat any wild plant. Good food doesn't have to come from the store or garden.

Analyze the selection to identify its main idea and details. Use a Web like the one here to organize your thoughts. Write the main idea in the center and the details in the outer ovals. Then answer the questions below.

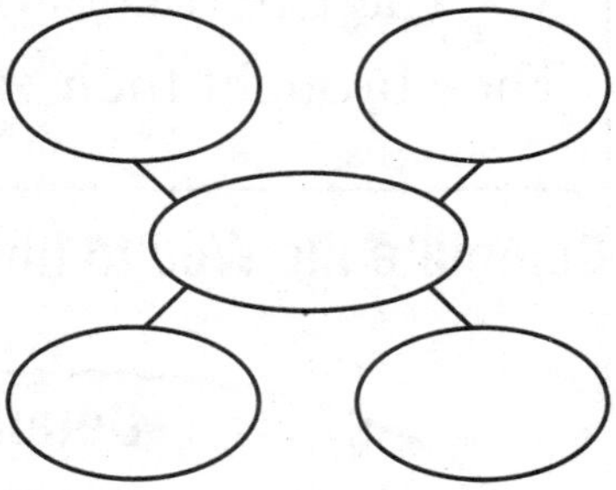

1. Where does food come from? Support your answer with text details from the selection.

____

____

2. What details does the author provide about wild foods to support the main idea?

____

____

____

Name ______________________ Date ____________

Compound Words

daydream	homeland	nightfall	landmark
campfire	lifetime	fly-fishing	

Each sentence shows a compound word in parentheses. Complete each sentence using the word in parentheses.

1. (daydream) I always
____
2. (campfire) We like to toast marshmallows
____
3. (homeland) The place where you
____
4. (lifetime) She had accomplished
____
5. (nightfall) Now that it is November
____
6. (fly-fishing) They went to the river
____
7. (landmark) You can find your way around by
____

Name ______________________ Date ____________

VCCV Pattern

Basic **Write the Basic Word that completes each analogy.**

1. *Happily* is to *joyously* as *rarely* is to ______________ .
2. *Shoe* is to *sneaker* as *spice* is to ______________ .
3. *Omelet* is to *eggs* as *house* is to ______________ .
4. *Give* is to *receive* as *lend* is to ______________ .
5. *Puddle* is to *ocean* as *dollar* is to ______________ .
6. *Quarterback* is to *football* as *goalie* is to ______________ .
7. *Carpenter* is to *house* as *photographer* is to ______________ .
8. *Mountain* is to *peak* as *ravine* is to ______________ .
9. *Dentist* is to *teeth* as *mechanic* is to ______________ .
10. *Safety* is to *security* as *peril* is to ______________ .

Challenge 11–14. **Write an e-mail to a friend about a movie you have seen recently. Describe a scene that you liked. Use three Challenge Words. Write on a separate sheet of paper.**

Spelling Words

1. million
2. collect
3. lumber
4. pepper
5. plastic
6. borrow
7. support
8. thirty
9. perfect
10. attend
11. canyon
12. traffic
13. fortune
14. danger
15. soccer
16. engine
17. picture
18. survive
19. seldom
20. effort

Challenge

occur
venture
challenge
rascal
splendid

Name ______________________ Date ____________

Spelling Word Sort

Sacagawea
Spelling: VCCV Pattern

Write each Basic Word beside the correct heading.

VC/CV Pattern: Double consonants	**Basic Words:** **Challenge Words:** **Possible Selection Words:**
VC/CV Pattern: Different consonants	**Basic Words:** **Challenge Words:** **Possible Selection Words:**

Challenge Add the Challenge Words to your Word Sort.

Connect to Reading Look through *Sacagawea*. Find words that have the VCCV pattern. Add them to your Word Sort.

Spelling Words

1. million
2. collect
3. lumber
4. pepper
5. plastic
6. borrow
7. support
8. thirty
9. perfect
10. attend
11. canyon
12. traffic
13. fortune
14. danger
15. soccer
16. engine
17. picture
18. survive
19. seldom
20. effort

Challenge

occur
venture
challenge
rascal
splendid

Name ____________________ Date __________

Proofreading for Spelling

Sacagawea
Spelling: VCCV Pattern

Find the misspelled words and circle them. Write them correctly on the lines below.

On their trip west, Lewis and Clark hired a French trader for his knowledge of Indian languages. Then they discovered that the trader's wife, Sacagawea, gave the crew more language suport than the trader. She was perfec for the job. Sacagawea would atend meetings between the explorers and Indians to be the interpreter. Even though the group did not meet much trafic on the trail, Sacagawea did not have time to be lonely. She would walk down the canyonn to colleck any food she could find for the more than thirte men to eat. When Sacagawea found a bush with what seemed like a milion berries on it, she couldn't pickure a better forchun. Her extra effert helped the crew servive the long journey. Lewis and Clark owed a lot to Sacagawea.

1. ____________
2. ____________
3. ____________
4. ____________
5. ____________
6. ____________
7. ____________
8. ____________
9. ____________
10. ____________
11. ____________
12. ____________

Spelling Words

1. million
2. collect
3. lumber
4. pepper
5. plastic
6. borrow
7. support
8. thirty
9. perfect
10. attend
11. canyon
12. traffic
13. fortune
14. danger
15. soccer
16. engine
17. picture
18. survive
19. seldom
20. effort

Challenge

occur
venture
challenge
rascal
splendid

Name ____________________ Date ____________

Abbreviations for People and Places

An **abbreviation** is a short form of a word. Most abbreviations begin with a capital letter and end with a period. Both letters of state name abbreviations are capital letters, and no period is used.

Person	Mr. Hideki Nomo
Place	55 Porter Blvd.
Place	Shoreline, WA 98155

Thinking Question
What parts of the address are shortened forms of words?

1–8. Write each group of words. Use an abbreviation for the underlined word or words.

1. Shoshone Trading Company ____________
2. Charles Pompy, Junior ____________
3. 92 Mountain Road ____________
4. Doctor May Dawson ____________
5. 195 Water Street ____________
6. Mister Robert Woods, Senior ____________
7. 16 Muddy Creek Drive ____________
8. Beavercreek, Oregon 97004 ____________

Name ____________________ Date ____________

Sacagawea
Grammar: Abbreviations

Abbreviations for Mailing Addresses

An **abbreviation** is a short form of a word. Use abbreviations when writing street names and states in a mailing address. Abbreviate words such as *road* or *avenue* with a capital letter and end with a period. Write both letters of state name abbreviations with capital letters, and do not use periods.

Road	Rd.	Court	Ct.
Street	St.	Post Office	P.O.
Avenue	Ave.	Boulevard	Blvd.

Thinking Question
What parts of an address can I make shorter? How can I shorten the whole word?

Write each mailing address using abbreviations.

Full Address	Abbreviated Address
1. Mister Pedro Saravia The Total Pet Supply Company 9302 Riverside Drive Toledo, Ohio 43601	
2. Miss Alexis Parker The Press Building 14 Paper Lane Seattle, Washington 98104	
3. Gregory Nulman President, Choice Restaurants Post Office Box 269 Brooklyn, New York 11216	

Name ______________________ Date ______________

Abbreviations for Time and Measurement

An **abbreviation** is a short form of a word. The abbreviations for days and months begin with a capital letter and end with a period. Some other abbreviations for time and measurements begin with a lowercase letter and end with a period.

time	**measurement**
Wed., Aug. 26	165 mi., 4 yd.

Thinking Question
What parts can I make shorter? How can I shorten the whole word?

1–10. Write these groups of words, using correct abbreviations.

1. 8,000 feet ______________
2. 1 hour, 45 minutes ______________
3. Tuesday, January 7, 1806 ______________
4. Monday–Friday ______________
5. 3 yards, 11 inches ______________
6. April 30, 1803 ______________
7. November 24, 2011 ______________
8. Thursday, February 27, 1805 ______________
9. 7 hours, 15 minutes ______________
10. March 10, 1922 ______________

Name ______________________ Date ____________

Irregular Verbs

Present	Past	Past with Helping Verb
begin	began	(has, have, had) begun
give	gave	(has, have, had) given

The Special Verb *be*	
Present Tense	**Past Tense**
Dad <u>is</u> reading about Lewis and Clark. My parents <u>are</u> in the den.	Meriwether Lewis <u>was</u> an army captain. Both explorers <u>were</u> captains.

1–8. Write the correct form of the verb in parentheses to complete each sentence.

1. The explorers __________ by the campfire. (past tense of *sit*)
2. Their dog __________ at their feet. (present tense of *be*)
3. The explorers __________ dinner earlier. (past tense of *eat* with helping verb)
4. After dinner, the men __________ stories about the past. (past tense of *tell*)
5. They __________ happy to reach the Pacific Ocean. (future tense of *be*)
6. Lewis __________ pictures of animals and plants in his diary. (past tense of *draw*)
7. The expedition __________ its winter camp in early May. (past tense of *leave*)
8. They __________ for their supplies in cash. (past tense of *pay*)

Name ______________________________ Date ____________

Conventions

Each group of words has two incorrect abbreviations. Use proofreading marks to correct the abbreviations.

1. Mr. and mrs Tom Charbonneau, Jr.

   1804 Hidatsa Dr.

   Sioux City, Ia., 51101

2. Frid., Febr'y. 14

3. 55 mls per hour on the Fort Mandan expy

4. mond., octob 22

5. Doc. Michelle Mitchell

   431 Expedition boulv'd

   Bethel, ME 04217

6. 17 In, 3 ft., 4 yrd.

Name ____________________ Date __________

Focus Trait: Ideas

Choosing Interesting Details

Good writers try to use details that will interest the reader. The details should support the main idea, or message, of the story.

With Uninteresting Details	Without Uninteresting Details
My dad took me to see a champion swimmer at our swimming pool. **The pool is next to the bank.** He was scheduled to show up at nine o'clock sharp, **two hours after the pool opens.**	My dad took me to see a champion swimmer at our swimming pool. He was scheduled to show up at nine o'clock sharp.

Read the next sentences. Cross out the details that are not important or interesting. Then rewrite the sentences.

1. My brother and I are on the swim club, so we usually go to the pool at eight o'clock. Anyway, at nine the Olympian was going to meet and greet the public. Then he would sign autographs.

____

____

2. I was ready a half hour early, and I had everything I needed: my camera, my autograph book, my swimming trunks, and a towel. If my hero decided to go for a quick swim, I wanted to be ready to get in the pool! I like my blue swimming trunks best.

____

____

____

Rewrite the next sentences on a separate sheet of paper. Use sensory words to make the underlined details more interesting.

3. When we got into the car, Dad's car wouldn't start. It made me so mad! By the time we got to the pool, my favorite athlete was leaving. Then he looked at me, and I knew he would stop to talk.

Name ______________________ Date __________

Theme

Read the selection below.

A Home for Melvin and Peanut

Brittany and her twin brother Josh decided to adopt some pets. Brittany got a dwarf hamster named Melvin, and Josh got a gerbil he named Peanut. To have the right cages and right food for each animal, the twins had read books and compared notes.

The twins learned how to make a home for their new pets. They put them into a clear tank with a mesh top to keep them from escaping. The holes in the mesh allowed the animals to breathe. Next, they put a layer of wood chips on the bottom of the tank and hung a water bottle with a metal spout on the side of the tank. Then they placed a heavy bowl in the tank for food. Gerbils and hamsters like to climb, so they put rocks in the tank, too. Since gerbils and hamsters also like to run, the twins put in an exercise wheel. Josh got a piece of cardboard for Peanut to chew, too.

Brittany decided to get some vegetables, fruits, mealworms, and crickets for Melvin. Her brother added some cheese and bread for his gerbil. All their research helped the twins make Melvin and Peanut comfortable in their new home.

Use the Inference Map to explain details from the text that will help you understand the lesson that the characters learn. Then write the theme in the bottom box.

Detail	Detail	Detail

Theme

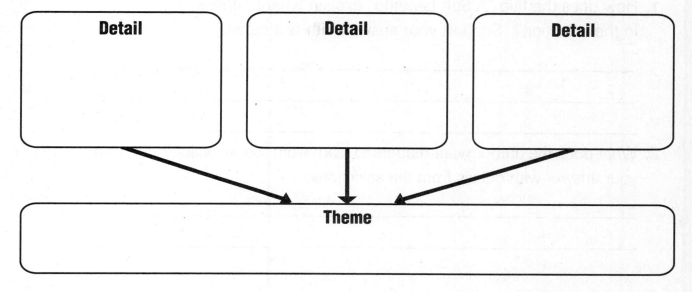

Name ______________________________ Date ______________

Theme

Read the selection below.

A Soft Landing

I never knew life could be so easy! I began life in a cardboard box in a dirty alley. My cat littermates and I ran for our lives from dogs and huge boxes on wheels.

Then someone caught me and put me in a metal cage. I was in a big square box all day and all night. They fed me and washed me. They kept me away from dogs, but I missed my family. All the cats there were in cages and frightened.

Lots of people came to visit. Sometimes the people let me out of the cage for a while. Then, one day, they unlocked my cage! They put me in an even smaller cage and carried me out of the building to one of the boxes on wheels!

We all traveled until we came to a nice, big place. It was clean and bright with soft furniture and carpeting. It had cats and people. Food and water were waiting for me, and there was not a box in sight! Boy, did I get lucky! Life can be good.

Use an Inference Map like the one here to explain details from the selection and determine its theme. Then answer the questions below.

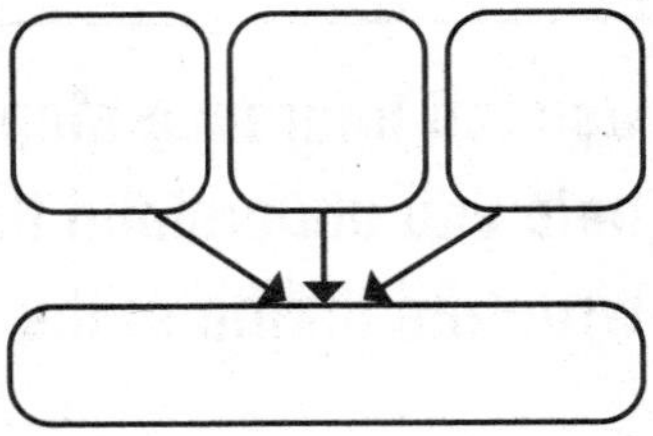

1. How does the title “A Soft Landing” explain what happens in the selection? Support your answer with text details.

____

____

____

2. What does the author want readers to learn from this selection? Support your answer with details from the selection.

____

____

Name ______________________ Date __________

Multiple-Meaning Words

figure	might	cover	racket
block	corner	pet	combination

Each sentence below contains a multiple-meaning word. Read each sentence. Fill in the circle next to the definition that fits the way the word is used in the sentence.

1. Alma was able to figure out a hard math problem.
   ○ **A.** understand ○ **B.** shape
2. The two friends lived on the same block.
   ○ **A.** get in the way of ○ **B.** a section of a street
3. He used all his might to pick up the heavy box.
   ○ **A.** maybe ○ **B.** strength
4. I will put my desk in the corner of the room.
   ○ **A.** place where two walls meet ○ **B.** to trap
5. The music was a combination of rock and hip-hop sounds.
   ○ **A.** numbers used to open a lock ○ **B.** a mix or blend of things
6. You should cover your head with a hat when it is cold.
   ○ **A.** a blanket ○ **B.** to put something on top of something else
7. My friend asked if he could pet my dog.
   ○ **A.** to stroke an animal ○ **B.** an animal kept by humans
8. I left my racket at a friend's house.
   ○ **A.** something used to play tennis ○ **B.** a loud noise

Name ______________________ Date ____________

VCV Pattern

Basic **Read the paragraph. Write the Basic Word that best replaces the underlined word or words in each sentence.**

Moving to a new place was an (1) important occasion in my life. I was only a (2) person who studies when my family shot into space. We flew to the (3) heavenly body Zondora. The shuttle flight from Earth to Zondora was very (4) fast. We stayed in a hovering (5) resort. The workers there were (6) respectful and helpful. Zondora has large lava pits and (7) icy plains. It has a large shield to (8) protect against anything that could harm the planet. If the shield is threatened, a (9) device that makes a loud noise blares. The people (10) join together to keep Zondora safe.

1. ______________ 6. ______________

2. ______________ 7. ______________

3. ______________ 8. ______________

4. ______________ 9. ______________

5. ______________ 10. ______________

Challenge 11–14. **Your brother and your best friend are on opposing teams of a football game. Write a journal entry that tells how you cheered for both teams. Use four of the Challenge Words. Write on a separate sheet of paper.**

Spelling Words

1. event
2. humor
3. rapid
4. music
5. relief
6. planet
7. detail
8. unite
9. frozen
10. figure
11. siren
12. polite
13. hotel
14. protest
15. punish
16. defend
17. relay
18. habit
19. student
20. moment

Challenge

rumor
jealous
license
image
rival

Name ______________________ Date ____________

Spelling Word Sort

Write each Basic Word beside the correct heading.

VC/V: Divide after the consonant	**Basic Words:** **Challenge Words:** **Possible Selection Words:**
V/CV: Divide before the consonant	**Basic Words:** **Challenge Words:** **Possible Selection Words:**

Challenge Add the Challenge Words to your Word Sort.

Connect to Reading Look through ***The World According to Humphrey***. Find words that have the VC / V and V / CV spelling pattern on this page. Add them to your Word Sort.

Spelling Words

1. event
2. humor
3. rapid
4. music
5. relief
6. planet
7. detail
8. unite
9. frozen
10. figure
11. siren
12. polite
13. hotel
14. protest
15. punish
16. defend
17. relay
18. habit
19. student
20. moment

Challenge

rumor
jealous
license
image
rival

Name ______________________ Date ____________

Proofreading for Spelling

Find the misspelled words and circle them. Write them correctly on the lines below.

What a releef to be back at school! If only I could talk, I would ask Mrs. Brisbane for a momint of her time to protes the weekend's arrangement at the Thomases. Don't get me wrong now. The family treated me nicely, and they did not punich me when water spilled inside my cage. They actually thought it was an exciting ivent. Mr. Thomas thinks he has a great sense of humer, but here's a small deteil that I'll only share with Mrs. Brisbane: His jokes are the corniest on the planit. Mrs. Thomas is very pollite, but her taste in muzic is simply awful. And she also has a very bad habet of serving frozin pizza that isn't cooked through. "Look at our little hamster go!" Mrs. Brisbane said. "He's running a relae race on his wheel. I think he's glad to be back."

1. ____________ 8. ____________
2. ____________ 9. ____________
3. ____________ 10. ____________
4. ____________ 11. ____________
5. ____________ 12. ____________
6. ____________ 13. ____________
7. ____________

Spelling Words

1. event
2. humor
3. rapid
4. music
5. relief
6. planet
7. detail
8. unite
9. frozen
10. figure
11. siren
12. polite
13. hotel
14. protest
15. punish
16. defend
17. relay
18. habit
19. student
20. moment

Challenge

rumor
jealous
license
image
rival

Name ______________________ Date ____________

Comparative Forms of Adjectives

A **comparative adjective** compares one person, place, or thing to another. To form a comparative adjective, you can usually add *–er* to the adjective. If the adjective ends in *y*, change the *y* to *i* before adding *–er*.

adjective	**comparative adjective**
Josh is tall.	Jacob is taller than Josh.
The weather is dry today.	The weather is drier today than yesterday.

Thinking Question
Are there two persons, places, or things being compared? Does the adjective end in –er?

1–4. Write the comparative form of the adjective in each sentence.

1. I think that spring feels (warm) ____________ than winter.
2. My dog seems hungry, but your dog looks ____________ .
3. Maddie is short, but Cindy is ____________ .
4. Her song is lovely, but I think your song sounds ____________ .

Some comparative adjectives are formed by adding the word *more*. Usually longer adjectives form the comparative this way.

Joe is more polite than Henry.

5–8. Write the comparative form of each adjective.

5. Sally felt (miserable) ____________ when she knew she had the flu.
6. The company is (efficient) ____________ than its competitor.
7. Will you feel (comfortable) ____________ sitting here?
8. Tonight's dinner tastes (delicious) ____________ than last night's.

Name ______________________ Date ____________

Superlative Forms of Adjectives

When we use adjectives to compare **more than** two persons, places, or things, we use the superlative form of the adjective. To form a **superlative adjective**, add *–est* or write *most* before the adjective.

Adjective	Comparative	Superlative
happy	happier	happiest
complex	more complex	most complex

Emily is luckier than Mary, but Alyssa is the luckiest of all.

Without a map, Gregory is more lost than Lew, but Edwin is the most lost.

Thinking Question
Are there more than two persons, places, or things being compared? Does the adjective end in –est?

1–5. Write the correct form of the adjective in parentheses to complete the sentence.

1. A rose is pretty, but Tom thinks an orchid is (pretty) ______________.

2. Susan says that of all the flowers, the peony is the (pretty) ______________.

3. This tulip is the (bright) ______________ shade of red I've ever seen.

4. Carrie told him that lavender smells (wonderful) ______________.

5. Trees grow the (tall) ______________ of all plants.

Name ______________________ Date ____________

Comparative and Superlative Forms of Adverbs

Adverbs often work with verbs and tell how, when, or where an action happens. They are used with action verbs, and many end with *–ly*. A **comparative adverb** compares the action of two or more things. The word *more* is often used. A **superlative adverb** compares the action of more than two things. The word *most* is often used.

Adverb	Comparative	Superlative
slowly	more slowly	most slowly
soon	sooner	soonest
promptly	more promptly	most promptly

Thinking Question
Does the adverb end in -ly? Is the word more *or* most *added?*

Use a comparative or superlative adverb for each blank below. Use the list on the right to help you complete the sentences.

1. Although many musicians were loud, Donald played the trumpet __________.
2. Sarah could add numbers __________ than her brother.
3. Jerry ran __________ than his best friend.
4. Of all my friends, Carmin lives __________.
5. Marty worked __________ on his project than his partner.
6. Jeremy answered the question __________ of the three contestants.

louder
loudest
more quickly
most quickly
more completely
most completely
closer
closest
harder
hardest
faster
fastest

Name ____________________ Date __________

Kinds of Adjectives

What kind	The **small** turtles had **brownish-green** shells and **short** legs.
How many	Ms. Roland rescued **some** turtles by the side of the road.
After *be*	The turtles were **helpless**.

1–4. Write each adjective and the word each adjective describes.

1. The young turtles tried to cross the busy, dangerous road.

____

____

2. Ms. Roland spotted the three turtles on her long walk.

____

____

3. She is kind to all animals so she carried them to safety.

____

____

4. The tiny creatures had wandered from the green, grassy marsh across the wide road.

____

____

Name ______________________ Date __________

Using Comparative/Superlative Forms to Provide Details

Using more exact comparative and superlative adjectives and adverbs can make your writing more interesting.

Less Exact	More Exact
Dinner smells better than lunch.	Dinner smells spicier and more delicious than lunch.
The big box is the heaviest.	The big box is the most impossible to fit!

Rewrite each sentence to make it more interesting. Try to use more exact adjectives and adverbs.

1. My favorite star is brighter than a light bulb.

____

2. It is maybe the brightest star in the world.

____

3. Don't you think the sun shines more clearly than your star?

____

4. The sun probably shines the strongest in the universe.

____

5. The sun's role in our lives is bigger than the moon's.

____

6. Sun energy is even better than wind energy.

____

Name ______________________ Date __________

Focus Trait: Ideas

You can make your ideas clearer if your paragraph has a topic sentence. Remove unimportant or unnecessary details to help support the main idea better.

Read the paragraph below. Circle the sentence that would make the best topic sentence to start the paragraph. Underline two details that do not belong in the paragraph.

One of the earliest toothbrushes was called the "chew stick." It was made from a twig about the size of a pencil. One end of the twig was pointed. The other end was chewed until it became soft and brushlike. People brushed with the chewed end. They cleaned between their teeth with the pointed end. New Orleans dentist Levi Spear Parmly (1790–1859) is credited as the inventor of modern dental floss. You might be surprised to learn that people have been using toothbrushes for thousands and thousands of years. The Chinese were the first to make and use toothbrushes with bristles. The handle was carved from bone or bamboo. The bristles were made from animal hair and then attached to one end of the handle. These stiff bristles did a better job cleaning teeth than the chew stick. The first nylon toothbrush was called Doctor West's Miracle Toothbrush.

Name ______________________ Date ____________

Cause and Effect

I Could Do That!
Comprehension:
Cause and Effect

Read the selection below.

Elizabeth Cady Stanton

Elizabeth Cady Stanton was a leader of the women's rights movement in the United States. Her work helped get women in the U.S. the right to vote.

Elizabeth was born in 1812. Her father was a New York congressman and judge. When she finished school, Elizabeth studied law in her father's office. She grew upset at how unfair the laws were for women and began speaking up for women's rights.

In 1854, Elizabeth was asked to speak before the New York state legislature. Thanks to her speech, married women in New York won many of the same rights as their husbands.

In 1870, Elizabeth joined Susan B. Anthony and other women to work for women's voting rights. She spent many years traveling the country to win support for their cause.

Until she died in 1902, Elizabeth kept writing and speaking about women's rights. In 1878 she wrote an important paper about giving women the right to vote. The paper was given to Congress each year. In 1920, women finally won the right to vote.

Complete the Flow Chart to show a chain of effects connected to a single cause in Elizabeth Cady Stanton's life.

Cause:

Effect:

Effect:

Effect:

Name ______________________ Date ____________

Cause and Effect

Read the selection below.

She Didn't Run—She Walked

Sojourner Truth was a slave who was not afraid to stand up for what was fair. One day her owner promised he would free her if she spun a certain amount of wool. Then she got hurt and spun less wool than expected, so the owner changed his mind.

That wasn't fair. So she made a plan. She worked until she had spun all the wool the owner had wanted. Then she left. Sojourner was proud of how she left. She didn't run away. She walked. Sojourner found a family who kept her safe until she could become free legally. To earn her keep, she worked for the couple. They paid her wages for her work. That was fair.

Once she was free, Sojourner wanted to help her children become free. Then an owner illegally sold her son into further slavery. That wasn't fair. So Sojourner fought him in court. Even though she was a woman and a former slave, she was not afraid to fight for what was right and fair.

Use a Flow Chart like the one shown here to identify cause-and-effect relationships in the selection. Then read and answer the items below.

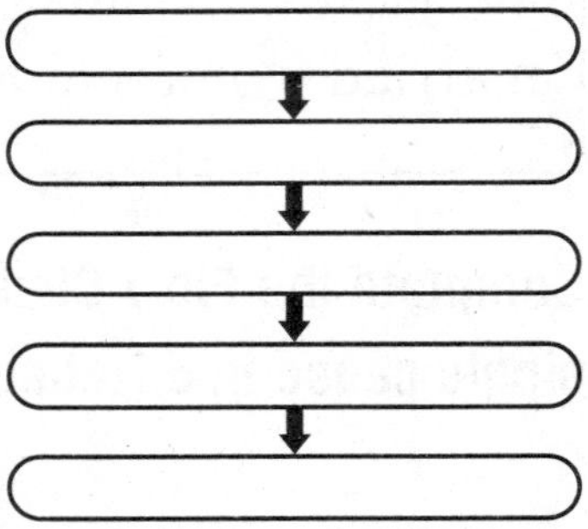

1. Identify a cause-and-effect text structure in the selection. Use details from the selection to support your answer.

____

____

____

2. Explain how the cause-and-effect text structure you identified can help you locate and recall information. Use selection details to support your answer.

____

____

____

Name ______________________ Date __________

Using a Dictionary

frame	frequent	friction
freeze	freshwater	Friday

Use a dictionary to help you answer each question about the words listed above.

1. What is the etymology, or word history, of the word *Friday?*

____

____

2. What is the past-tense form of *freeze?*

____

3. What part of speech is the word *frequent?*

____

4. Which syllable of *friction* is emphasized?

____

5. Use the word *frame* as a noun in one sentence and as a verb in another.

____

____

____

6. Draw a line between each syllable of the word *freshwater*.

____

Name ______________________ Date ____________

VCCV and VCV Patterns

Basic Complete the puzzle by writing the Basic Word for each clue.

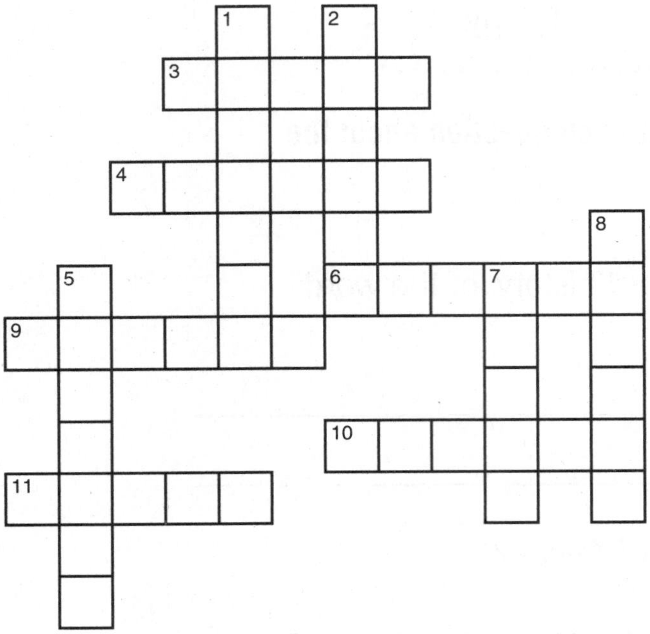

Across

3. in front of
4. having a space or opening inside
6. shiny, white metal
9. something given in return for a worthy act
10. sixty seconds
11. in math, to take away from

Down

1. something that protects or covers
2. very well known
5. person qualified to treat people's teeth
7. to believe to be of worth
8. not working properly

Spelling Words

1. dentist
2. final
3. finish
4. narrow
5. shelter
6. ahead
7. corner
8. hollow
9. divide
10. famous
11. recent
12. silver
13. capture
14. cabin
15. dinner
16. minus
17. minute
18. value
19. reward
20. broken

Challenge

decent
secure
standard
frontier
stampede

Challenge 12–14. You just watched a movie called *On the Range with Cowboy Ed*. Describe a scene from the movie. Use three Challenge Words. Write on a separate sheet of paper.

Name ______________________ Date ____________

Spelling Word Sort

Write each Basic Word beside the correct heading.

VC / CV Pattern: Divide Between the Consonants	**Basic Words:** **Possible Selection Words:** **Challenge Words:**
V / CV Pattern: Divide Before the Consonant	**Basic Words:** **Challenge Words:** **Possible Selection Words:**
VC / V Pattern: Divide After the Consonant	**Basic Words:** **Possible Selection Words:**

Spelling Words

1. dentist
2. final
3. finish
4. narrow
5. shelter
6. ahead
7. corner
8. hollow
9. divide
10. famous
11. recent
12. silver
13. capture
14. cabin
15. dinner
16. minus
17. minute
18. value
19. reward
20. broken

Challenge

decent
secure
standard
frontier
stampede

Challenge Add the Challenge Words to your Word Sort.

Connect to Reading Look through *I Could Do That!* Find words that have the VCCV or VCV patterns on this page. Add them to your Word Sort.

Name ______________________ Date ____________

Proofreading for Spelling

I Could Do That!
Spelling: VCCV and VCV Patterns

Find the misspelled words and circle them. Write them correctly on the lines below.

Susan B. Anthony was a famus woman at the end of the nineteenth century. In 1872, she broke the law by casting a vote in a presidential election. She knew that the resent Civil War had shown the valew of voting, a reaward that should be given to all people, not just men. She would devide her time between big cities and small towns. Susan wanted to captore the attention of women and convince them of their rights. Women would finich household chores early to host a tea or invite friends to diner just to discuss what Susan had to say. Susan would speak anywhere—a big meeting hall or a small kabin. Everywhere she went, there were crowds. Some women waited in line around the cornur for hours, while others stood along the nerrow hallways to catch Susan's finel words about civil and political rights.

1. ______________ 7. ______________
2. ______________ 8. ______________
3. ______________ 9. ______________
4. ______________ 10. ______________
5. ______________ 11. ______________
6. ______________ 12. ______________

Spelling Words

1. dentist
2. final
3. finish
4. narrow
5. shelter
6. ahead
7. corner
8. hollow
9. divide
10. famous
11. recent
12. silver
13. capture
14. cabin
15. dinner
16. minus
17. minute
18. value
19. reward
20. broken

Challenge

decent
secure
standard
frontier
stampede

Name ______________________ Date ____________

Contractions with *not*

I Could Do That!
Grammar: Negatives

A **negative** is a word that makes a sentence mean *no*. A **negative contraction** is made with a verb and the negative word *not*. An apostrophe takes the place of the letter *o* in each contraction with *not*.

contraction with *not*
Esther isn't at home, but she may be at the hat shop.

Thinking Question
What word is a contraction made with a verb and the negative word not?

1–8. Write the contraction for the underlined word or words in each sentence.

1. There are not any blue hats in the window today. ____________
2. This hat does not have a ribbon. ____________
3. That small cowboy hat will not fit Mr. Fox's head. ____________
4. There were not many customers today. ____________
5. The seamstress cannot find her sewing needle. ____________
6. Please do not sit on my hat. ____________
7. Ms. Kelly did not buy the hat with red stripes. ____________
8. Esther had not made a hat this large before. ____________

Using Negatives

The words *no*, *no one*, *nobody*, *none*, *nothing*, *nowhere*, and *never* are negatives. A contraction with a verb and the word *not* is also a negative. When making a negative statement, make sure to use just one negative.

positive
I understand the candidates' opinions.

negative
I don't understand the candidates' opinions.
I understand none of the candidates' opinions.

Thinking Question
What word will change the sentence to a negative meaning? Does the sentence still make sense?

1–6. Use a negative to change the meaning of the sentence from positive to negative. Write the negative sentence on the line below.

1. Anybody in the fifth grade can run for class president

   ____

2. Roger is running for class president.

   ____

3. Tom has asked Roger if he can be his vice president.

   ____

4. Myung-Yun always likes to help make campaign posters.

   ____

5. Everyone is excited about the school elections this year.

   ____

6. The class president can do something about all of the issues that bother students.

   ____

   ____

Name ______________________ Date ____________

Avoiding Double Negatives

I Could Do That!
Grammar: Negatives

Words such as *not*, *no*, and *never* are negatives. Using two negatives together is called a **double negative**. Never use two negatives together in a sentence.

double negative

My mother won't tell nobody how she voted.

corrected sentences

My mother won't tell anybody how she voted.
My mother will tell nobody how she voted.

Thinking Question
What two negatives are used together in the sentence?

1–8. Write the correct word shown in parentheses to complete the sentence.

1. There (is, isn't) no presidential candidate that my parents completely support. ____________
2. That candidate hasn't said (anything, nothing) about the important issues. ____________
3. He doesn't support (any, none) of the laws to help the environment. ____________
4. Don't vote for (anyone, no one) without learning his or her political views. ____________
5. Doesn't (anybody, nobody) agree with that candidate's views? ____________
6. Isn't there (anywhere, nowhere) I can get better information about the candidates? ____________
7. The voters (have, haven't) no choice but to support the new law. ____________
8. This candidate (has, hasn't) never been honest with the voters. ____________

Name ______________________ Date ____________

I Could Do That!
Grammar:
Spiral Review

Kinds of Adverbs

How	I carefully packed my luggage into the wagon.
When	Father was finally moving our family to California.
Where	We were traveling there with several other families.
Negative	I could hardly wait to see our new home.

1–8. Underline each adverb. Write the verb it describes.

1. The wagon train rode steadily across the prairie. ____________
2. We sadly waved goodbye to our old friends. ____________
3. Sometimes the wagons crossed shallow rivers and streams. ____________
4. Dad had stored our gear and supplies inside. ____________
5. We had barely left when my sister fell asleep. ____________
6. Mom had never wanted to leave our old home. ____________
7. The sun was setting slowly on the horizon. ____________
8. My sister and I rarely had the chance to see a sunset on the prairie. ____________

Name ______________________ Date ____________

I Could Do That!
Grammar: Connect to Writing

Proofreading

Proofreading can help you make certain that you have used contractions and negatives correctly in your writing.

incorrect with proofreading marks
Learning to sew ~~wasn't~~ [was] never difficult for Esther.
correct
Learning to sew was never difficult for Esther.

1–6. Correct the use of contractions or double negatives in each sentence. Write the sentence correctly on the line below.

1. Esther doesnt' like that dress pattern.

____

2. Esther never sewed nothing before she was eight.

____

3. She couldn't find no silk for Ms. Kelly's dress.

____

4. Sewing these pants wont take long.

____

5. There isn't no one in town who sews better than Esther.

____

6. The stitching on this shirt isnt neat and even.

____

Name ______________________ Date ____________

I Could Do That!
Writing: Write to Inform

Focus Trait: Sentence Fluency
Using Transition Words

Cause-and-Effect Sentences	Transition Added
When Esther was a girl, only men could vote. Her mother could not vote for president.	When Esther was a girl, only men could vote. **Therefore**, her mother could not vote for president.

A. Read each pair of sentences. Connect the sentences using a cause-and-effect transition word or phrase.

Cause-and-Effect Sentences	Transition Added
1. Esther made nice clothes. Women paid her to make clothes for them.	Esther made nice clothes. __________ women paid her to make clothes for them.
2. Esther heard Susan B. Anthony speaking out about women's rights. She wanted to help women get the vote, too.	Esther heard Susan B. Anthony speaking out about women's rights. __________ she wanted to help women get the vote, too.

B. Read each pair of sentences. Connect the sentences using a transition word or phrase.

Pair/Share **Work with a partner to brainstorm how to add transition words or phrases to make the sentences read smoothly.**

Cause-and-Effect Sentences	Transition Added
3. Esther liked to do things for herself. She painted the sign for her hat shop.	
4. People thought that Esther was too young to run a business. They were shocked to see her open a hat shop.	

Name ______________________________ Date ____________

Text and Graphic Features

Read the selection below.

Yosemite National Park

One of the most popular national parks in the United States is Yosemite National Park. The park is in east-central California. The area of the park is 1,189 square miles, and it is set along the *Sierra Nevada*.

The park is famous for its tall mountains and valleys. *The highest mountain is Mount Lyell, which is 13,114 feet tall.* The valleys have rock walls made from granite. *The largest is El Capitan. It rises up to 7,569 feet.*

People come to Yosemite to climb the mountains and to hike the trails. Along the trails, hikers can see animals such as mule deer, squirrels, chipmunks, and black bears.

If you are ever in California, go visit Yosemite National Park!

Major Features
alpine wilderness, giant sequoia trees, Yosemite Valley

Use the Column Chart to show the location and purpose of the text and graphic features used in the selection.

Text or Graphic Feature	Location	Purpose

Name ______________________________ Date ____________

Text and Graphic Features

Read the selection below.

Pine Tree Identification Guide

Introduction

There are approximately 115 species of pine trees worldwide. Thirty-five of them grow here in the United States. Sometimes it's hard to tell one tree from another. This guide will help you identify some of the more common pine trees by looking at where they grow, their height, needles, and cones.

Eastern White Pine

Range: northeastern United States
Height: 80–100 ft.
Needles: Occur in bundles of five
Cones: Curved, 4–8 in. long

Norway Spruce

Range: northern United States
Height: 80–100 ft.
Needles: stiff, less than an inch long, sharp pointed tips
Cones: 4–6 in. long, cylindrical

Pinyon Pine

Range: southwestern United States
Height: 10–30 ft.
Needles: 1–2 in. long; occur in bundles of 2
Cones: 1–2 in. long; oval shaped; very thick scales containing edible seeds

Conclusion

Pines trees are economically important as a source of lumber and other useful products. They are also beautiful ornamental plants. It's fun to learn about them.

Use a Column Chart to explain text and graphic features in the selection. Then answer the questions below.

1. If you see a pine tree with needles that occur in bundles of five, what kind of tree is it?

____

2. Why are some words in italics in the text?

____

3. What kind of information is found after the word *Cones* in bold for each tree?

____

Name ______________________ Date ____________

Prefixes: *pre-*, *inter-*, *ex-*

prearrange	interact	intermingle	exit
precaution	international	exclaim	intercontinental

Each sentence shows a word in parentheses with the prefix *pre-*, *inter-*, or *ex-* in parentheses. Complete the sentence using each word in parentheses.

1. (prearrange) I will call you to

   ____

2. (precaution) Buckling your safety belt is

   ____

3. (interact) When you start at a new school

   ____

4. (international) The world-famous film actor was

   ____

5. (intermingle) He doesn't like it when

   ____

6. (exclaim) When she sees that scary movie

   ____

7. (exit) Take the highway, and make sure you

   ____

8. (intercontinental) The family traveled from North America to South America

   ____

Name ______________________ Date __________

VCCV Pattern

Basic Write the Basic Word that each sentence describes.

1. No one else knows this.
   ____
2. Cats and dogs have these.
   ____
3. You buy this to see a movie in the theater.
   ____
4. Someone who writes a book is called this.
   ____
5. You can hang this on a wall for decoration.
   ____
6. You can put sand in this at the beach.
   ____
7. People travel into outer space using this.
   ____
8. This is a type of food to eat.
   ____
9. This protects your clothes when you cook.
   ____
10. This is to pick things up and put in one place.
    ____

Challenge 11–14. You have been invited to a friend's party, but you can't attend because you're going to your family reunion that day. Write a letter to your friend explaining why you can't attend the party. Use four Challenge Words. Write on a separate sheet of paper.

Spelling Words

1. poster
2. secret
3. whether
4. author
5. rocket
6. bushel
7. agree
8. bucket
9. ticket
10. declare
11. chicken
12. clothing
13. apron
14. whiskers
15. degree
16. gather
17. achieve
18. rather
19. bracket
20. machine

Challenge

regret
nephew
method
decline
vibrate

Name ____________________ Date __________

Spelling Word Sort

The Ever-Living Tree
Spelling: VCCV Pattern

Write each Basic Word beside the correct heading.

V/CCV: Divide before the consonant blend or digraph	**Basic Words:** **Challenge Words:** **Possible Selection Word:**
VCC/V: Divide after the consonant blend or digraph	**Basic Words:** **Challenge Words:** **Possible Selection Words:**

Spelling Words

1. poster
2. secret
3. whether
4. author
5. rocket
6. bushel
7. agree
8. bucket
9. ticket
10. declare
11. chicken
12. clothing
13. apron
14. whiskers
15. degree
16. gather
17. achieve
18. rather
19. bracket
20. machine

Challenge

regret
nephew
method
decline
vibrate

Challenge Add the Challenge Words to your Word Sort.

Connect to Reading Look through ***The Ever-Living Tree: The Life and Times of a Coast Redwood.*** Find words that have the VCCV spelling pattern. Add them to your Word Sort.

Name ______________________ Date ____________

Proofreading for Spelling

Find the misspelled words and circle them. Write them correctly on the lines below.

In 1903, Colonel Charles Young was ordered to take his troops to Sequoia National Park. He would rathar have stayed in San Francisco, where the temperature rarely registered a degre under 45 in the winter. But whehter or not he wanted to go, he had to agre to the U.S. Army orders. Traveling on horseback for 16 days, Young and his troopers arrived in Sequoia. They brought clotheng and food. To make sure there was enough to eat, each man had to gathar a bushal of fruit and fill a buket with water. The supplies were so heavy the braket on the shelf broke. The men had no mashine to fix it. Hammer and nails would do. Young and his men were able to acheive their goal of making the wagon road long enough for people to be able to get to the park. Colonel Young, the first African-American superintendent of a national park, could deklare his work a success.

1. ____________ 7. ____________
2. ____________ 8. ____________
3. ____________ 9. ____________
4. ____________ 10. ____________
5. ____________ 11. ____________
6. ____________ 12. ____________

Spelling Words

1. poster
2. secret
3. whether
4. author
5. rocket
6. bushel
7. agree
8. bucket
9.. ticket
10. declare
11. chicken
12. clothing
13. apron
14. whiskers
15. degree
16. gather
17. achieve
18. rather
19. bracket
20. machine

Challenge

regret
nephew
method
decline
vibrate

Name ______________________ Date ____________

Using Quotation Marks

A **direct quotation** tells a speaker's exact words. Use quotation marks (“ ”) before and after a direct quotation. Do not use quotation marks unless you give a speaker's exact words.

direct quotation

“What do you want to do today?” Dad asked.

Thinking Question
What words tell exactly what the speaker said?

1–6. Write each sentence. Add quotation marks where they are needed. Write *correct* for those sentences that do not need quotation marks.

1. Let's go for a nature walk, Joan replied.

____

2. That's a great idea! Michael exclaimed.

____

3. Would you like to go the Redwood forest? Dad asked.

____

____

4. Mom explained that Redwoods are the largest living trees in the world.

____

____

5. They are also some of the oldest living organisms on Earth, Joan added.

____

____

6. Joan asked Michael if he was looking forward to the nature walk.

____

____

Name ______________________ Date ____________

Capital Letters, Spacing, and Punctuation in Quotations

Use capital letters and punctuation to write direct quotations correctly. Always capitalize the first word of a quotation. Use a comma to separate a quotation from the words that tell who is speaking. Put end marks inside the last quotation marks.

When a quotation starts a sentence, put a comma at the end of a statement. Use the usual end punctuation for questions and exclamations.

direct quotation
Angela exlaimed, "What a big tree!"
"The redwood is a unique tree," Jee agreed.
"Do you think we can climb it?" asked Angela.

Thinking Question
What kind of sentence is this quotation? Where does the quotation come in the sentence?

1–5. Write the quotations correctly.

1. shall we look for something to eat the woodpecker asked

   ____

2. the chipmunk asked do you see any acorns

   ____

3. bugs sound good to me said the woodpecker.

   ____

4. the chipmunk exclaimed that sounds absolutely awful

   ____

5. most birds eat worms and bugs said the woodpecker

   ____

Name ______________________________ Date ______________

Writing Dialogue

Dialogue uses quotations to tell a speaker's exact words. Quotation marks go around the words spoken, and a comma separates the dialogue from the rest of the sentence. Indent the first line of a speaker's dialogue.

"Don't go into the woods alone," Jerry warned.

Consuelo laughed, "I wouldn't do that! It's too easy to get lost without a ranger to act as a guide."

Thinking Question
Where does one speaker's dialogue end? Where does a new speaker's dialogue begin?

Activity **Write the dialogue correctly on the lines below. Put the quotation marks where they belong, and punctuate and capitalize each sentence correctly.**

what do you want to do today Arturo asked.
I want to hike in the redwood forest replied Rose.
Arturo wondered what do you want to see there.
There are all kinds of animals in a redwood forest said Rose.
Oh I hope we don't see a skunk cried Arturo.
Rose laughed and answered we'll probably smell one first.

____

____

____

____

____

____

____

____

____

Name _______________________________ Date ______________

Prepositions and Prepositional Phrases

Preposition	Prepositional Phrase
from	A dark brown seed falls from the giant tree.

1–5. Underline the prepositional phrase once and the preposition twice in each sentence.

1. The seed sprouts beneath the dirt.
2. Its roots spread through the soil.
3. The sun shines brightly above the tiny seedling.
4. Rain falls and soaks the ground around the young tree.
5. The tree reaches its branches toward the sunny, blue sky.

6–8. Combine each pair of sentences by moving the underlined prepositional phrases. Write the new sentence on the line. Capitalize and punctuate quotations correctly.

6. Martha said the Sequoia is rooted firmly. It is rooted firmly in the ground.

____

____

7. This amazing tree grows slowly explained Mark. It grows for hundreds of years.

____

____

8. The full-grown trees stand together. They stand beside the river.

____

Name ______________________ Date ____________

Word Choice

A Quotation with *said*	A More Exact Word for *said*
"You could be the Christopher Columbus of space," Toni said.	"You could be the Christopher Columbus of space," Toni joked.

1–6. Rewrite the sentence. Add capital letters and punctuation. Replace *said* with a more exact word. Write the new sentence on the line.

1. Jenny said I plan to be an astronaut when I grow up

____

2. wow! that's an awesome goal to have Cooper said

____

3. Fran said look It's a bird It's a plane it's Jenny the Astronaut

____

4. you're not the least bit funny Jenny said to Fran

____

5. Jenny said exploring space would be a dream come true

____

6. Fran said I get airsick, and I'm afraid of heights for me it would be a nightmare

____

____

Name ______________________________ Date ______________

Writing Clear Directions

Procedural writing explains how to do something. Good procedural writing includes a clear purpose, the materials needed, steps that are easy to follow, and a conclusion.

Vague	Clear
I like making tree rubbings and then collecting leaves from the same tree.	You can follow these steps to make a tree rubbing for your scrapbook.
To make a tree rubbing, I use paper and something that writes in color.	You will need a white piece of paper and a crayon in your favorite color.

Rewrite the vague steps in the correct order on the right. Change or add words to make the directions clearer.

Vague Steps	Clear Steps
Place the paper against the tree. Rough bark makes an interesting rubbing, so pick your tree carefully! Rub the tree with your marker, and watch the pattern of the bark show up. Rubbing too hard will make the paper rip.	______________________________ ______________________________ ______________________________ ______________________________ ______________________________ ______________________________ ______________________________ ______________________________

Now rewrite the vague conclusion below.

Pair/Share **Work with a partner to brainstorm a fitting conclusion for the tree rubbing activity.**

Vague Conclusion	Clear Conclusion
I always collect some leaves from the tree, too, but few people think of making tree rubbings.	

Name ______________________ Date ____________

Compare and Contrast

Read the selection below.

Whales Are Not Fish!

Fish and whales both swim in the sea. They have two eyes and both have fins and tails. However, the tail of a fish is vertical, and a whale's tail is horizontal. Fish and whale fins are different, too. Whales have bumps on their fins. This actually makes them go faster. Scientists have copied this design to make better engines!

A main difference between whales and fish is the fact that whales are mammals. While fish have gills, whales have lungs like you and me. They must come up to the surface of the water to breathe. They open a blowhole at the top of their heads to take in air. The blowhole is a watertight cover that helps them let out air and quickly takes it back in before they go under the water again.

Fish lay eggs. Because whales are mammals, they give birth to live young. Whales also care for their young. We are still learning about how whales communicate with each other and how they travel.

Complete the Venn Diagram below to compare and contrast whales and fish.

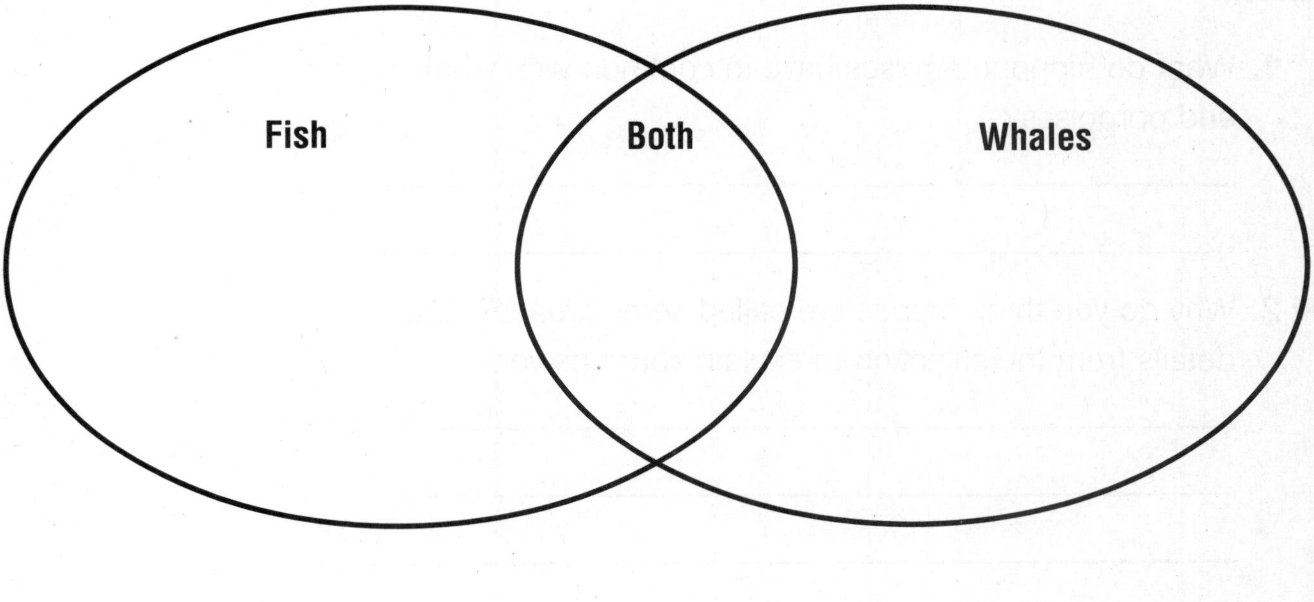

Name _______________________ Date ___________

Compare and Contrast

Read the selection below.

Hippos

The hippopotamus lives in rivers and lakes in Africa. Hippos remain cool during the hot day by staying in the water or mud. Female hippos even give birth in the water. At dusk, hippos come out of the water to graze for food. For this reason, the hippopotamus is called semi-aquatic. The word aquatic means "related to water."

Even though they look like they might be related to pigs, hippos are actually more closely related to whales and porpoises. Whales, porpoises, and hippos share a common ancestor and history of development. They are all mammals. While hippos are not ocean animals, they do love water. Unlike its relatives the whale and porpoise, however, the hippo has four legs instead of fins.

One way the hippo is similar to whales and porpoises is its speed. Hippos are surprisingly fast and can run faster than humans.

Use a Venn Diagram like the one shown to compare and contrast hippos with whales and porpoises. Then answer the questions below.

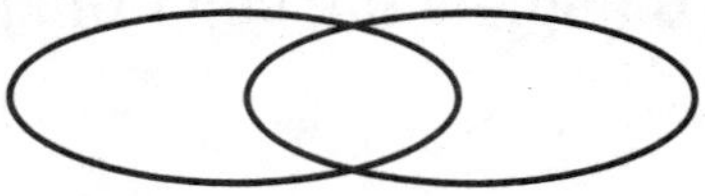

1. What do hippopotamuses have in common with whales and porpoises?

____

____

2. Why do you think hippos are called *semi-aquatic*? Use details from the selection to explain your answer.

____

____

____

Name ______________________ Date ____________

Suffixes *-ed, -ly*

wrapped	frequently	displayed	exhausted
normally	naturally	fairly	suffered

Complete each sentence using a word from the box.

1. It snows ______________ in cold places like Alaska.
2. I would not ______________ be so excited, but today is my birthday.
3. It is important to divide a treat ______________ so that everyone gets the same amount.
4. After running ten miles, she was ______________ .
5. During the spelling bee, he ______________ the embarrassment of being on stage.
6. The books were ______________ in the store window.
7. The actor read his lines very ______________ .
8. ______________ in a warm coat, I went out into the cold December snow.

Name ______________________ Date ____________

VCCCV Pattern

Basic **Write the Basic Word that belongs in each group.**

1. example, model, ____________________
2. stock, inventory, ____________________
3. describe, clarify, ____________________
4. locate, live, ____________________
5. traveler, seeker, ____________________
6. beast, creature, ____________________
7. empire, monarchy, ____________________
8. midpoint, halfway, ____________________
9. lone, solo, ____________________
10. sportsperson, player, ____________________
11. finish, conclude, ____________________
12. in place of, rather than, ____________________

Challenge 13–15. Write an e-mail message to your friend telling about an art exhibit you have seen—perhaps at an art museum, an art fair, or a school art exhibit. Use three Challenge Words. Write on a separate sheet of paper.

Spelling Words

1. hundred
2. supply
3. single
4. middle
5. explain
6. surprise
7. pilgrim
8. sandwich
9. instead
10. complete
11. monster
12. settle
13. address
14. farther
15. sample
16. although
17. turtle
18. athlete
19. orchard
20. kingdom

Challenge

fortress
instant
exclaim
mattress
sculptor

Name ____________________ Date __________

Spelling Word Sort

Write each Basic Word beside the correct heading.

VC/CCV Pattern: Divide before consonant blend or digraph	**Basic Words:** **Challenge Words:** **Possible Selection Words:**
VCC/CV Pattern: Divide after consonant blend or digraph	**Basic Words:** **Challenge Words:** **Possible Selection Words:**

Challenge Add the Challenge Words to your Word Sort.

Connect to Reading Look through ***Owen and Mzee: The True Story of a Remarkable Friendship***. Find words that have the VCCCV patterns on this page. Add them to your Word Sort.

Spelling Words

1. hundred
2. supply
3. single
4. middle
5. explain
6. surprise
7. pilgrim
8. sandwich
9. instead
10. complete
11. monster
12. settle
13. address
14. farther
15. sample
16. although
17. turtle
18. athlete
19. orchard
20. kingdom

Challenge

fortress
instant
exclaim
mattress
sculptor

Name ______________________ Date ____________

Owen and Mzee
Spelling: VCCCV Pattern

Proofreading for Spelling

Find the misspelled words and circle them. Write them correctly on the lines below.

This is a story about a rare hawksbill tirtle whose adress is Hanauma Bay Nature Preserve in Hawaii. The turtle was seen with a hook caught in its left flipper. Everyone assumed the turtle would die so it was a surprize when a scuba diver spotted it swimming farthur out in the bay. Divers were able to rescue the hawksbill, altheugh the vet's X-ray showed a sengle rusty fishing hook embedded in the animal. The vet decided to cut away as much of the hook as possible insteed of removing it. After the hawksbill was treated with antibiotics, it was released back into Hanauma Bay with "HB" painted on its shell. Several hundrid people visit the bay daily. Some will bring a sandwitch and fruit from a nearby orcherd. They hope to catch a glimpse of "HB" swimming in the midle of the bay.

1. ____________
2. ____________
3. ____________
4. ____________
5. ____________
6. ____________
7. ____________
8. ____________
9. ____________
10. ____________
11. ____________

Spelling Words

1. hundred
2. supply
3. single
4. middle
5. explain
6. surprise
7. pilgrim
8. sandwich
9. instead
10. complete
11. monster
12. settle
13. address
14. farther
15. sample
16. although
17. turtle
18. athlete
19. orchard
20. kingdom

Challenge

fortress
instant
exclaim
mattress
sculptor

Commas with Introductory Words

When you write, use a comma with the **introductory words** *yes, no,* and *well* to show a pause.

comma with an introductory word
Well, the giant tortoise eats both plants and animals.

Thinking Question
Does the sentence begin with yes, no, *or* well*? Where should a comma be used to show a pause?*

1–5. Write the sentence correctly. Add commas where they are needed.

1. Yes giant tortoises sleep inside their shells.

____

____

2. No they don't walk very fast, although their legs are strong.

____

____

3. Well their legs have to hold up those very heavy shells.

____

____

4. Yes these tortoises are only found in Asia.

____

____

5. No the Aldabra Giant Tortoise is not the largest tortoise in the world.

____

____

Name ______________________ Date ____________

Commas with Names

Use a comma or commas to set off the name of a person being addressed directly.

person being addressed by name
Where do hippos live, Mr. Wilcox?
Can you imagine, Victor, having a hippo as a pet?

Thinking Question
What person is being addressed directly? Where should a comma or commas be used to set off the person's name?

1–5. Write the sentence correctly. Add commas where they are needed.

1. Carmen the natural habitat of the hippo is Africa.

____

2. Did you know Todd that hippos can talk to each other underwater?

____

____

3. Tasha hippos spend most of their day in the water.

____

4. Hippos do not sweat Carmen so they use mud and water to stay cool.

____

____

5. We are going to watch this video about hippos now Walter.

____

____

Name ______________________ Date ____________

Commas in a Series

When you write, use a comma to separate the words in a series. Remember, a series may contain single words or phrases.

We saw tortoises, hippopotamuses, and birds.
There are sea lions, sea otters, fur seals, and elephant seals at the zoo.

Thinking Question
Which words or phrases are in a series? How are commas used to separate the items in a series?

1–5. Add commas where they are needed. Write the sentence correctly on the line.

1. I am asking Manuel Sue and Keith to work on my science project with me.

   ____

   ____

2. Otters orcas and sea lions are all mammals.

   ____

3. People who drill dump or dig up the sea floor are not allowed in the sanctuary.

   ____

   ____

4. The otter flipped flopped and almost fell into the water.

   ____

5. A layer of fat a thick coat of fur and a dry spot in the sun all help sea mammals to stay warm.

   ____

   ____

Name ______________________ Date ____________

Writing Titles

Book: Tortoises and Turtles	**Magazine:** Time	**Newspaper:** The City Journal
Story: "Will You Be My Friend?"	**Poem:** "To a Dear Friend"	**Article:** "Ten Things You Should Know about Hippos"

1–4. Write each title correctly in the space below.

1. a guide to african wildlife
(book)
____

2. climbing kilimanjaro
(poem)
____

3. the silent song of the cobra
(story)
____

4. the johannesburg daily times
(newspaper)
____

5–6. Write each sentence correctly in the space below.

5. Bertram did you read the article sea ecosystem?
____

6. Yes the teacher has several copies of water wonders magazine.
____

Name ______________________ Date ____________

Conventions

Proofreading can help you make certain that you have used commas correctly in your writing. Using commas makes your writing clear and easy to understand.

Incorrect with proofreading marks

Mark: You know, Dad‸ the population of hippos in Africa has shrunk tremendously.

Dad: That's a serious problem‸ Mark.

Correct

Mark: You know, Dad, the population of hippos in Africa has shrunk tremendously.

Dad: That's a serious problem, Mark.

Activity **This part of a script has 15 missing commas. Add a comma or commas to each part in the script.**

Mark: Yes I agree. Did you know Dad that people are the greatest threat to the hippo population?

Dad: No I wasn't aware of that.

Mark: Well it's true. Hippos are killed for their fat their ivory teeth and because they eat so much grass.

Dad: Is anything being done to save the hippos Mark?

Mark: Yes some of the areas where hippos live are protected.

Dad: Well that makes sense. I think Mark that we should do our part to save the hippos.

Mark: That's a great idea Dad! Let's get a hippo for a pet!

Dad: No let's not. You were kidding weren't you Mark?

Name ______________________ Date ____________

Focus Trait: Ideas

Finding the Best Information

Source	Information
Encyclopedia	Articles about many different topics
Atlas	Maps of places all over the world
Internet	Web sites of organizations as well as electronic reference materials
Interviewing an expert	Unique information
Newspaper and magazine articles	Up-to-date information on different topics
Nonfiction books	Facts about real people, places, and things

1–3. Answer the following questions about using sources to find the best information.

1. Maggie is researching tortoises. She wants to answer the question, *Where do tortoises live?*

a. Which source could Maggie use? ______________

b. What other question could she answer by using this source?

____

2. Luis is researching how zoos are run. He wants to answer the question, *How many people work at the zoo in my city?*

a. Which source should Luis use? ______________

b. What other question could he answer with this source?

____

3. Nina is researching Kenya. She wants to answer the question, *What ocean is closest to Kenya?*

a. Which source should Nina use? ______________

b. What other question could she answer with this source?

____

Name ______________________ Date ____________

Author's Purpose

Read the selection below.

The Adventures of Jules Verne

If you like science fiction and adventure stories, read Jules Verne. Verne was one of the world's first science fiction writers. He wrote stories about adventures with modern technology.

Around the World in 80 Days tells the story of a rich man named Phineas Fogg, who bets a friend that he can travel around the world in eighty days. He plans to use trains, steamships, and even a hot air balloon. The book, published in 1873, tells of Fogg's adventures in different parts of the world.

Another of Verne's famous books, *20,000 Leagues Under the Sea,* is the story of a professor who goes looking for a sea monster that has been sinking ships. The sea monster turns out to be a submarine called the *Nautilus*. The professor and his servant enter the submarine and realize that the captain is responsible for the attacks. Then, they try to escape.

Both of these books are exciting adventure stories that sometimes describe machines that hadn't been invented at the time. Many of Verne's ideas later came true.

Complete the Inference Map to show text details and identify the author's purpose for writing. Write complete sentences.

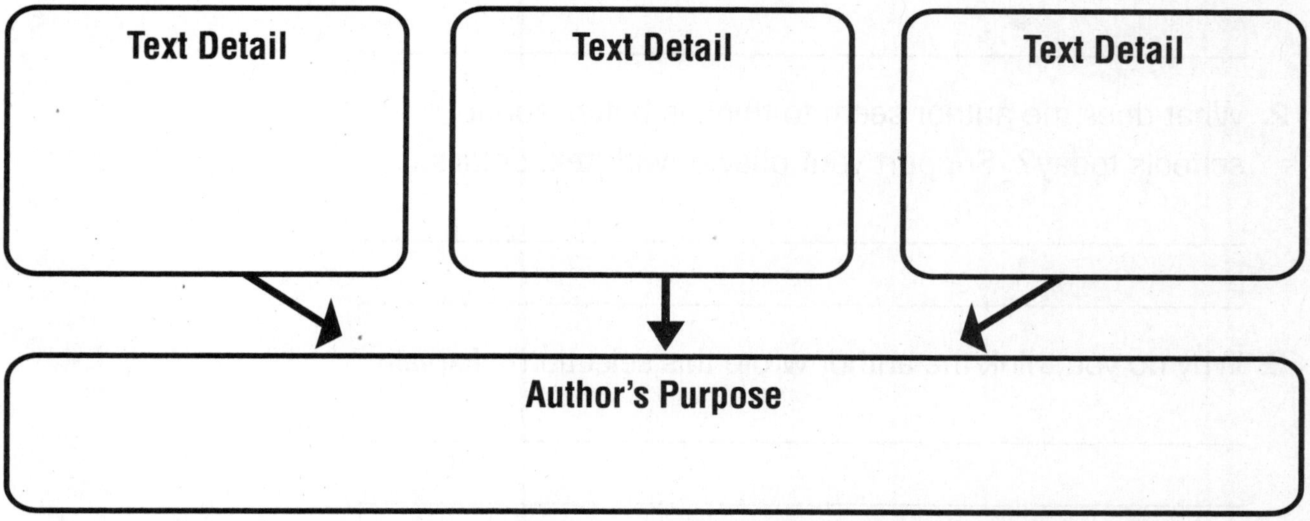

Name ______________________ Date ____________

Author's Purpose

Read the selection below.

The Progress of the American School

Most students in the United States today go to several different schools. Some begin school as early as age four. Others begin preschool even earlier. Most go on to a different school for kindergarten and elementary school. Many attend a new school for middle school or junior high, and then yet another school for high school. Each school is tailored to the needs of the age group of its students.

In nineteenth-century America, however, preschool did not exist. Kindergarten was uncommon. And everyone else went to the same school. Often, they went to school in the same room!

To keep order, teachers had to be very strict. Because they had few books, they had their students memorize facts. School may have been boring and dull, but people learned what they needed to get by.

Use an Inference Map like the one here to organize your thoughts. Analyze the selection to determine the author's viewpoint and purpose. Then answer the questions below.

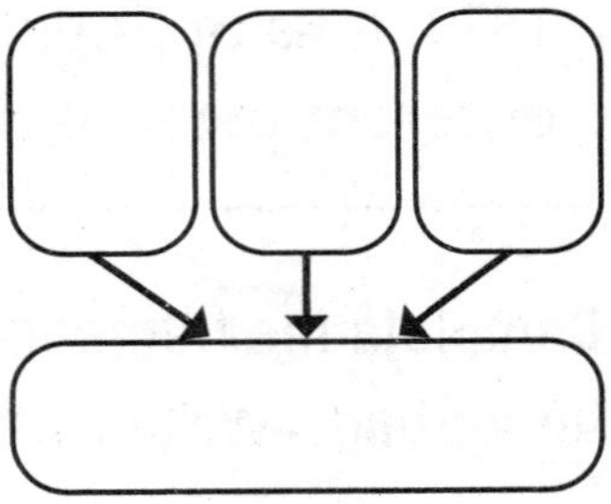

1. What in the title shows the author's view of school?

____

____

2. What does the author seem to think is better about schools today? Support your answer with text details.

____

____

3. Why do you think the author wrote this selection? Explain.

____

____

Name ______________________ Date ____________

Greek and Latin Word Parts: *meter, therm, aud, fac*

The words in the box each have a part that comes from Greek or Latin. In Greek, *therm* means "heat" and *meter* means "measure." In Latin, *aud* means "to hear" and *fac* means "to make" or "to do."

thermometer	barometer	audible	manufacture
thermos	chronometer	audience	factory

Activity **Write the correct word from the box to complete each sentence.**

1. When the concert ended, the orchestra stood and bowed to the ______________.
2. The captain used a ______________ to help determine the position of the ship at sea.
3. The company will ______________ and sell computers.
4. Check the ______________ outside to see if you need a sweater.
5. Mr. Wilson makes chocolate candy at his ______________.
6. The weather forecast predicts rain, because the ______________ reading shows a drop in air pressure.
7. Every morning my dad fills his ______________ with hot coffee.
8. With everyone talking at once, Solomon's voice was barely ______________ above the noise.

Name ______________________________ Date ____________

The Fun They Had
Spelling: VV Pattern

VV Pattern

Basic Write the Basic Words that fit the clues to complete the crossword puzzle.

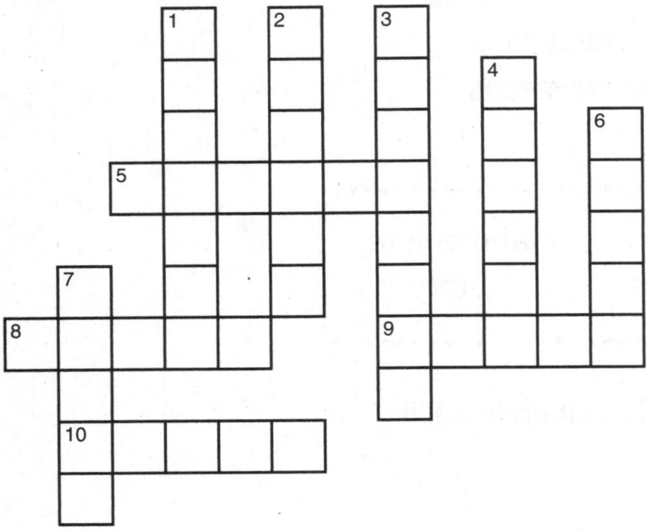

Across

5. piece of rock flying through space

8. tape that records TV programs

9. where cowhands show skills

10. equipment used to receive signals

Down

1. study of natural things

2. food made from grain

3. second month of the year

4. punctuation mark

6. large musical instrument

7. daily written record

Challenge 11–14. You are asked to be student teacher for your geography class today. Give instructions to the class about a writing assignment in which they describe the features of the region in which they live. Use four of the Challenge Words. Write on a separate sheet of paper.

Spelling Words

1. idea
2. lion
3. usual
4. radio
5. liar
6. poem
7. India
8. piano
9. January
10. quiet
11. poet
12. science
13. diary
14. violin
15. period
16. February
17. cereal
18. video
19. meteor
20. rodeo

Challenge

variety
gradual
geography
diagram
punctuate

Name ____________________ Date __________

Spelling Word Sort

Write each Basic Word beside the correct heading.

VV Pattern with two syllables: Divide between the vowels	**Basic Words:** **Possible Selection Words:**
VV Pattern with three syllables: Divide between the vowels	**Basic Words:** **Challenge Words:**
VV Pattern with four syllables: Divide between the vowels	**Basic Words:** **Challenge Words:** **Possible Selection Words:**

Challenge Add the Challenge Words to your Word Sort.

Connect to Reading Look through *The Fun They Had*. Find words that have the VV patterns on this page. Add them to your Word Sort.

Spelling Words

1. idea
2. lion
3. usual
4. radio
5. liar
6. poem
7. India
8. piano
9. January
10. quiet
11. poet
12. science
13. diary
14. violin
15. period
16. February
17. cereal
18. video
19. meteor
20. rodeo

Challenge

variety
gradual
geography
diagram
punctuate

Name ______________________ Date ____________

Proofreading for Spelling

Find the misspelled words and circle them. Write them correctly on the lines below.

It was in Janeary that Talia got the idear to enter the Galactic Music Contest. She wrote a composition for her violen using a pome for inspiration. It was early Febuary when she heard.

"Mamma, guess what?" said Talia, smiling. "I placed in the contest. I have to go to Indea for the final competition. I may get to see a lyin there!"

"That's wonderful news," said Mrs. Simms as she handed Talia the sereal.

Talia left the next morning on the shuttle. Everyone was quiat and focused on the captain's vidio. She explained that in the usueal way, after blast-off, they would shut off the engines to conserve fuel and switch to solar power. As Talia looked out the window, she saw a metear streak past her. To her, that was a sign of good luck!

1. ____________ 7. ____________
2. ____________ 8. ____________
3. ____________ 9. ____________
4. ____________ 10. ____________
5. ____________ 11. ____________
6. ____________ 12. ____________

Spelling Words

1. idea
2. lion
3. usual
4. radio
5. liar
6. poem
7. India
8. piano
9. January
10. quiet
11. poet
12. science
13. diary
14. violin
15. period
16. February
17. cereal
18. video
19. meteor
20. rodeo

Challenge

variety
gradual
geography
diagram
punctuate

Name ______________________ Date ____________

Capitalization and Writing Titles

Capitalize important words in the titles of movies, books, chapters, and articles in a newspaper or magazine. Short words such as *in*, *if*, *of*, *a*, and *the* are not capitalized unless they are the first word in the title.

When writing the title of a shorter work, such as a story or news article, use quotation marks. When writing the title of a longer work, such as a book, magazine, or movie, underline the title.

book title	**story**
A Pizza for Jin	"The Diary of a Mouse"

Thinking Question
Is this title capitalized correctly? Does the title name a long work or a short work?

1–5. Rewrite each sentence. Add capital letters, underlining, and punctuation where they are needed.

1. The headline in Friday's newspaper read "clowns lead parade."

____

____

2. the little mermaid is my little sister's favorite movie.

____

____

3. Jesse's story about his trip to Mexico was called "crossing the border."

____

____

4. benson elementary wins trophy was the front page headline in the school paper.

____

____

Name ______________________ Date __________

End Punctuation

The punctuation at the end of a sentence helps to show its meaning. Use a period (.) at the end of a statement or a command. Use a question mark (?) at the end of a question and an exclamation mark (!) to show strong feeling.

declarative	I like to play basketball.
imperative	Hand me the ball, please.
interrogative	What is the score?
exclamatory	What a great game!

Thinking Question
What kind of sentence am I reading? Does the sentence tell something, ask a question, or show excitement?

1–8. Add the correct end mark for each sentence. Write *declarative*, *interrogative*, *imperative*, or *exclamatory* on the line.

1. A voice command can make the mechanical dog walk and sit ______________
2. Insert a quarter into the machine ______________
3. How many centuries have passed since the Revolutionary War ______________
4. The building inspector will be here next week ______________
5. Your picture is amazing ______________
6. What a waste of time this is ______________
7. How much progress have you made with your work ______________
8. Try not to miss your bus ______________

Name ______________________ Date ____________

Lesson 25
PRACTICE BOOK

The Fun They Had
Grammar: Proper Mechanics

Using Apostrophes

When you join two words to make a contraction, use an **apostrophe (')** to represent the letters left out. You should also use an apostrophe to show ownership with a possessive noun.

contraction do not becomes don't
possession shoe of the girl becomes the girl's shoe

Thinking Question
Why is there an apostrophe in this word? Does the word show a possessive or a contraction?

1–5. Write the contraction for the underlined words.

1. Laeticia does not want to be a cheerleader this year. ________
2. Mark said that he is coming with us to the game. ________
3. They are working on the school paper as reporters. ________
4. I did not swim in the race, did you? ________
5. I am going to win first place in the art contest. ________

6–10. Circle the correct word in parentheses to complete each sentence.

6. (Carls, Carl's) hat is on the table.
7. The (womens's, women's) packages were full of gifts.
8. (Nancy's, Nancies) boat is named *Good Times*.
9. Mrs. (Sanchezes, Sanchez's) son is a pilot in the Air Force.
10. The wood carving is (James's, Jameses)

Name ______________________ Date ____________

Lesson 25
PRACTICE BOOK

The Fun They Had
Grammar: Spiral Review

Writing Abbreviations

Titles	Doctor	Dr.	Senior	Sr.
Addresses	Road	Rd.	Company	Co.
Months	March	Mar.	November	Nov.
Days	Tuesday	Tues.	Saturday	Sat.
States	Alabama	AL	Wisconsin	WI
Time	Hour	hr.	minute	min.
Measurement	Feet	ft.	Inch	in.

Rewrite these groups of words, using correct abbreviations for the underlined word or words.

1. Miami, Florida ____________
2. Sunday, December 9, 1951 ____________
3. a length of 35 feet ____________
4. 465 Maple Street ____________
5. Doctor Sanjay Walsh, Junior ____________
6. Post Office Box 2157 ____________
7. Mechanical Supply Corporation ____________
8. 32 minutes, 15 seconds ____________
9. Jibby's Rare Book Company ____________
10. 1458 Greenview Boulevard ____________
11. 4176 Seaport Avenue ____________

Name ______________________ Date ____________

Writing Carefully

Incorrect Mechanics	Correct Mechanics
At last! the day of the science fair has finally arrived and everyones excited. mr. joness class will present it's project first? Our class will be last.	At last! The day of the science fair has finally arrived, and everyone's excited. Mr. Jones's class will present its project first. Our class will be last.

1–4. Rewrite the sentences on the lines below. Use the correct capitalization and punctuation.

1. dont forget to bring treats to school on Friday. they are for Miss Smiths birthday party

____

____

2. simons boots were covered with mud they were also filthy and smelly

____

____

3. be careful didnt I tell you the sidewalk was slippery its covered with ice, too

____

____

4. kim wrote a scary story about an imaginary friend named Bindi its called the secret staircase

____

____

Name ____________________ Date __________

Focus Trait: Word Choice
Using Synonyms to Paraphrase

Original Sentence	Paraphrased Sentence
Bees have round, hairy bodies and wasps have bodies that are less round and hairy.	Bees are rounder and hairier than wasps.

1–4. Rewrite each sentence in your own words. Use synonyms and other ways of rewording.

1. Furniture was fastened to classroom floors so that it could not be moved.

   ____

   ____

2. Almost all of the youngsters carried their lunches to school and had their meal in the classroom.

   ____

   ____

3. Children enjoyed having conversations with their buddies.

   ____

   ____

4. School was a place where children could study and have fun.

   ____

   ____

Name ______________________ Date __________

Final Schwa + /r/ Sounds

Basic: Write the Basic Word that best fits each clue.

1. One of five digits on each hand: __ __ ◯ __ __ __
2. A person who acts in a play: __ __ __ __ ◯ __
3. A kind act that helps a friend: __ __ ◯ __ __
4. To disturb: __ __ __ __ ◯ __
5. Provides power to a car: ◯ __ __ __ __
6. A sign with words or a design: ◯ __ __ __ __ __
7. A body temperature higher than normal: __ ◯ __ __ __
8. Shows your reflection: __ __ __ ◯ __ __
9. Treats people who are sick: ◯ __ __ __ __ __
10. To come into: ◯ __ __ __ __
11. Part of a shirt that fits around your neck: ◯ __ __ __ __ __
12. Sprays water to clean: __ __ __ __ ◯ __
13. A person's state of mind: __ __ ◯ __ __ __
14. Person who begs for a living: ◯ __ __ __ __ __
15. Can be worn for warmth: __ __ ◯ __ __ __ __
16. Hard work: __ __ __ __ ◯

Now write the circled letters in order to name two months of the year.

Answer: __ __ __ __ __ __ __ __ and __ __ __ __ __ __ __ __

Challenge 17–18: Write a sentence using two of the Challenge Words. Write on a separate sheet of paper.

Spelling Words

Basic

1. enter
2. banner
3. sugar
4. shower
5. motor
6. collar
7. labor
8. finger
9. mirror
10. beggar
11. favor
12. bother
13. fever
14. doctor
15. temper
16. actor
17. polar
18. sweater
19. traitor
20. whenever

Challenge

calendar
error
popular
barrier
director

PRACTICE BOOK

**The Girl Who
Loved Spiders**

Spelling: Final Schwa + /r/
Sounds

Word Sort

Write each Basic Word next to the correct heading.

final /ər/ spelled *ar*	Basic Words: Challenge Words:
final /ər/ spelled *er*	Basic Words: Challenge Word: Possible Selection Words:
final /ər/ spelled *or*	Basic Words: Challenge Words: Possible Selection Word:

Challenge: Add the Challenge Words to your Word Sort.

Connect to Reading: Look through "The Girl Who Loved Spiders." Find words that have the final schwa + /r/ spelling patterns. Add them to your Word Sort.

Spelling Words

Basic
1. enter
2. banner
3. sugar
4. shower
5. motor
6. collar
7. labor
8. finger
9. mirror
10. beggar
11. favor
12. bother
13. fever
14. doctor
15. temper
16. actor
17. polar
18. sweater
19. traitor
20. whenever

Challenge
calendar
error
popular
barrier
director

Name ______________________ Date ____________

Lesson 26
PRACTICE BOOK

The Girl Who Loved Spiders
Spelling: Final Schwa + /r/ Sounds

Proofreading for Spelling

Find the misspelled words and circle them. Write them correctly on the lines below.

I pulled the coller of my sweeter up around my ears. Even though I had a fevre, I still felt cold. I needed a docter. Instead a polor bear walked up to me and said, "Whennever I look in the miror, I see shugar. Is that normal?" The bear was wearing a red shirt and blue jeans. I reached out my hand to touch him. He felt real. Maybe I was sicker than I thought.

I told him he shouldn't bothar me with silly questions. Then I asked if he was real or an actur. He lost his tempir and called me a trator to the cause. He held up a bannor that said "Bears Should Rule the World," wagged his fingir at me, and left. Then the door opened and a rabbit in a jumpsuit came in and started talking. I pulled a blanket over my head and went to sleep.

1. ______________ 8. ______________
2. ______________ 9. ______________
3. ______________ 10. ______________
4. ______________ 11. ______________
5. ______________ 12. ______________
6. ______________ 13. ______________
7. ______________ 14. ______________

Spelling Words

Basic
1. enter
2. banner
3. sugar
4. shower
5. motor
6. collar
7. labor
8. finger
9. mirror
10. beggar
11. favor
12. bother
13. fever
14. doctor
15. temper
16. actor
17. polar
18. sweater
19. traitor
20. whenever

Challenge
calendar
error
popular
barrier
director

Making Comparisons

<u>Comparative adjectives</u> are used to compare two things. <u>Superlative adjectives</u> are used to compare more than two things.

Adjective	Comparative	Superlative
slow	slower	slowest
cute	cuter	cutest
fast	faster	fastest
happy	happier	happiest

Thinking Question
How many persons, places, or things are being compared?

A turtle is *slower* than a lizard.

A snail is the *slowest* of the three.

Circle the correct form of the adjective to complete each sentence. Write C if the adjective is the comparative form. Write S if the adjective is the superlative form.

1. Jana is (tall, taller) than her sister Sasha. ________
2. My little sister is the (cutest, cuter) baby in the whole world. ________
3. Kelli insisted that ghost stories are (scariest, scarier) to read than biographies. ________
4. That is the (funnier, funniest) joke I have ever heard. ________
5. Matt is a (fastest, faster) runner than Saleem, but Juan is the (fastest, faster) runner of the three boys. ________

Name ______________________ Date __________

Making Comparisons with *More* and *Most*

With long adjectives, use **more** to compare two persons, places, or things. Use **most** to compare three or more.

The ant is **more** interesting than the grasshopper.
The ant is the **most** interesting of all insects.

Thinking Question
How many persons, places, or things are being compared?

1–5. Rewrite each sentence, adding either *more* or *most* to the adjective in parentheses.

1. The _____ things I learned to do when I moved to Florida were to always wear shoes, to always shake out my shoes, and to watch my step when walking. (important)

____

____

____

2. Spiders are _____ in Florida than in New York. (plentiful)

____

3. I think the _____ part about moving is making new friends. (difficult)

____

____

4. I think running road races is ____ than looking for bugs. (satisfying)

____

____

5. What is the _____ insect to be found in the area where you live? (common)

____

____

Name ______________________ Date ____________

Comparing with *Good* and *Bad*

Some adjectives need to change forms when they are used to compare things.

The adjectives *good* and *bad* are two examples.

Adjective	Comparative	Superlative
good	better	best
bad	worse	worst

Thinking Question
How many persons, places, or things are being compared?

Getting out of school early is good. Weekends are better. Summer break is best of all.

1–5. Complete the sentence by writing the correct form of the adjective shown in parentheses.

1. The ____________ news I heard was that 120 amphibian species are now extinct. (bad)
2. David was happy that his second paper was _________ than his first. (good)
3. What is the _________ book you have ever read? (good)
4. I liked the first book _________ than the second. (good)
5. The _________ part of our museum trip was the ride home. (bad)

Name ______________________________ Date ____________

Lesson 26
PRACTICE BOOK

The Girl Who Loved Spiders
Grammar: Spiral Review

Correct Adjectives

- The words *a, an,* and *the* are special adjectives called **articles.**

Articles	
Use *a* if the next word begins with a consonant sound.	Ron found **a** giant beetle.
Use *an* if the next word begins with a vowel sound.	**An** ant is a social insect.
Use *the* if the noun names a particular person, place, or thing.	**The** grasshopper landed right on Maria's book.

- Capitalize adjectives formed from proper nouns.

Wayne studied insects with a **Chinese** teacher.

1–5. Rewrite the sentences, supplying the correct article.

1. Roberto wrote ___ report on dragonflies.

____

2. _____ class visited a museum last Thursday.

____

3-4. The spider is ____ arachnid and not ___ insect.

____

5. I want to learn everything I can about ____ moth.

____

6–8. Rewrite the sentences, correcting errors in the use of proper adjectives.

6. The canadian guide told us what to look for.

____

7. The arabian horse has great energy and intelligence.

____

8. For a solid week the group investigated the mexican coast.

____

____

Name ______________________ Date ____________

Sentence Fluency

Combine two short, choppy sentences into one sentence to make sentences flow smoothly.

Sentence 1	Sentence 2
The elephant is the biggest animal in the zoo.	The elephant is also the most magnificent animal.

The elephant is the biggest and most magnificent animal in the zoo.

1–3. Combine these short, choppy sentences to make one sentence.

1.

Sentence 1	Sentence 2
The Taipan snake has the most poisonous venom of any snake in Australia.	It also has the longest fangs.

____

____

2.

Sentence 1	Sentence 2
The largest shark on the Australian coast is the Great White.	It is also the scariest shark.

____

____

3.

Sentence 1	Sentence 2
My science teacher, Mrs. Welles, is the most interesting teacher I have ever had.	She also is the most knowledgable.

____

____

Name ______________________ Date ____________

Focus Trait: Word Choice

Details for writing about spiders

Topic	***Exact Details***
Spiders	spiderweb, threads, silk, scary, fascinating, spin, dewdrops

List three or more details that you might use in a poem or other type of writing about the topics below. Include interesting word choice.

Topic	**Exact Details**
Ladybug	
grasshopper	
dragonfly	
honeybee	

Name ____________________ Date __________

Final Schwa + /l/ Sounds

Basic: Read the paragraphs. Write the Basic Words that best complete the sentences.

It was an exciting and **(1)** day. Ana arrived at a bicycle race. She stopped to **(2)** at the colorful balloons and streamers decorating the starting line. A **(3)** of ten other racers were standing by their bicycles.

"Don't be nervous," Ana told herself. "This will be **(4)** compared to all the training that I did."

Ana remembered to tie her shoelaces so they would not **(5)** in her bicycle wheels. The last time that had happened, Ana hurt her **(6)**. Ana used a **(7)** to wipe mud off the shiny **(8)** bicycle frame.

At the starting line, Ana prepared to **(9)** fast. She and the other racers burst forward. It was going to be a **(10)** for the prize!

1. ____________________ 6. ____________________
2. ____________________ 7. ____________________
3. ____________________ 8. ____________________
4. ____________________ 9. ____________________
5. ____________________ 10. ____________________

Challenge 11–12: Your English teacher asks you to write about your favorite subject, which is math. Use two of the Challenge Words. Write on a separate sheet of paper.

Spelling Words

Basic

1. title
2. towel
3. battle
4. pedal
5. metal
6. simple
7. eagle
8. special
9. total
10. trouble
11. nickel
12. gentle
13. barrel
14. model
15. tangle
16. ankle
17. marvel
18. juggle
19. squirrel
20. riddle

Challenge

cancel
decimal
material
pretzel
triangle

Name ______________________ Date ____________

Lesson 27
PRACTICE BOOK

Amphibian Alert!
Spelling:
Final Schwa + /l/ Sounds

Word Sort

Write each Basic Word next to the correct heading.

Final /l/ or /əl/ spelled *el*	**Basic Words:** **Challenge Words:**
Final /l/ or /əl/ spelled *al*	**Basic Words:** **Challenge Words:** **Possible Selection Word:**
Final /l/ or /əl/ spelled *le*	**Basic Words:** **Challenge Word:** **Possible Selection Words:**

Challenge: Add the Challenge Words to your Word Sort.

Connect to Reading: Look through "Amphibian Alert!" Find words that have the final schwa + /l/ spelling patterns on this page. Add them to your Word Sort.

Spelling Words

Basic

1. title
2. towel
3. battle
4. pedal
5. metal
6. simple
7. eagle
8. special
9. total
10. trouble
11. nickel
12. gentle
13. barrel
14. model
15. tangle
16. ankle
17. marvel
18. juggle
19. squirrel
20. riddle

Challenge

cancel
decimal
material
pretzel
triangle

Name ____________________ Date ____________

Proofreading for Spelling

Amphibian Alert!
Spelling:
Final Schwa + /l/ Sounds

Find the misspelled words and circle them. Write them correctly on the lines below.

In 1799, a French army officer named Pierre-Francois Bouchard was working near the city of Rosetta in Egypt. Bouchard and his men saw many ancient things, including a moddel of a house made of a mettal that looked like nikel. For fun, the men would juggil small stones. One day Bouchard found a stone slab that was different from the others. He was very gentil with it as he used water from a nearby barel to wash off the layers of dirt.

Bouchard saw strange symbols. The treuble was that he did not know what they meant. Bouchard took the stone to scholars. They all had to marvell at it, but they were unable to understand it. Was that a reddle or the titil of a play? Was the bird an eagel? Was that little creature a flying squerrel? More than 20 years passed before anyone could translate the Rosetta Stone.

1. ____________ 7. ____________
2. ____________ 8. ____________
3. ____________ 9. ____________
4. ____________ 10. ____________
5. ____________ 11. ____________
6. ____________ 12. ____________

Spelling Words

1. title
2. towel
3. battle
4. pedal
5. metal
6. simple
7. eagle
8. special
9. total
10. trouble
11. nickel
12. gentle
13. barrel
14. model
15. tangle
16. ankle
17. marvel
18. juggle
19. squirrel
20. riddle

Challenge

cancel
decimal
material
pretzel
triangle

Name ______________________ Date __________

Lesson 27
PRACTICE BOOK

Comparing with Adverbs

Amphibian Alert!
Grammar: More Comparisons

Short Adverbs
Comparative adverbs: Add *-er* to short adverbs to compare two actions.
Superlative adverbs: Add *-est* to compare three or more actions.

Thinking Question
Does the adverb compare two actions? Does the adverb compare three or more actions?

Adverb	Comparative	Superlative
late	later	latest
hard	harder	hardest
fast	faster	fastest
well	better	best

Brad arrived to school later than Jake, but Amelia arrived latest of all.

Circle the correct form of the adverb to complete each sentence. Write C if the adverb is the comparative form. Write S for the superlative form.

1. John arrived (earliest, earlier) than Dave to the amphibian display. ________
2. Of his team, Sean worked the (faster, fastest) repairing the frog terrariums. ________
3. Lena sang the (louder, loudest) of all the helpers. ________
4. If team A works (hardest, harder) than team B, it will finish the display by noon. ________
5. Of all the guides at the amphibian display, Marta explains tadpoles (better, best). ________

Name ______________________ Date ____________

Comparing with Adverbs

For most adverbs that end in *-ly*:

- use *more* to compare two actions.
- use *most* to compare three or more actions.

Thinking Question
Does the adverb end in -ly? How many things does the adverb compare?

Adverb	Comparative	Superlative
quickly	more quickly	most quickly
skillfully	more skillfully	most skillfully
easily	more easily	most easily

A horse runs more quickly than a human. Cheetahs run the most quickly of all animals.

1–5. Write the form of the adverb shown in parentheses that correctly completes the sentence.

1. Do you think turtles can swim ______________ than frogs? (quickly)
2. The third doctor cared for the injured newt ______________. (skillfully)
3. Jason handles the salamanders ______________ than Bill. (carefully)
4. Of all the helpers, Aiden works the ______________. (quietly)
5. Alan identified amphibians ______________ than Mitsuo after taking a class. (easily)

Name ______________________ Date ____________

Comparing with Adverbs

Circle the correct word in parentheses to complete each sentence.

1. Dennis smiles (wider, widest) of all his friends.
2. "I think clothing dries (most, more) quickly in warm air than in cold," said Dana.
3. I shop at Bloom's Market (more, most) frequently than I shop at Lynn's Market.
4. Of all the fruits sold at Bloom's market, the bananas will (more, most) likely sell out first.
5. When teams choose players, Beth is (most, more) readily chosen than Brianne because she runs (faster, fastest).

Name ____________________ Date __________

Negatives

- A word that makes a sentence mean "no" is called a *negative*.
- The words *no*, *no one*, *nobody*, *none*, *nothing*, and *never* are negatives.
- The word *not* and **contractions** made from *not* are also negatives.
- Never use two negatives together in a sentence.

Incorrect	Correct
There **weren't no** fish in the pond.	There **weren't any** fish in the pond. There **were no** fish in the pond.
I **won't never** give away my frog.	I **won't ever** give away my frog. I **will never** give away my frog.

1–4. Write the negative on the line provided.

1. Nobody wanted to leave. ____________________
2. I can't finish this assignment on time. ____________
3. Before this class, I had never studied reptiles. ________
4. I had no interest in learning about newts. __________

5–8. Rewrite the sentences, correcting errors in the use of negatives.

5. Jason can't go nowhere until he finishes his chores.

____

6. Before taking this class, Pete didn't know nothing about reptiles.

____

____

7. I don't like nothing about insects.

____

8. Jim doesn't never want to miss a class again.

____

Name ______________________ Date ____________

Conventions: Proofreading

Use proofreading marks to cross out errors and insert corrections.

Sentence with Errors	Corrected Sentence
Elena's performance was worser than Ralph's.	Elena's performance was ~~worser~~ worse than Ralph's.

1–5. Use the proofreading marks to fix the convention errors in the sentences below.

1. Of the five books I read on mammals, this was the worse.
2. Among the 50 essays submitted, Jose's essay was judged the better.
3. Of all my grades, my grade in science was the better.
4. Of the three team members, Kara works the faster.
5. Jenna studied more harder than I did.

Name ______________________________ Date ____________

Focus Trait: Voice

Amphibian Alert!
Writing Trait: Voice

Flat Voice	***Interesting Voice***
I found a salamander. I was surprised.	I lifted the log. Wow! There was a bright yellow salamander underneath!

Read each sentence. Rewrite it, giving it interest and feeling.

Flat Voice	**Interesting Voice**
1. My dad and I saw a frog in the pond.	
2. I don't like people throwing things in the pond.	
3. The bullfrogs made funny sounds.	
4. I didn't like holding the toad.	

Name ______________________ Date ____________

Three-Syllable Words

Basic: Write the Basic Word that best replaces the underlined word or words.

Dear Grandma,
Our family (1) trip to Washington, D.C., was great! Mom, Dad, Rick, and I had a good time (2) jointly. We saw (3) a few places, including the (4) building that holds books of Congress. (5) An additional place we visited was the White House. The (6) leader of the United States wasn't there. (7) But, we saw a lot of other things during the tour. For (8) instance, we saw a painting of Abraham Lincoln in the State Dining Room. I wasn't allowed to use my (9) photographic device, or I would have taken pictures for you. My (10) preferred place was the Smithsonian. Washington, D.C., is full of (11) stories from the past.
Love,
Matt

1. ____________
2. ____________
3. ____________
4. ____________
5. ____________
6. ____________
7. ____________
8. ____________
9. ____________
10. ____________
11. ____________

Challenge 12–13: An astronaut is speaking at your school about her recent shuttle ride through space. You get to talk to the astronaut after her speech. Write a sentence about your talk, using two Challenge Words. Write on a separate sheet of paper.

Spelling Words

Basic
1. library
2. another
3. hospital
4. example
5. deliver
6. history
7. however
8. several
9. vacation
10. important
11. victory
12. imagine
13. camera
14. potato
15. remember
16. together
17. memory
18. favorite
19. continue
20. president

Challenge
internal
ornament
interview
universe
article

Name ______________________ Date ______________

Word Sort

Write each Basic Word beside the correct heading.

First syllable stressed	**Basic Words:** **Challenge Words:** **Possible Selection Words:**
Second syllable stressed	**Basic Words:** **Challenge Words:** **Possible Selection Words:**

Challenge: Add the Challenge Words to your Word Sort.

Connect to Reading: Look through "Museums: Worlds of Wonder." Find words that have three syllables with first and second syllables stressed. Add them to your Word Sort.

Spelling Words

Basic

1. library
2. another
3. hospital
4. example
5. deliver
6. history
7. however
8. several
9. vacation
10. important
11. victory
12. imagine
13. camera
14. potato
15. remember
16. together
17. memory
18. favorite
19. continue
20. president

Challenge

internal
ornament
interview
universe
article

Name ______________________ Date __________

Proofreading for Spelling

Find the misspelled words and circle them. Write them correctly on the lines below.

In 1906, Hiram Bingham had had enough of studying the history of the Incas in Peru in the libary at Yale. He knew they were importint to the history of South America for severle reasons. He decided to take a working vacashun to South America. Not wanting to rely on his memery, he took many notes and a kamera so he could remembir all the facts when he went to delivir a speech about his travels.

In 1911, Bingham returned to Peru to lead anether expedition and continew his quest for knowledge about the Incas. One can only imajin his surprise when he discovered Machu Picchu, the "lost city of the Incas." The expedition turned out to be a huge personal victry for Bingham. The ancient stone city, hidden by five hundred years of jungle growth, is considered by some to be the greatest surviving exampel of Incan architecture.

1. ______________
2. ______________
3. ______________
4. ______________
5. ______________
6. ______________
7. ______________
8. ______________
9. ______________
10. ______________
11. ______________
12. ______________
13. ______________
14. ______________

Spelling Words

1. library
2. another
3. hospital
4. example
5. deliver
6. history
7. however
8. several
9. vacation
10. important
11. victory
12. imagine
13. camera
14. potato
15. remember
16. together
17. memory
18. favorite
19. continue
20. president

Challenge

internal
ornament
interview
universe
article

Name ______________________ Date ____________

Possessive Pronouns with Nouns

- A **possessive pronoun** is a pronoun that shows ownership.
- **Possessive pronouns** can replace possessive nouns in a sentence.

Possessive Pronouns	
my	its
your	our
her	their
his	

The teacher gave her students **the students'** tickets to the museum.
The teacher gave her students **their** tickets to the museum.

Thinking Question
Are there possessive nouns in the sentence? Do any of them need to be replaced to avoid repetition?

1–5. Rewrite each sentence with the correct form of the possessive pronoun in parentheses.

1. Max and I went to see <u>Max's</u> favorite exhibit. (my, his, our)

____

2. We observed a dinosaur fossil and read about the <u>fossil's</u> discovery. (our, their, its)

____

3. We learned about dinosaurs, including <u>dinosaurs'</u> habits and diets. (its, her, their)

____

4. Mary told me that <u>Mary's</u> brother would love the exhibit, too. (my, her, their)

____

5. Marcus and I found <u>Marcus's and my</u> class in the museum shop. (its, our, her)

____

Name ______________________ Date ____________

Possessive Pronouns that Stand Alone

Thinking Question
Is the possessive pronoun followed by a noun?

Some possessive pronouns are placed before nouns. Others are used by themselves and stand alone.

Possessive Pronouns That Stand Alone	
mine	hers
yours	ours
his	theirs

The tickets to the exhibit are **ours.**

1–4. Write the possessive pronoun that stands alone on the line.

1. Is the ticket to the polar bear exhibit hers? ____________

2. The airplane ticket is mine. ____________

3. Since we have tickets but cannot attend, would you like to use ours? ____________

4. The teacher will give you yours. ____________

5–6. Rewrite each sentence on the line so that the possessive pronoun stands alone.

5. Which report is your report? ______________________________

6. The report about trees is my report.

____

Name ______________________ Date ____________

Possessive Pronouns

- Some possessive pronouns are placed before nouns.
  Jeff left his backpack on the school bus.
  My books are in Mom's car.
- Other possessive pronouns are used by themselves and stand alone.
  I think the museum tickets are yours.
  The red skates in the locker are mine.

1–6. Replace the underlined word or words with the correct possessive pronoun.

1. Jill's inline skates are sitting on Jill's porch. ____________
2. "The backpack with reflector strips is my backpack," I said. ____________
3. Jane can't find Jane's shoe. ____________
4. Which one of the lunches is your lunch? ____________
5. The three boys rode the three boys' bikes to school. ____________
6. If Ned has my jacket, then I have Ned's jacket. ____________

Name ______________________ Date ____________

Writing Quotations

- **Quotation marks** show a speaker's exact words.
- **Capitalize** the first word of a quotation.
- Place **quotations marks** before and after the speaker's exact words.
- Use a **comma** to set off words that tell who is speaking.
- When the quotation comes first, place a **comma** inside the last quotation marks.
- If the quotation is a question or an exclamation, place a **question mark** or **exclamation mark** inside the last quotation marks.

  Ms. Winger said, "Listen to your guide carefully."

1–8. Rewrite the quotations, correcting the punctuation errors.

1. "Have you ever been to the City Museum" asked Chloe.

   ____

2. Yes, I have replied Aiden.

   ____

3. Charlie said "I hope we see dinosaurs".

   ____

4. Marta exclaimed "the Enchanted Caves are so awesome"!

   ____

5. "I like Art City better" said Danielle.

   ____

6. Mr. West suggested "let's go see the World Aquarium now."

   ____

7. This will be fun! exclaimed Sam.

   ____

8. I will have so many things to tell my family, said Luis.

   ____

Name ______________________ Date ____________

Sentence Fluency

To avoid repeated possessive nouns, replace them with possessive pronouns.

Sentence with Repeated Possessive Nouns	Sentence with Possessive Pronouns
Jose wanted Jose's mom to chaperone Jose's field trip to the museum.	Jose wanted his mom to chaperone his field trip to the museum.

1–5. Rewrite each sentence, replacing repeated possessive nouns with possessive pronouns to improve sentence flow.

1. Today, the fourth graders will have fun on the fourth grader's first field trip.

   ____

2. Sarah told about Sarah's visit to the museum.

   ____

3. Kayla saved a piece of Kayla's favorite cake for Kayla's mother.

   ____

4. Pam showed Pam's project to the class.

   ____

5. By running in the museum, Tim broke one of the rules that Tim's teacher had given to Tim's class.

   ____

   ____

Focus Trait: Organization

A well-organized paragraph contains:
- a topic or main idea;
- details that support the main idea;
- a sequence of ideas or events that usually happen in order of first, next, and last;
- a conclusion that restates the main idea.

Use a separate sheet of paper. Organize the sentences below in an order that makes sense.

1. I told everyone that it was the best birthday present ever!
2. After the dishes were washed, we hurried out to the car.
3. First, Mom and Dad woke me up at seven o'clock.
4. Then, I saw the big sign above the bike store.
5. The drive to Bill's Bike Shop seemed to take forever.
6. Dad made my favorite breakfast, but I was too excited to eat very much.
7. Finally, I would get to see my new trail bike and take it for a test ride.
8. It was Saturday, and my birthday wish was about to come true!

Name ______________________ Date ____________

Words with Silent Consonants

Basic: Write Basic Words on the lines provided that will best complete the sentences.

My aunt's job is to keep the water pipes in people's homes running smoothly. She is a (1) ____________. She has to (2) ____________ down and work under sinks. Sometimes she has to (3) ____________ into small spaces to find the (4) ____________ to the plumbing problem. She often has to use tools from her toolbox to (5) ____________ pipes together. Working with tools, my aunt has to take care not to scrape a (6) ____________ or a wrist. She carries a radio in her toolbox because she likes to (7) ____________ to music as she works. The music helps keep her (8) ____________ and relaxed as she does her job. Her customers (9) ____________ her and praise her work. She says being a plumber is a good, (10) ____________ job to have.

Challenge: You've watched a documentary film about the building of the Egyptian pyramids. Write a review of the film for your class. Use two of the Challenge Words. Write on a separate sheet of paper.

Spelling Words

Basic

1. half
2. comb
3. mortgage
4. honor
5. fasten
6. kneel
7. wreath
8. calm
9. answer
10. handsome
11. wrinkle
12. listen
13. fetch
14. yolk
15. climb
16. honest
17. knuckle
18. plumber
19. limb
20. folktale

Challenge

tomb
glisten
design
hasten
wrestle

Name ________________________ Date ____________

Save Timber Woods!
Spelling: Silent Consonants

Word Sort

Write each Basic Word next to the correct heading.

/m/ spelled *mb*	Basic Words: Challenge Words:
/n/ spelled *kn*	Basic Words:
/ô/ spelled *ho*	Basic Words:
/r/ spelled *wr*	Basic Words: Challenge Word:
silent *l, t, d,* or *w*	Basic Words: Challenge Words:
Other silent consonants	Challenge Word:

Challenge: Add the Challenge Words to your Word Set.

Spelling Words

Basic

1. half
2. comb
3. mortgage
4. honor
5. fasten
6. kneel
7. wreath
8. calm
9. answer
10. handsome
11. wrinkle
12. listen
13. fetch
14. yolk
15. climb
16. honest
17. knuckle
18. plumber
19. limb
20. folktale

Challenge

tomb
glisten
design
hasten
wrestle

Name ______________________________ Date ____________

Lesson 29
PRACTICE BOOK

Proofreading for Spelling

Save Timber Woods!
Spelling: Silent Consonants

Find the misspelled words and circle them. Write them correctly on the lines below.

After college, Chef Alice Waters went to France, where she was impressed by the honist food she ate, from an omelet made with the freshest egg yoke to fish cooked the day it was caught. She learned that the French were often willing to spend haff of their income for quality produce. Since 1971, Alice has owned Chez Panisse, a California restaurant famous for the quality of its food. People have been known to komb the woods and neel in mud beneath the lim of a tree to fetsh Alice a mushroom with an ugly wrinkil and incredible flavor. Other people grow herbs and make a wreth of them for Alice. She has worked hard to teach children about growing and eating fresh food. Today there are children in local schools who prefer to lisen to Alice talk about gardening than hear a folktail about a handsum prince.

1. ______________ 7. ______________
2. ______________ 8. ______________
3. ______________ 9. ______________
4. ______________ 10. ______________
5. ______________ 11. ______________
6. ______________ 12. ______________

Spelling Words

1. half
2. comb
3. mortgage
4. honor
5. fasten
6. kneel
7. wreath
8. calm
9. answer
10. handsome
11. wrinkle
12. listen
13. fetch
14. yolk
15. climb
16. honest
17. knuckle
18. plumber
19. limb
20. folktale

Challenge

tomb
glisten
design
hasten
wrestle

Name ______________________ Date ____________

Using *I* and *me*

- Use the pronoun *I* as the subject of a sentence.
  Lucas and I learned so much!
- Use the pronoun *me* after ***action verbs*** and after the words *to, with, for,* or *at.*
  The council gave **David and me** their complete attention.
  Will you come with **me** to the meeting?
- When you talk about yourself and another person, always name yourself last.

Thinking Question
Is the pronoun the subject or the object of the sentence?

1–6. Rewrite each sentence with the correct word(s) in parentheses.

1. (Dominic and I, Dominic and me) wanted to save the forest.

____

2. Eileen told (I, me) what was happening to the forest.

____

3. Carlos and (I, me) realized the deer had nowhere to go.

____

4. Deer often visited (me and my family, my family and me).

____

5. My brother and (I, me) have seen them look for food.

____

6. (He and me, He and I) watched the deer quietly through the window.

____

Name ______________________ Date __________

Subject and Object Pronouns

- **Subject pronouns** are used as the subject of a sentence. They tell whom or what the sentence is about.
- **Object pronouns** follow action verbs or the words *to, for, with, in,* or *at.*

Subject Pronouns	Object Pronouns
I, you, he, she, we, it, they	me, you, him, her, it, us, you, them

We gave the information to **her**, and **she** told **them** about the forestry class.

Thinking Question
Does the pronoun tell who or what does the action? Does the pronoun follow an action verb or the words to, for, with, in, *or* at?

1–5. Rewrite each sentence, using the correct pronoun in parentheses.

1. Isabel read (we, us) the article about the housing development.

____

2. Olivia and (he, him) could not believe what they heard.

____

3. (They, Them) want to cut down huge parts of the forest.

____

4. To (we, us), the forest should be used for hiking and camping.

____

5. Since animals cannot speak, we will speak for (them, they).

____

Name ______________________ Date ______________

Reflexive Pronouns

A **reflexive pronoun** is used when the subject and object of a sentence are the same person/thing or people/things. We use reflexive pronouns with the word *by* to mean alone or without help.

Subject Pronouns		Reflexive Pronouns
I	it	myself
you	we	yourself
he	you (plural)	himself
she	they	herself
		itself
		ourselves
		yourselves
		themselves

I will take care of *myself* someday. *I* like to walk to school *by* myself.

1–8. Fill in the blanks with the correct reflexive pronoun.

1. Jane made ______________ a sandwich.
2. Be careful, Lisa. Don't cut ______________ with the knife.
3. "I think I will build a clubhouse by ______________," said Paul.
4. We blamed ______________ for getting lost in the museum.
5. Please boys, make ______________ feel at home.
6. The girls made five dozen cupcakes by ______________.
7. The dog saw ______________ in the mirror and barked.
8. Jack made ______________ a pizza for lunch.

Name ______________________ Date ____________

Save Timber Woods!
Grammar: Spiral Review

Commas in Sentences

Use a comma to set off these types of words and phrases:

- the words *yes, no,* and *well* or proper names when they begin a sentence

  No, feeding deer human food is not a good idea.
- introductory phrases and clauses

  If you want to see deer, you have to be still.
- the name of a person directly addressed in a sentence.

  Don't blame the deer, Becky, for being hungry.

1–5. Rewrite the sentences, adding commas where they are needed.

1. No I do not want deer in our yard.

   ____

2. The poor deer lost their homes Alanna.

   ____

3. Well my family is losing our favorite tree.

   ____

4. We should get the facts Denzel before we decide.

   ____

5. Because we left home late we arrived after the park closed.

   ____

6–8. Rewrite the following script. Add three missing commas where they are needed.

Eliot: Well that went better than I expected
Maria: Eliot you were great!
Gerald: What can we do now to raise money guys?

Name ______________________ Date ____________

Save Timber Woods!
Grammar: Connect to Writing

Sentence Fluency

Repeating words in writing is uninteresting and awkward. To avoid using a noun over and over again, replace it with a pronoun.

Sentence 1	Sentence 2
Caleb didn't like the deer eating his tree.	Caleb scared it away.

Caleb didn't like the deer eating his tree. **He** scared it away.

1–3. Replace the repeated noun with a pronoun to improve sentence fluency.

1.

Sentence 1	Sentence 2
Nicole told her friends about the problem.	Nicole wanted to help.

____

____

2.

Sentence 1	Sentence 2
Last year the deer were safer.	The deer had more land.

____

3.

Sentence 1	Sentence 2
The people of our community have a problem.	The people of our community need to work together.

____

____

Name ______________________ Date ____________

Save Timber Woods!
Writing Trait: Ideas

Focus Trait: Ideas Focusing on Addressing Objections

Good writers think about how their audience will react to their ideas. In a persuasive essay, they try to address any objections ahead of time. This writer addressed the objection by the developer about building houses on Timber Woods.

Idea: *We should save Timber Woods from being destroyed.*
Possible Objection: *We want to build more houses on the Timber Woods land.*
Revised sentence: *Homes could be built where the Smithfield warehouses are instead of Timber Woods.*

1–3. Read the idea and the possible objection. Rewrite the sentence so that it addresses the objection. You can refer to "Save Timber Woods!" to find information to answer it.

1. Idea: Cutting down the forest will cause a lot of problems.

Possible Objection: It costs too much money for us to buy the land.

Revised sentence: ______________________________

____

2. Idea: Saving the woods is good for the local environment.

Possible Objection: The woods don't help the town in any way.

Revised sentence: ______________________________

____

3. Idea: Wildlife creatures belong in their natural environments.

Possible Objection: It's nice to see deer in my backyard.

Revised sentence: ______________________________

____

Name ______________________ Date ____________

Unusual Spellings

1–10. Complete the puzzle by writing the Basic Word for each clue.

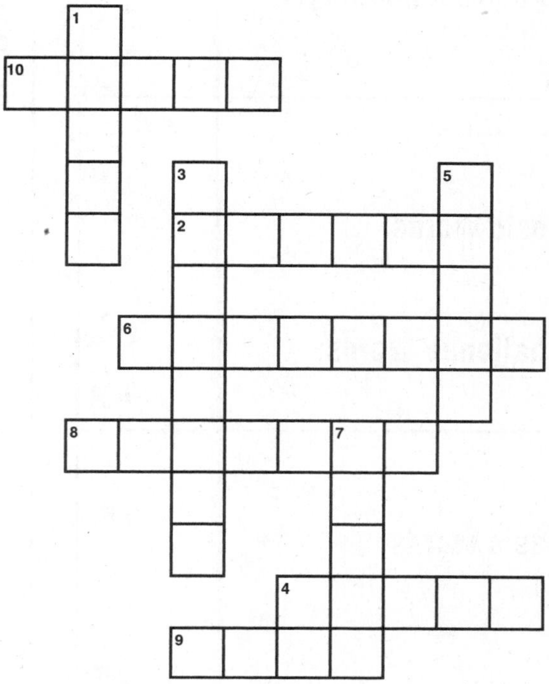

Across

2. a group working toward a common goal
4. to fill or cover with water
6. a weekly or monthly publication
8. in contact with
9. a group sharing common traits
10. to form an opinion without being sure

Down

1. someone who watches over or protects
3. enjoyable or attractive
5. past of "to have as its meaning"
7. a way of doing something

11–12. Create two book titles: one about a trip to the ocean bottom in a colorful vessel and one about a collection of humorous poetry. Use two of the Challenge Words. Write on a separate sheet of paper.

Spelling Words

Basic

1. meant
2. routine
3. style
4. flood
5. month
6. pleasant
7. guess
8. women
9. either
10. against
11. disguise
12. sweat
13. magazine
14. guard
15. receive
16. wonder
17. league
18. type
19. ceiling
20. money

Challenge

plaid
onion
guarantee
rhyme
submarine

Name ______________________ Date ____________

Mystery at Reed's Pond
Spelling: Unusual Spellings

Word Sort

Write each Basic Word next to the correct heading.

Unusual Spellings with One Syllable	**Basic Words:** **Challenge Words:**
Unusual Spellings with Two Syllables	**Basic Words:** **Challenge Word:**
Unusual Spellings with Three Syllables	**Basic Words:** **Challenge Words:**

Challenge: **Add the Challenge Words to your Word Sort.**

Spelling Words

Basic

1. meant
2. routine
3. style
4. flood
5. month
6. pleasant
7. guess
8. women
9. either
10. against
11. disguise
12. sweat
13. magazine
14. guard
15. receive
16. wonder
17. league
18. type
19. ceiling
20. money

Challenge

plaid
onion
guarantee
rhyme
submarine

Name ______________________ Date ____________

Proofreading for Spelling

Find the misspelled words and circle them. Write them correctly on the lines below.

I was following my rootine for the munth, practicing with the bowling leegue after work. I'm an amateur detective, so I gess I'm always on the lookout for trouble. I arrived at the bowling alley early, and I noticed two strange womin. I couldn't help but wonnder if ether of them was the tipe to bowl. I didn't think so. The tall one wore a disgize. I looked up and began to swet with fear. There was a figure hanging from the seiling. I turned to run.

The tall woman leaned right agenst my face. "You can't go," she said. "I didn't recieve my monie yet." Shaking, I asked her what she ment. She laughed and told me she needed to be paid for the mystery party. Then I realized the figure was just a decoration. It's a good thing I'm just an *amateur* detective.

1. ____________
2. ____________
3. ____________
4. ____________
5. ____________
6. ____________
7. ____________
8. ____________
9. ____________
10. ____________
11. ____________
12. ____________
13. ____________
14. ____________
15. ____________

Spelling Words

Basic

1. meant
2. routine
3. style
4. flood
5. month
6. pleasant
7. guess
8. women
9. either
10. against
11. disguise
12. sweat
13. magazine
14. guard
15. receive
16. wonder
17. league
18. type
19. ceiling
20. money

Challenge

plaid
onion
guarantee
rhyme
submarine

Contractions with Pronouns

- Pronouns can be combined with some verbs to form **contractions.**
- An **apostrophe** replaces the letter or letters that are left out.

  I'm going to study that turtle until **it's** engraved in my memory.
- Contractions for the pronouns *he, she,* and *it,* when used with the verbs *is* and *has,* are the same *(he's, she's, it's).*

Thinking Question
What two words can I combine to make a contraction?

1–5. On the line, write the contraction for the underlined words.

1. We are observing nature with our class. ____________
2. They have taken many notes about the pond. ____________
3. You will have time to observe everything. ____________
4. Adrian said he had never seen a turtle like that. ____________
5. You are responsible for your actions. ____________

6–10. On the line, write the two words that make up each underlined contraction.

6. Lea thinks we've solved the mystery. ____________
7. What do you think they'll do with the red turtles? ____________
8. You've seen the boy put the red turtle in the pond. ____________
9. Mr. Roberts says that it's important to take care of the pond. ____________
10. I've done enough research on turtles to know that this answer is wrong.

____

Name ____________________ Date __________

Pronouns and Homophones

Mystery at Reed's Pond
Grammar: Contractions with Pronoun

- **Homophones** are words that sound alike but have different spellings and meanings. Some pronoun contractions are homophones.

Homophones	Meaning
it's its	it is belonging to it, of it
they're their there	they are belonging to them in that place
you're your	you are belonging to you

You're very kind to animals and their habitats.
They're enjoying your book on turtles.

Thinking Question
What sentence clues can I use to figure out the meaning and correct spelling of the homophone?

1–6. Read each sentence. Write the correct homophone in parentheses.

1. We found a cracked egg (their, there). ____________
2. The egg should have been in (it's, its) nest. ____________
3. (They're, There) observing the young turtles in the pond. ____________
4. (Your, You're) correct about the effects of pollution. ____________
5. (Your, You're) computer gave us the information we needed. ____________
6. (Its, It's) hard to believe that the boy did not want to keep his pet turtles.

____

Name ______________________ Date ____________

Using Pronouns

- Pronouns can be combined with some verbs to form contractions.
- An apostrophe replaces the letter or letters that are left out.
  Example: I am = I'm
- Contractions for *he, she,* and *it* when used with verbs *is* and *has* are the same.
  Example: he is = he's   he has = he's
- Some pronoun contractions are homophones.
  Example: it's = it is   its = belonging to it

1–5. On the line, write the contraction for the underlined words.

1. I am ready to write a report about my field trip.
   ____
2. My teacher says that I will have one week to finish it.
   ____
3. Sylvia said she has decided to do a photo essay as her report.
   ____
4. She said that it is going to be her best report ever.
   ____
5. Les thinks we are going to have fun reading our reports in class.
   ____

6–10. On the line, write the correct homophone for each sentence.

6. (Your, You're) going to visit the science museum next week.
   ____
7. (There, Their) will be students from the whole school district at the museum.
   ____
8. (Their, They're) going on the same guided tour as your class.
   ____
9. (It's, Its) going to be an amazing experience!
   ____
10. Don't forget to bring (you're, your) cameras.
    ____

Commas in Sentences

- A **series** is a list of three or more items with the word *and* or *or* before the last item.
- Use *commas* to separate the items in a series. Put a comma after each item except the last one.
- Some choppy sentences can be combined using a series.

  Snakes and lizards are reptiles. So are alligators and crocodiles.

  Snakes, lizards, turtles, alligators, and crocodiles are all reptiles.
- Use a comma to separate the **month and date from the year.**
- Use a comma to separate **city or town and its state.**

  I will be sixteen on August 4**,** 2010.

  The best park is in Yellowstone**,** Montana.

1–5 Rewrite the sentences, adding commas where they are needed.

1. The scales of a snake are cool dry and hard.

   ____

2. This park was opened on July 4 1949.

   ____

3. A turtle in danger can pull its head legs and tail into its shell.

   ____

4. Most turtles live in ponds lakes rivers or the ocean.

   ____

5. Next summer I'm going to ecology camp in Orlando Florida.

   ____

Combine the sentences using a series. Write the new sentence on the lines.

Both turtles and tortoises bask in the sun. They both have bony shells. Turtles and tortoises can withdraw inside their shells for protection.

____

____

Name ____________________ Date ____________

Conventions: Proofreading

Sentence with Errors	Corrected Sentence
Im sure their excited to have solved the mystery.	I'm sure ~~their~~ they're excited to have solved the mystery.

1–6. Use the proofreading marks to fix the convention errors in the sentences below.

1. Ive never solved a mystery before.

2. Its about time we helped animals by saving their habitats.

3. Youd never guess what my favorite pond animal is.

4. I love frogs because their so interesting.

5. Youll be glad that you did so much to help.

6. The western pond turtle is being squeezed out of it's habitat.

Name ______________________ Date ____________

Focus Trait: Sentence Fluency Using Different Kinds of Sentences

Writers can give the same information in different kinds of sentences.

The western pond turtle needs to have its home protected.

Question: Doesn't the western pond turtle deserve a safe home?

Exclamation: The western pond turtle must have a safe home!

1. If we work together, we can save the animals at Reed's Pond.

Command: ____

Question: ____

2. The red-eared slider should not be released in Reed's Pond.

Exclamation: ____

Command: ____

3. Saving the pond's native species is very important.

Question: ____

Exclamation: ____